Explorations
of
Intrapersonal Space

The Measurement of Intrapersonal Space by Grid Technique

Volume 1

Explorations
of
Intrapersonal Space

Edited by

Patrick Slater

Senior Lecturer, St. George's Hospital Medical School

JOHN WILEY & SONS

London · New York · Sydney · Toronto

Library of Congress Cataloging in Publication Data:

Main entry under title:

The Measurement of intrapersonal space by grid technique.

    Includes index.
    1. Psychometrics. 2. Least squares. 3. Personality assessment. I. Slater, Patrick. II. Title: Intrapersonal space by grid technique.
BF39.M38   155.2'83   76-8908

ISBN 0 471 01360 9

Typeset in IBM Journal by Preface Ltd., Salisbury, Wilts. and printed by The Pitman Press, Bath

LIST OF CONTRIBUTORS

S. JANE CHETWYND   *Research Fellow, Honorary Lecturer, St. George's Hospital Medical School, London S.W.17*

JEAN GRISTWOOD   *Formerly research worker, Institute of Psychiatry, London S.E.5*

JOHN GUNN   *Senior Lecturer, Institute of Psychiatry*

BASIL HONIKMAN   *Professor of Architecture, North Carolina State University*

ALAN LANDFIELD   *Professor of Psychology, University of Nebraska-Lincoln, Nebraska*

FAWZEYA MAKHLOUF-NORRIS   *Principal Clinical Phychologist, Runwell Hospital, Essex*

HUGH NORRIS   *Director, Alcoholic Rehabilitation Research Group, Department of Psychology, University of Birmingham*

JOHN ORLEY   *Department of Psychiatry, University of Oxford*

JOHN PALMER   *Research Officer in Epidemiology, Health Care Evaluation Research Team, Winchester*

STUART RILEY   *Lecturer in Marketing, University of Lancaster*

DOROTHY ROWE   *Principal Psychologist, Lincolnshire, Area Department of Clinical Psychology*

ANTHONY RYLE   *Director, University of Sussex Health Centre*

PHILLIDA SALMON   *Senior Lecturer in Child Development, Institute of Education, University of London*

JOHN SIMONS — *Research Fellow, Centre for Overseas Population Studies, University of London*

ELIZABETH SPINDLER BARTON — *Principal Psychologist, Meanwood Park Hospital, Leeds*

PETER STRINGER — *Lecturer in Psychology, University of Surrey*

TERRY WALTON — *Senior Clinical Psychologist, Scalebor Park Hospital, Yorkshire*

JAMES WATSON — *Professor of Psychiatry, Guys Hospital Medical School, London S.E.1*

CONTENTS

INTRODUCTION

EACH individual forms a microcosm of the known universe and a depository for all the ideas ever entertained about it. Here are everyone and everything that has attracted his interest or aroused his fears — in fact the whole extent and content of space and time as far as his mind can reach — and everything, too, that has found a place in his imagination — gods, saints, heroes, demons, monsters, Heaven and Hell, Utopias and El Dorados. Moreover, each private universe has its own processes of change, growth and decay, sudden and gradual.

One microcosm cannot be quite like any other. Each has a separate centre. To explore each is a separate undertaking. It is one that psychology must be prepared to undertake and be equipped for. We cannot claim to understand people in general if we do not understand one single person.

Maps giving distances and directions are an important part of the equipment in physical exploration; measurements are needed for constructing them; and methods for obtaining the measurements have to be studied. Similarly, methods of measuring the extent and direction of distances between points of reference in a private universe are prerequisite for mapping it and exploring it systematically.

Familiar methods may be adapted for the purpose. A battery of tests given to a class of children provides demographic data, recording their scatter in a test-space considered independent of the experimenter. If an informant, a teacher perhaps, rates the children on scales according to his own opinions though the data may be precisely similar in form, they are idiographic. They record the scatter of the children in the informant's microcosm. All such two-way arrays, demographic and idiographic alike, serve as coordinate systems within which the extent and direction of distances between different points can be measured.

Kelly (1955) recommended a way of obtaining an array of idiographic data which he called a repertory grid. In his Rep Test the informant is asked to name people who play various parts in his life at home, in school and at work. About twenty names fitted to the roles by the informant make up the elements. Then he is asked to compare the people named three at a time (the triad method), picking out one that is not like the other two and saying what the difference is — generous/ mean, brave/cowardly, strict/easy-going or whatever. The pair of terms thus elicited forms a bipolar construct which can be used to sort all the elements into those of one kind or the other. The number of constructs elicited depends on the informant; it seldom exceeds twenty in practice. The responses are recorded in the grid, which is a two-way table with a column for each element and a row for each construct, the entry in any cell showing how the construct applies to the element concerned.

This is only a simple example; the technique can be varied in a great many ways. The range of terms that can be used as constructs or as elements is limitless. Many can be used as either. For instance, the suitability of different kinds of clothing for different occasions could be evaluated either by taking the clothes as constructs and the occasions as elements, or vice versa. It is the manner in which they are used that distinguishes them. The constructs function as operators and the elements as operands. A grid must contain terms of both sorts, referring to a common topic, so that all the elements can be evaluated on all the constructs. Functions of either sort, or both, may be supplied by the interviewer or elicited from the informant, and the evaluations may be on any grading scale or may be made by ranking.

There is no universal standardized procedure. When a client comes to a consultant with a problem they may collaborate in choosing the elements and constructs for a grid that will help to elucidate it. The value of the grid so made will depend on its relevance to the client's personal problem, and it may never be needed again. Kelly contrasts the technique with objective tests in clinical use by pointing out that a psychologist uses tests as a construct system for comparing the patient with other people, while the patient using a grid applies his own construct system to his own elements and is himself the tester.

Though Kelly's personal construct theory (PCT) serves to explain the method and interpret the results, it cannot claim a monopoly of the technique. Other procedures that can be used to obtain data in the form of grids have been proposed by Moreno (1934), Stephenson (1935, 1936, 1953) and Stagner and Osgood (1941).

The last, extended by Osgood (1957), has become widely known as the semantic differential, constructs being described for the purpose as scales and elements as concepts. It is designed for making measurements in a common semantic space, not in the intrapersonal space of a particular informant. However, there is no difficulty in processing differentials as grids. Programs in the grid analysis package (see below) can be applied. The differential completed by each informant can be analysed separately or it can be combined with others to form a consensus grid, after which each differential can be compared with the consensus. Chapter 13 provides an example of this procedure.

Such ingenious methods of studying psychological variation within an individual will go to waste if the data collected are not analysed efficiently. Most investigators give very little attention to this subject. Stephenson (1953) and Osgood (1957) are exceptions, but even their methods suffer from undesirable and unnecessary limitations.

In 1964 the British Medical Research Council allowed the author a grant for methodological research with two objectives: (a) to develop a coordinated set of programs for analysing grids by computer and (b) to provide a service available without charge to qualified psychiatrists and psychologists in the United Kingdom to analyse such data for them. The two purposes were supplementary: the intake of data brought fresh insights into the possibilities of the technique and fresh problems for consideration, and the distribution of the results and discussions with users spread up-to-date information about the facilities offered by the service. Although it was not made generally available outside the U.K., trial sets of data have been accepted from many parts of the world. The number of grids analysed per year increased exponentially; it rose to 3000 in 1970 and had reached 10,000 by 1973.

The M.R.C. decided then that the service should be decentralized. Programs should be distributed to computing centres at universities and regional hospital boards throughout the U.K. It is hoped that before long anyone working with grids will have access to some local centre where they can be analysed by computer.

The programs now made available form the grid analysis package (GAP). They include INGRID, which applies principal component analysis to an individual grid, and various programs for comparing grids. How far grids can be compared depends on how closely they can be matched. Grids which are aligned by row and column are open to the most exhaustive comparisons and have been studied in greatest detail. Three programs applicable to them are included in the package, DELTA, SERIES and SEQUEL. DELTA compares two grids and extracts a grid of differential changes, then analyses it to find the dimensions where changes have been greatest. SERIES collates any number, produces a consensus grid and provides all the results needed for detailed analyses of variance. SEQUEL follows on from SERIES, and compares each individual grid with the consensus and defines the major dimensions of difference. These three programs are compatible with each other and with INGRID; grids can be transferred from one to another provided they are correctly aligned; a consensus grid can be analysed by INGRID, two consensuses can be compared by DELTA, and so on. The results are supplementary; there is no overlapping or inconsistency.

Grids aligned only by element can be combined by extending the number of constructs, and ones aligned only by construct can be combined by extending the number of elements. These alternatives are covered by the programs PREFAN and ADELA, which are included in the package, together with COIN (for which see Slater, 1972).

The general purpose of the programs is to provide measurements of distances in intrapersonal space and enable it to be mapped. They dissect the recorded data efficiently into independent parts, enabling the investigator to examine them as exhaustively as he desires. The procedures followed, including principal component analysis and analysis of variance, are employed simply as applications of the method of least squares. They do not depend on any assumptions, either psychological or statistical. Consequently, they are completely general; they apply to all data in the form of grids.

Some time ago an agreement was reached with John Wiley and Sons to publish a book on the subject, to be called *Intrapersonal Space* and subtitled 'The measurement of subjective variation by grid technique'. It was to consist of three parts: the first on the data, discussing the phenomena of intrapersonal space and methods of collecting numerical descriptions of them to be recorded as grids; the second on the analysis, describing the computing processes and explaining the reasons for adopting them; and the third on the results, giving examples to show the variety of the problems that can be investigated with grid technique and of the measurements that can be obtained.

The material assembled proved eventually too extensive to be published in a single volume. It will appear in two, with the common title *The Measurement of Intrapersonal Space by Grid Technique*. The papers on applications are in this volume and the methodological material will be in a separate volume entitled 'Dimensions of intrapersonal space'. I am extremely grateful to the contributors and feel proud and fortunate in presenting their papers.

The first eight chapters concern clinical applications of grids, indicating how they fit in with clinical work, how they can be adapted for use with children and mental defectives and what evidence they provide of mental disorders. The technique is also used to monitor changes in the mental state of a patient under psychiatric treatment and to assess psychiatrists' insight into the inner worlds of their patients. The remaining chapters illustrate other applications: there is a study of stereotyped habits of thought about the roles of women in society, of holiday-goers' opinions on the attractions of seaside resorts, of ways in which people think about the places where they live, of criminals' responses to stressful situations, of native Africans' beliefs about supernatural beings and of Javanese midwives' attitudes to birth control. The summaries have been added by me.

Different methods of analysis are also represented. Nearly all the contributors have referred their data to the M.R.C. service and their work provides examples of the use of most of the programs in the grid analysis package. Two detailed studies demonstrate the potentialities of INGRID and DELTA. Contributions referring to other methods have come from Riley and Palmer, who used a version of PREFAN modified and extended for market research work; Salmon, who quotes numerous investigations by people who have adopted methods not employed by the service; and Landfield, who makes exceptional use of incomplete grids and discusses the psychological significance of omissions. Hugh and Fawzeya Norris have developed their own ways of displaying results obtained from INGRID analyses of grids with certain contents in order to study how patients see the difference between 'myself as I am' and 'myself as I would like to be'.

The proof of the pudding is in the eating, as we all know well, and I hope it will be agreed similarly that the proof of grid technique is in its uses. If so, why not treat it like a pudding? First try the finished product, and if it is good enough enquire afterwards for the recipe with the requisite advice on ingredients and preparation. In short, it may not be a bad idea to begin with this book and then go on to the other.

PATRICK SLATER

References

Kelly, G. A. (1955). *The Psychology of Personal Constructs*, W. W. Norton, New York.

Moreno, J. L. (1934). *Who Shall Survive?* Nervous and Mental Disease Publishing Co., Washington, D.C.

Osgood, C. E. (Ed.) (1957). *The Measurement of Meaning*, University of Illinois Press.

Slater, P. (1972). 'The measurement of consistency in repertory grids'. *Brit. J. Psychiat.*, 121, 45–51.

Stagner, R., and Osgood, C. E. (1941). 'An experimental analysis of a nationalistic frame of reference'. *J. soc. Psychol.*, 14, 389–401.

Stephenson, W. (1935). 'Correlating persons instead of tests'. *Character and Personality*, 4, 17–24.

Stephenson, W. (1936). 'The foundations of psychometry: four factor systems'. *Psychometrika*, 1, 195–210.

Stephenson, W. (1953). *The Study of Behaviour: Q–Technique and Its Methodology*, University of Chicago Press.

1

GRID TECHNIQUE IN THE CONVERSATION BETWEEN PATIENT AND THERAPIST

Dorothy Rowe

Summary

The use of grid technique in a clinical setting is described. It makes an episode in a drama, with antecedents and consequences, not a self-contained experiment in an insulated cubicle. The patient comes to the therapist for help, and during the course of treatment the therapist may introduce a suitable grid to improve the communication between them. Its practical value will depend on what he can learn from it and how the results can be used for the benefit of the patient. Two cases are described. (P.S.)

I always feel discomforted whenever I use the words 'therapy' and 'therapist' in relation to my work. These words always seem slightly pretentious and self-indulgent. Pretentious because, no matter how we disguise it, there is the sense of the therapist having wisdom about life and self-indulgent because I am simply engaging in an activity I always enjoy — having a conversation. Yet, while it is a simple enjoyment, it is also one of the most important human activities and skills, the interchange of ideas. It is a skill that can only be learnt by practice, though we may polish our style through imitation, and, while we practise it, it is difficult to see what we are doing while we are doing it. Conversation is motion. When we set out to describe, to analyse a conversation, as I am proposing to do here, we pin the fluttering white butterfly to the table, put the bird in the cage and so lose some essential element of what we wanted to study. Perhaps if we could keep reminding ourselves that the butterfly once fluttered and the bird once flew, then we would not delude ourselves that the recorded words we are studying contain every essential element of the conversation.

Conversations come in all styles and content. One of the reasons for using a grid early in the conversation between client and therapist is that it suggests a style (I ask a lot of questions) and a content (how the client sees himself and his world). Another reason often given for using a grid is that it provides a baseline against which change can be measured. I have often used grids in this way, but subsequent conversations with clients who had done grids make me wonder whether there are not some types of grid which are not just simple yardsticks but are themselves instruments of change. When we stand a child against a wall to measure his height, we know that in the seconds he is against the wall his height is likely to change in some infinitesimal degree, but we also know that the wall and the tape measure play no part in creating that change. However, when we ask a client to consider the implicit pole of a core construct, to make differentiations about his loved ones of a kind always forbidden by his family's mores, we are asking him to undertake activities which may change him. When we ask a client to do a WAIS or EPI, we are asking him questions the answers of which he knows he knows or he knows he does not know. In giving a grid we may ask our client questions the answers of which he does not know he knows, and, when he discovers what he knows, this discovery changes him. Our present grid methods do not pick up this kind of change. The client may comment at the time, 'I don't know why I said "theoretical" is the opposite of "practical"' or 'I suppose I do feel guilty about my father. I've never really thought about it before', but other changes may occur without an overt sign. In researching here, we are not simply mapping an unexplored territory. It is a territory which changes under the explorer's foot. No step can be retraced, for wherever the explorer goes the territory is new to him. Aids like test—retest reliability and population norms which stood him well in other climes are of no use to him here, in the way that the concepts of Newtonian physics were of no use in studying particles at high speed. We can, of course, use grid technique like a questionnaire and not confront a client with more than he is prepared to tell us and himself, and this may at times be a useful thing to do — but not in therapy. Therapy is a search into the unknown, and the grid can suggest a direction to travel. While the therapist must never abandon his concepts of reliability and validity, our touchstones in the search for truth, as he is dealing with change he may have to find other ways of applying these concepts.

In ordinary conversation, how do we determine the reliability and validity of the ideas expressed by the person conversing with us? We may note a discrepancy between what he says and what we know him to do. He may describe himself as being a hard worker, yet we have observed that he is invariably late for work. Hence we regard his ideas as unreliable. We may observe the ways in which his set of ideas differs from our own and, believing our own ideas to be as close to the truth as humanly possible, we regard his ideas as invalid. (If his ideas are sufficiently different from ours we may regard him as mad, the epitome of unreliability and invalidity.) We can apply the same methods in assessing the reliability and validity of the grids we give, but, if we are working within a personal construct theory framework, there will be a difference in the way we interpret discrepancies from the way discrepancies are ordinarily interpreted. Discrepancies between the words and actions of one person or between one person's set of ideas and another's are not, to the personal construct theorist, inexplicable gaps or human foolishness. For the personal construct theorist there is a continuity between a man's words and his actions, between the construct system by which he orders his world and the actions he performs in his world. When we observe a discrepancy between a man's words and his actions, then we are simply lacking the necessary information to see how the two are connected. The man who describes himself as a hard worker, but arrives late for work may consider that he puts in more work in a short day that his colleagues do in a full day, and that there is, for him, no discrepancy between his words and actions. Of course, for him the term 'hard work' may have an entirely different meaning and set of associations within his system from that of his observer, but if his observer is a personal construct theorist he knows that each person has his own personal construct system developed out of his own experience.

Each man has his own truth, and madness, like beauty, lies in the eye of the beholder.

When we give a client a grid, we ask him to make some statements about himself. If we want to know how reliable and valid these statements are, we need to talk with him further to check how well we understood him. A good starting place for this discussion is at a point of discrepancy between the client's construct system and the therapist's own system, as I found in a conversation I had with a boy called David.

David's father had asked me to have a chat with David who was causing his parents considerable distress since he had got into the habit of taking any money which was left lying round the house and even taking money out of his mother's purse without her permission. Whenever he was found out, he was very contrite and promised not to do it again, but invariably did. I thought that he might have been annoyed at being sent along to see me, but he was pleasant and charming – a thoroughly likeable young man. He said he did not know why he took the money and he wished he could stop himself, but he could not. He said he would be pleased if I could help him. So we began by doing a grid. He chose a list of elements which included himself, his ideal self, his parents, brothers, girlfriend, his schoolmates, several teachers and a school prefect, Jim, with whom he did not get on very well. It became clear that David belonged to a group of lads whose efforts to enliven a boring school were unappreciated by the teachers. His mates and his girlfriend seemed 'more important to him than gaining his 'O' levels, although he was interested in art and hoped to go to an art college to become a teacher. His constructs included 'understanding', 'artistic', 'mature', 'self-confident' and 'spoilt'.

A simplified graph of the analysis of David's grid is shown in Figure 1.1. Here component 1 is defined by the constructs 'understanding' versus 'self-confident' and component 2 by the constructs 'mature' versus 'spoilt'. Self and ideal self are

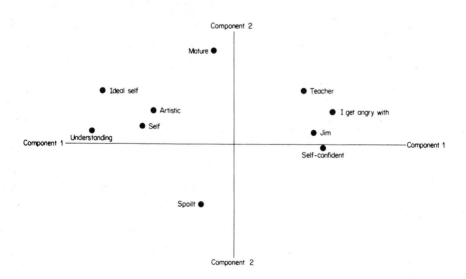

FIGURE 1.1   Graph of the analysis of David's grid

fairly close together at the 'understanding' end of component 1, while Jim is at the 'self-confident' end.

On the second occasion When David and I met, I explained how a grid is analysed and showed him the graph of his grid. He said he thought it was a fair representation of the way he saw things.

There were some part of the graph that puzzled me, that is, did not fit my construct system. For me, the constructs 'mature' and 'self-confident' would be correlated since I see self-confidence increasing with maturity. Moreover, I expect that adolescents wish to become more self-confident and so I would expect that an adolescent's ideal self would come out closer to 'self-confident' than 'self'. But, according to David' graph, he wished to become even less self-confident than he was. This was the point at which I began questioning David in the way we call laddering. All of our conversation was recorded on tape and this is how it went.

'What, for you, is the opposite of self-confident?' I asked.

'Being shy,' he replied.

Pointing to the graph I asked, 'If this is shy over here, you've described yourself as being shy, and also your ideal self, the person you'd like to be, as being shy. So it seems that you'd prefer to be a shy person. Is that right?'

'Yes.'

'Why is it important to you to be a shy person rather than a self-confident person?'

'People who are self-confident, not many people like them. They boast about themselves — they're big-headed.'

'So by being a shy person you feel you're a likeable person. But, why is it important to you to be a likeable person?'

'Wouldn't like to go around with people hating me, talking about me behind my back.'

'Some people don't mind being disliked — they're not worried by being disliked. What is it that worries you?'

'I don't mind it too much, but I wouldn't want to be like Jim — everyone hated him because he was too self-confident. I wouldn't want to be like that.'

'So if somebody is self-confident then people talk about him behind his back . . . and if you think that you're being talked about behind your back, how does this make you feel?'

'I don't know, I've never been in that position, but I wouldn't know what to say if I thought they were talking behind my back. They wouldn't want me there.'

'So by being a shy person you can be sure that other people will like you and behave towards you in the way that they think about you; they'll be quite honest with you because they like you . . . what happens in a situation where you're entitled to be self-confident. Now suppose in most groups you know more about art — suppose you had a great success — you produced work which was immediately acclaimed as being great art, how would you feel about this?'

'I don't think I'd tell them.'

'You wouldn't draw it to their attention in any way?'

'I think I would, but not by telling them.'

'So it's pretty important to you not to appear successful?'

'Yes.'

The importance he placed on being liked came out further as we explored the implications of other constructs he had used. I introduced the notion of being respected and asked, 'Are people who are always liked always respected?'

'No,' he said.

'Why not?'

'Respected — means being something special.'

'If you had to choose between being a person who was liked or being a person who was respected, which would you prefer?'

'Being liked — if a person knew he was respected, that would make him self-confident.'

'So if you became a respected person you would be in danger of becoming self-confident and so not be liked?'

'Yes . . . If I'm not liked I feel uncomfortable.'

Presumably, we learn our notions of being liked and respected from our parents. I asked David, 'If I said to your father which would you prefer, to be liked or respected, what would he say?'

'A bit of both.'

'If he had to make a choice, which would he choose?'

'I really don't know. It might be respected.'

'Now with your mother, what would she choose?'

'A bit of both.'

'But if she had to make a choice.'

'She'd be liked.'

So, whatever his parents may have thought they had taught him about being the kind of person who is respected or the kind of person who is liked, what David had learned from his life's experience is that it is safer to be a likeable person than a respected person. At his stage in life it was safer and, therefore, more pleasant to belong to a group of peers, to take their opinions seriously and to join in their social activities, than to accept the loneliness of studying for examinations and to risk rejection by his peers by becoming the respectable schoolboy so admired by teachers and parents. His behaviour developed logically, sensibly, from his construct system, but one problem remained. If one sets out to be a likeable fellow one needs not only engaging charm, which David had in plenty, but also sufficient finance to maintain one's social life. David needed money to go to the coffee bar, discotheque or cinema, and for records and cigarettes. His parents gave him fifty pence a week and refused to increase this sum. It was, indeed, dangerous to take odd sums of money from home, but it was even more dangerous not to be able to pay one's way in a social life which was essential to one.

David and I decided to take the matter back to his parents. We arranged a meeting of the four of us. First, I asked his parents to write down the answers to my question, 'If you had to choose between being liked and and being respected, which would you choose?' Both of them wrote down 'being liked'. They were then unable, in the conversation which followed, to assume that pose of extreme respectability which parents of adolescents often feel constrained to adopt and they came to agree that David's financial situation needed reviewing. This was done to David's satisfaction.

Unfortunately, not all my conversations have such neat endings. It is much easier to demonstrate the direct relationship between a person's construct system and his behaviour than it is to change his construct system or, as in David's case, to effect

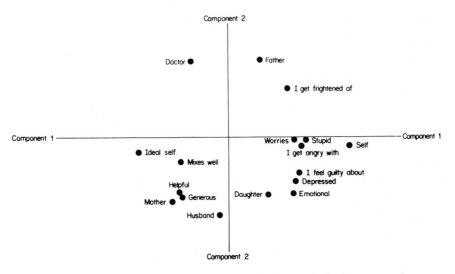

FIGURE 1.2   Graph of the analysis of Mrs. King's grid

some changes in his world so that his construct system fits it more happily. Work with grids has certainly increased our understanding of why depressed people keep on being depressed. When I first started to work with grids, I met a woman who organized her world very simply into good people and bad people. The good people were poorly; the bad people were well. She operated this system without much change over many years, despite the excellent ministrations of doctors to cure her depression and to solve her family problems (Rowe, 1971). Further conversations with depressed people have led me to the belief that the construct system of a depressed person turns on some version of the proposition that suffering is virtuous. This idea is so embedded in our culture that it is not easy to persuade a person holding this idea that he could suffer less and still be virtuous.

One such person I talked with was Mrs. King, whose case notes were inches thick by the time she was forty. These notes contained accounts of every standard treatment for depression interspersed with accounts of operations for various largely hypochondriacal complaints. One advantage of using a grid early in the conversation with such a client is that it establishes that the conversation we are to have will be different from the conversation she has learned to have with doctors. She completed a grid of fourteen elements and twelve constructs. A simplified diagram of the analysis of her grid is shown in Figure 1.2. This shows the separation of self and ideal self often found with depressed people, with self being associated with negative feelings and ideal self with unattainable attributes and an idealized mother and husband. The conversation which followed the doing of this grid showed how necessary it was for her to become depressed and also that there was one major construct on which her husband and her mother differed, a construct central to her predicament but not shown on the grid.

First I asked, 'What for you is the opposite of emotional? What words would you use to describe someone who wasn't emotional?'

'Tough, I suppose,' she replied.

'Would you prefer to be an emotional person or a tough person?'

'Well, it's certainly no joy being emotional, where I am at the moment, so I suppose I'd sooner be tough.'

'Why do you think it better to be a tough person?'

'Well, I mean, if anybody says anything, I always get upset over it, I always seem to take everything the wrong way and get upset over things. I always wish I was tougher and could, you know, let things slide instead of taking it hard.'

'So tough people let things slide.'

'Mmm.'

There was a pause and then I asked, 'Why is it important to let things slide?'

'Well, you get upset over things and then you brood on them, and they upset you and you end up getting depressed over them, whereas if you let things slide you can forget about them and, er, say me and my husband had a row, well I can be hung up for days, where the next day he's forgotten about it, so I think it would be better if I could get up and forget about these things instead of brooding about them.'

'Why is it important to forget about these things?'

'Well, I suppose they're best forgotten. If you have a row with somebody there's no point in keeping it up. I suppose it's best forgotten.'

'Why?'

'Don't know really.' She was silent for some moments and then said, 'There's no point in going over a row, it doesn't do much good.'

'Yet this is what you do, isn't it?'

'Well, yes, I do, I brood over it. And it doesn't do any good. It just makes me ill.'

'Yes.'

There was a long pause and then she said, 'So I think if you could forget about things like my husband does, it would be happier all round.'

'You say that but you don't really believe it.'

'Well, you see my husband's got a job where he works in a butcher's shop, so therefore if we have a row he can't go to work with a miserable face. He's got customers to serve and, you know, he just can't be miserable. So I suppose, well, he's in such a lot of company all day and he gets on well with his job, well, I think that's how he forgets things so easily. Whereas I'm at home, and I keep thinking of things that have been said, and I just brood over them, so I think that if you can get out and forget about these things you're better off.'

'So he's better off than you, because he . . .'

'He is, yes.'

'At first you were saying it's good, it's the right thing to forget about having a row, and then I asked you but why, and you thought about it and said, well, my husband does this . . . but then he's only able to do this because . . .'

'He is, yes.'

'He's got people around him, and a job, a lot of people coming in, being pleasant, making jokes.'

'That's what it is, you see.'

'Yes, so he's not really doing it because it's the right and proper thing to do, he's doing it because he's able to do it.'

'Yes.' There was a long silence and then she said, 'I'm not able to do it, well, you see, say we have a row and we're going to a dance, well, he can put on a face then and forget about it, but deep down I haven't forgot about it and I want to keep bringing it up with me husband, but he won't see, he just says, "Oh, forget about it" and that's it. He won't argue the point about things.'

'When you want to talk about something and he says, "Oh, forget about it", how do you feel then?'

'Well, you feel that bottled up you could scream, because he just won't talk about these things. He just doesn't seem to understand it, because he was brought up in a big family, and he was brought up pretty rough and had to stand up for himself a lot. Where I was brought up I was an only girl, and I was very close to my mother and I think I was brought up more sheltered.'

'So you say he was brought up rough and you were brought up sheltered.'

'Yes. Me and me mother was so close. We was very close.'

'Which do you think is better, to be brought up rough or to be brought up sheltered?'

'I don't know really. You've got to be a bit tough with your children, but then you've got to love them as well. I can't always show that to my children. That's why I feel guilty about it.'

'It's best if a person's brought up in between brought up rough and brought up sheltered. If a person's brought up rough, what sort of things will go wrong?'

'Well, I can't see anything's gone wrong in my husband's case.'

'Just sort of generally?'

'Well, if they're brought up real rough they start doing wrong things and getting mixed up with rough crowds.'

'Why is it important that a person shouldn't be brought up in too sheltered a way?'

'Well, I think you get too attached.'

'What's wrong with getting too attached?'

'Well, like me, I was so attached to my mother . . . and the times I wish she was still here to talk to, you know . . . you miss them so much . . . here, she's been dead quite a few years now, but you still miss them so. So, I don't think you want to be too sheltered.' There was a long pause and then she said, 'Ten years, ten years this month.'

'When you say you miss your mother, what sort of feeling do you get then?'

'You just feel you've lost something, somebody you can talk too — you can't talk things over with my husband. He's good and all that, but you just can't talk to him.'

'Is there anyone you can talk to?'

'No, not really.'

'Does this make you feel very lonely?'

'Yes, I'm afraid I do feel very lonely.'

She went on and talked more about the death of her mother. I commented, 'You describe her as being a good woman and your husband as being a good husband and you describe them both as being close, so you saw your husband as being like your mum.'

'Yes.'

'And then, he's not like your mum.'

'No, I just can't get through to him.' She described how she and her husband quarrel because she refuses to let him make love to her when she is depressed. It seemed to me that perhaps she was trying to force him to be her mother, and, of course, one does not have sex with one's mother.

We went on to talk about how she suffered from pains in the chest which the doctors told her were imaginary but which, she feared, heralded a death from heart attack in the same way that her father had died. Some years ago, she had quarrelled with her father and told him she hoped he would die. He had walked out the door and done just that. Now she was plagued with these pains which her husband refused to take seriously. She wished that she were a tougher person, 'able to answer people back and get things off me chest instead of bottling them up.'

I asked, 'The people who answer back and get things off their chest, what sort of people are they?'

'They have their say and that's it. When they've had their say they don't worry about things.'

'Why is it important not to worry?'

'Well, you've got to worry sometimes, but the way I worry, I worry about bad things and I make myself ill doing it, but you've got to worry to a certain extent, because if your children was ill and you didn't worry they'd get worse and you'd do nothing about it.'

'If you're a person who worries, you do things to look after the people that you care about. A person that doesn't worry ... that person mightn't look after somebody they care about.'

She went on to describe two occasions on which she had worried about her children against the advice of her husband and through her worrying and taking the child to a doctor a disaster had been averted. Now, of course, she was worrying about dying in the same way as her father had died. People told her that she was wrong to worry, but if worrying did avert a disaster, then she should go on worrying, even if it did mean being depressed.

So, starting from the grid, we explored a construct system, the bare bones of which are shown in Figure 1.3. Here the alternative implications of 'being brought up sheltered' and 'brought up rough' are to be lonely or to mix in rough crowds (do

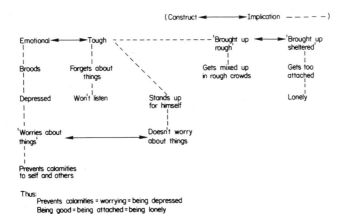

FIGURE 1.3 Relationships among constructs and their implications in Mrs. King's construct system

bad things), while the alternatives of being emotional and being tough are preventing calamities, worrying and being depressed as against not worrying and not listening to (caring for) other people. So, being lonely and depressed is the logical and necessary outcome, for should we not all try to be good and try to prevent calamities befalling us and those we love?

This kind of conversation, or therapy, which starts with a grid has as its aim making overt the covert constructs and their implications. Sometimes, when the client puts into words a set of constructs by which he has ordered his world and so produced painful results, the very ridiculousness of his point of view forces itself upon him and he is able to abandon or alter his schema. But sometimes the set of constructs are too important, too central to the client to admit of change. Then he has to face the fact that the predicament of which he complains is not the result of a visitation beyond his control but is a predicament of his own choosing. When a depressed woman finally says, 'But I like being a martyr', she knows she is saying, 'I choose to be depressed'. Once she defines her predicament as the outcome of a choice she has made, she can then define herself as being in control of her life and as being able to make other choices.

The essential feature of this kind of conversation is that the therapist, starting with the grid, tries to learn and to work in the client's own language and does not try to teach the client his language by using terms like 'depressive illness' or 'resistance', derived from his favourite theory. Such a conversation should be more readily understood by others who may inquire about it, since the language used is usually our simple common language. In the study of how human beings live their lives there is no need to create a special language. Common experience should be describable in our common language.

Reference

Rowe, D. (1971). 'Poor prognosis in a case of depression as predicted by the repertory grid'. *Brit. J. Psychiat.*, **118**, 297—300.

2

GRID MEASURES WITH CHILD SUBJECTS
Phillida Salmon

Summary

This comprehensive survey of the use of grids with children begins by comparing grid technique with other methods of assessing personality in children such as standardized tests, questionnaires, rating scales and projective techniques, indicating where its advantages lie and what its limitations are. Then every stage in the procedure is reviewed: introducing the topic, choosing the elements and constructs for the grid, getting it filled in and interpreting it. Examples of appropriate procedures are quoted from researches with children. Incidentally, they illustrate the flexibility of the technique; if the materials and the method of presentation are suitably chosen, grids can possibly be given to normal children as young as four and also to subnormal children from an early age. Some areas are indicated where further research is needed. (P.S.)

The case for grid measures with children

Although psychologists have probably been as often concerned to assess personality in children as in adults, it seems true to say that methods of personality assessment are less satisfactory where the subject is a child. As far as British research work is concerned, the method most often used has almost certainly been the questionnaire or inventory. Some useful information has undoubtedly been obtained from studies employing this sort of measure, but certain serious problems do seem implicit in the assessment of children by questionnaire — problems which set limits to its usefulness. The most obvious of these problems has to do with the fact that in most measures of this type the subject must read through a number of questions or statements, and although the wording of questionnaires for children has been simplified as far as possible, a reading age of eight years is normally required. This clearly excludes not only normal children younger than eight, in whom many investigators have been interested, but also children older than this but backward in reading — the typical CGC 'case', in fact, whose personality is of vital interest to the clinic's psychologist. Just as serious a problem, and one which probably vitiates this type of measure for a greater number of children, derives from the fact that it is of the paper-and-pencil type. To very many school-age children, any such exercise is boring and dull; to still others, it is actually a feared and hated activity. Where this is the case, the response given by the subject is likely to be careless, stereotyped or deliberately misleading, and although these tendencies can sometimes be detected by checks on response bias or through the use of buffer items, so avoiding 'false positives', the resulting record reveals little about the personality of the child, or shows whether his responses were due to his wish to baffle or mislead the investigator or were the outcome of simple lack of comprehension.

Measures of the questionnaire kind have on the whole been designed for group rather than individual administration. In contrast, those assessment procedures which have risen from clinical needs are typically designed for individual administration. Because of this, they have succeeded rather better in escaping the problems entailed in a highly standardized and inflexible assessment situation. These individually administered techniques can perhaps be categorized under the two headings of rating scales and projective techniques. With regard to the first, probably the most widely used scales in this country, whether in research or clinical contexts, are the Vineland Social Maturity Scale and the various Bristol Social Adjustment Guides. Both types of scale involve the rating of an individual child, by someone who knows him well, on a variety of aspects of behaviour defined carefully by the scale. The fact that such scales are typically filled in by adults reduces the likelihood that the verbal content or the task itself will be beyond the respondent's comprehension, while the fact that the investigator is normally at hand to clarify things if necessary means that the rater's difficulties are unlikely to go unrecognized, as can so easily happen in the classroom filling-up of questionnaires.

Although rating scales avoid the most obvious problems involved in questionnaires or inventory measures of personality, they introduce certain difficulties of their own. Of all measures, rating scales seem to offer the greatest opportunities for biases of all kind to flourish. Whether parent or teacher, the rater is unlikely to be an unbiased observer of the child rated, particularly since so many of the items can be seen as indirect measures of the wisdom and efficacy of rearing or teaching methods. Inevitably, the door is thereby opened to all the attitudes of defensiveness, repression, wishful thinking, distortion, and so on, so well documented in relation to maternal reporting. Unlike questionnaires, rating scales do not normally incorporate measures of such biases. A different, but potentially equally vitiating, type of bias is the one emphasized by Cronbach — the difficulty which most people have in using any scale in a statistically proper way. This perhaps derives from the difficulty which many people have with the concept of an average; rating scales, which tend to define behaviours in such terms as 'more than most children' or 'normally for his age', are likely to be demanding the conceptually impossible of many of their raters, although this fact will not be clear from the ratings obtained. And whereas the biases likely to arise in questionnaires are at least the subject's own, in rating scales they are those of another person entirely and cannot even be argued to show an aspect of the subject's personality!

Projective techniques stand in contrast to both questionnaire and rating scale measures of children's personality in that they typically employ non-verbal material for the child to respond to. For this reason, these techniques are neither limited to children with reasonably good educational skills and attitudes, as with questionnaires, nor are they so likely as rating scales to elicit attitudinal biases, not being as easy to 'see through' as verbal statements. Again, as individually administered procedures *par excellence*, they can encompass an almost limitless degree of flexibility, thus avoiding the problems of fixed wording entailed by questionnaires and, to a lesser extent, by rating scales. Because of their freedom from rigid channelling of the child's responses and the opportunity they seem to offer him for revealing the aspects of experience which are salient, troublesome or fulfilling for him as a unique individual, projective techniques have a strong appeal to many psychologists concerned with assessing children's personalities, particularly those who, like clinical psychologists, are interested not in normative aspects but in highly individual outlooks. What is more, they are mostly much enjoyed by children.

Yet, attractive as projective techniques of personality assessment may be, they seem likely to entail grave difficulties for their users. These relate to the interpretation of the subject's response rather than to its elicitation. Projective techniques tend to fall into two groups: those that have a clear and relatively comprehensive system of interpretation and those, much more numerous, that have little in the way of an interpretative system, or at least have a great many loose ends. Both types seem to present their own kind of difficulty. In the case of techniques involving a standard scoring system, interpretation seems typically to rest upon far-fetched, if intriguing, links between particular aspects of response and their supposed symbolic significance. This can result in reducing the witness of the subject's response to a few simple categories. What is perhaps even more disturbing to many psychologists about such interpretations is that the relationships and concepts on which they rest are often resistant to operational definition and thus to experimental test. Where techniques leave a great deal of the interpretation to the judgement of the particular clinician, he is likely to feel that the standard material involved in the technique is no more useful than any other stimulating material which he might have chosen and that his interpretation is no freer of subjectivity than an interview might have been. Thus, projective techniques for assessing personality in children seem to fall between two stools: on the one hand, they oblige the psychologist to use a system of interpretation based on frequently obscure and usually questionable assumptions and, on the other, they throw him back on his own resources without the help of precise or quantifiable indices.

Considering the types of measure discussed so far, there seems to be a dilemma between two sorts of approaches, each of which is to some extent unsatisfactory. On the one hand, there are normative procedures yielding precise information, the validity of which can be established, but, like a psychometric Procrustes, forcing the child to fit a few predetermined dimensions which may well be irrelevant, or at least at a tangent, to his particular outlook, problems and developmental directions. On the other hand, there are projective techniques which allow the child the opportunity for spontaneous and personal response and seem potentially to offer insight into his unique subjective world, but which, in trying to make sense of such information, either reduce it to limited and dubious categories or provide inadequate guidelines to help the investigator out of the chaos of a mass of raw data. The choice seems to be between the arbitrary imposition of meaning on the child in the interests of precision and quantifiability, and woolliness or subjectivity of interpretation in the interests of idiographic validity. Yet, here, repertory grid technique can be claimed to offer a median way out of the dilemma.

Repertory grid technique arose out of personal construct theory, the fundamental tenet of which is that human beings make their own interpretations of events. The technique is therefore aimed at examining, as extensively and sensitively as possible, the subject's phenomenological world, just as are projective techniques. Kelly made no distinction between people on grounds of age and did not, unlike some theorists, give children a second-class citizenship in the matter of construing. He insisted, indeed, that right from birth human beings are engaged in construing events and that the discriminative bases on which even the youngest infant can be seen to act are not qualitatively different from the conscious, verbally labelled distinctions which adults use.

Although repertory grid technique shares with projective techniques the focus upon the subject's unique subjectivity world and though, again like these techniques, it is a variable assessment procedure rather than a standardized test, here the similarity ends. Because the technique consists essentially of a sorting task of one kind or another, the results lend themselves to statistical analysis. Data yielded by the test are therefore 'hard' and, though making proper sense of the results will depend on the good judgement and imaginativeness of the investigator, the nature of the data will prevent the technique from being merely a projective test for the tester — a charge which has been levelled at certain other assessment procedures. A further protection against undue subjectivity in the interpretation of results derived from this technique lies in the clearly stated and relatively comprehensive assumptions about personality in the theory of which this assessment procedure is an integral part.

Thus, repertory grid technique appears to offer the flexibility and individual focus characteristic of projective techniques, while also retaining the precision and quantifiability of standardized tests. That it avoids many other theoretical and practical problems and that it is a technique particularly well suited to the assessment of children will, it is hoped, become clear as each aspect of its construction, administration and interpretation is discussed in the following sections.

Methods of using repertory grids with children

Before discussing the various aspects of grid administration with child subjects, it will be as well to consider what limits, if any, are likely to exist in its application. Despite the fact, referred to earlier, that even the youngest of infants can be said to have constructs and thus, in theory at least, to lend himself to grid procedures, in practice it is difficult to see how these procedures could be applied with pre-verbal children. Although both elements and constructs can be defined in non-verbal terms, some form of verbal communication is likely to be needed in order to convey to the subject the sorting procedure he is being asked to engage in. It is, therefore, the possession by the child of a certain minimum of at least receptive language which makes the application of grids a feasible prospect. This requirement in turn implies lower limits of age and intelligence, which have not as yet been put to the test. By two years of age, most children have probably acquired sufficient language to be able to understand the procedures involved in simple forms of the grid. Certainly, meaningful results have been obtained with four-year-olds (Allison, 1972). Again, subnormality as such does not preclude the use of grids, as Wooster's (1970a) study showed, but children at the lower end of severe subnormality, in so far as this entails virtually no linguistic skills, could probably not be given grids without an enormous amount of ingenuity on the part of the tester.

The various stages in grid administration and analysis will now be discussed in the order in which they would normally arise for someone concerned to assess an individual child or a group of children. For each stage, some general suggestions will be made, with evidence from existing studies where this is available.

Testing purposes

It seems logical to begin a discussion of ways of using grid procedures with children by considering for what kinds of purpose the investigator would be likely to find such procedures particularly relevant and worth the investment of time and effort which may be involved.

Probably the major kind of question, whether arising in a research or a clinical context, for which repertory grid technique is least suited is a normative one. Where the investigator is interested to find out how a particular child or group of children stands in relation to 'most children of this age' or 'children from working class backgrounds', other techniques of assessment are probably more appropriate to his needs. This is not to say that grids have not been used to answer this kind of question; they have been so used. But there are two reasons why they are less satisfactory than other kinds of assessment procedure where the question is of this type. The first is that few studies have had the resources to establish norms of construing for more than a small sample of the normative group; an investigator therefore has usually only inadequate norms against which to compare his own findings. The second, and more important, reason why grid techniques are unsuited to this type of question is that the main assumption on which they are built is that the constructions placed by individuals on the events in their lives are personal and constantly changing, and thus cannot legitimately be predicted in advance by the investigator.

The unsuitability of grid technique for answering essentially normative questions does not imply that it is inappropriate for the assessment of group differences. The assumption of shared content which is usually entailed in studies of this kind does not violate the theoretical position from which the technique arose, since Kelly's commonality corollary expressed the principle of common areas of construing. This kind of assessment procedure, however, unlike most others, does require that the areas built into the assessment are elicited from members of the kind of groups involved, and their relevance carefully tested with reference to the subjects within the groups being studied, rather than decided beforehand on the basis of studies with other groups or themes which the investigator himself considers appropriate.

Designed, as grid technique is, to be tailored to the particular individual on a particular occasion, its most appropriate usages are probably those arising out of questions about intra-individual relationships. Here, several kinds of study are involved. The most obvious is the individual case study. The technique lends itself to the assessment of the unique subjectivity world of a particular child on a particular occasion. Within the clinical context, the themes in terms of which a child is currently structuring his life, the way he sees himself and the important figures in his world, the areas which he seems to have difficulty in making sense of — all this is likely to emerge from a sensitive use of grid technique. The relevance of such information, in terms of determining the directions of treatment for children with personal difficulties and assessing change, makes the technique a particularly suitable one for the clinical psychologist working with children.

Another aspect of studying intra-individual relationships is the large one of ontogenetic change. Because grid technique can incorporate unique content, it can be used to assess changes over time within the same individual. Again, because it lends itself to the assessment of structural qualities as easily as those of content, structural changes derived from non-comparable content can be compared across large numbers of children. Thus, although each child within a large group construed the area of people in different terms, it might still be possible to show increasing complexity of construing with age across the whole group. The whole question of psychological change is, in fact, one for which repertory grid technique seems uniquely appropriate among assessment procedures. On the theoretical side, the definition of Man as 'a form of motion' expresses the emphasis given to the idea of continual change and development. In practice, too, the technique lends itself to registering changes, since information can be derived from consecutive forms of the grid in which both elements and constructs have been altered to accommodate new concerns and axes of reference on the part of the subject. (This, incidentally, also enables the technique to escape the problem of 'practice effects'.) This sensitivity to psychological change on the part of the technique places it in great contrast to questionnaire measures, for example. The dimensions selected by investigators constructing questionnaires are precisely those which can be applied across a very wide sample of subjects. Further, since such questionnaires are typically developed from within a theoretical framework which assumes the stability of basic personality characteristics, the dimensions incorporated within the tests are those which change little with age.

The adaptability of grid technique to individual situations also means that it can be used for the assessment of interpersonal relationships. The assumption of common areas of construing, noted earlier, is perhaps particularly relevant to the field of personal interaction, where each individual involved must have some understanding of the other's subjective world if communication is to be effective and mutually satisfying. This is an area of study which is much neglected, perhaps because the usual techniques or personal assessment involved fixed, standardized dimensions which cannot hope to show the fluctuating and highly individual dimensions of meaning which interpersonal relationships are likely to involve. Although, as yet, little work seems to have been carried out within this field, an attempt will be made later to show the sort of approach which might be adopted.

Although repertory grid technique has so far been discussed exclusively with reference to personality assessment, it is in fact equally relevant to the assessment of cognitive aspects of children, and this seems a suitable moment to mention this type of usage. There is, conventionally, a distinction between 'personality' and 'cognition', but it is one which does not obtain within personal construct theory, from which grid technique was derived. Conceptualization in its broadest sense is the area which the technique is designed to assess, and, clearly, this links together the aspects of people traditionally separated under the headings of personality and thinking, or intelligence. Apart from the fact that investigators who have been interested in personality have usually examined the child's construing of himself and other people, while those concerned with cognition have tended to look at the child's conception of the physical world, it is difficult to distinguish between the two types of study. Indeed, with claims like those of Little (1968) that certain adults and children are 'thing-specialists' while others are 'person-specialists', the definition of personality is being presented in terms of cognition, or vice versa.

The particular purposes for which grid technique seems suited within the cognitive field are, in general, similar to those within the field of personality assessment. Contrasting the technique with, for example, standard measures of intelligence, its flexibility and individual tailoring make it unsuitable for the sort of normative purposes for which IQ tests tend to be used, but enable it to avoid the charges so often levelled at these, of failing to assess divergent and creative thinking. As in studies of interpersonal relationships, grids can also be tailored to measure the exchange of meanings and the child's acquisition of publicly agreed dimensions of meaning, within the field which we call education. Finally, as in the personality sphere, changes in construction are particularly likely to emerge from this kind of assessment approach. Here again, there is a marked contrast with more traditional measures. The stability of intelligence throughout the life span is a cardinal principle underlying the construction of intelligence tests, so that tests showing changes over time are branded as unreliable; the focus of construct theory, on the other hand, is upon the way people's constructions change as they encounter new events. In so far as such an approach promises the assessment of the kinds of qualitative change stressed in the theoretical position of Piaget, for example, this technique is likely to be attractive to investigators interested in the processes of cognitive growth.

Introducing the grid

It is difficult to state any detailed procedures for introducing grids to children, because of the many different ways in which these can be presented, according to the age of the subjects involved and the kinds of purpose for which the technique has been chosen. The subject may be a pre-school child or an adolescent, the grid may be administered individually or to a group of children, elements may consist of physical objects or verbal labels, constructs may be elicited or supplied, the subject's task may be to order the elements in some physical way or to record judgements clerically, and, finally, the sorting may be a simple yes/no allocation or a more elaborate judging procedure. Obviously how the task is introduced to the child will depend upon these and other different forms of it.

However, certain general principles transcend the variety in detail of repertory grid technique; these principles imply certain ways of introducing the task to the children which are different from those required by most other psychological assessment procedures. One such principle concerns the degree to which the purposes of the procedures can be revealed to the subjects of them. With personality questionnaires, one would not normally wish to tell the subject that the aim of the procedure is to establish how neurotic, dominant or masculine he is; this is partly because to do so would be likely to arouse anxiety in most subjects and partly because a subject's knowledge of the purpose of the test might lead him to give false answers. Similarly, tests of intelligence are not usually presented as such (however much the subject may suspect that that is what they are), because of the threat that would be felt by many people faced with such a test. Grid technique, however, can be safely presented to the subject as precisely what it is: an assessment of the way an individual sees things. It can truthfully be said that there are no right or wrong answers and that every person's responses will be different from everyone else's. This, of course, does not mean that grids should be introduced in quite these terms to every child; to very young children, such remarks would mean little. What it does mean is that if any explanation is given in advance to the child it can be a truthful one and that if, as usually happens with older children, the subject is curious about just what the point of the task is it can be explained, even to the extent of demonstration.

A second important principle of grid procedure, which has implications for how it should be introduced to children, is the fact that, as a task, it is not likely to be outside the subject's capacity. Although the sorting of elements on constructs may require effort and thought on the part of the child, it will not be beyond him if the grid has been properly devised. In some cases, this should be said to the child before he begins, since many school children have unfortunately learned to be wary of any semi-formal task demanded of them. Usually, however, the nature of the procedure and its inherent interest for children make such assurances unnecessary. It is sufficiently unlike most classroom tasks not to arouse the anxieties of the child who feels inadequate and inhibited when faced with the usual paper-and-pencil type of test. With young children, again, the attractiveness of the physical objects or pictures, which are likely to make up the elements, will probably ensure that the procedure is experienced as an enjoyable game rather than an excessively demanding or frustrating activity. Although the situation is by no means one of free play, the restrictions it imposes do not seem to be experienced as irksome by even quite young children. Thus, for most child subjects, grids can safely be introduced as enjoyable and interesting.

Allowing that there can be no standard terms of introduction or instruction, it may nevertheless be helpful to consider the way that grid procedure might be introduced to two contrasting types of subject. The first case is a five-year-old child to be tested individually; the second is a group of fourteen-year-old adolescents within a school class.

Let us imagine that, for the first child, a grid has been devised to assess his construing of people. The elements are ten brightly coloured stand-up models set in a row on a low table at which the child is sitting, with the examiner at the other side. The models depict, realistically, people of both sexes and various ages, clothes and attitudes. Constructs have been elicited from the child by chatting with him about the people depicted and asking him, where necessary, to say what a person would be like if he were 'not like that', in order to establish opposite poles. Again, the child has been asked to elaborate constructs by being asked such questions as 'Who else do you know who is . . . (the child's label)?', 'What does he do that shows he's . . . ?' and 'What else does a . . . person do?'.

The grid is now introduced to the child by saying, 'Now look again at all of these people here on the table. Here's the first one. Is he a . . . person or is he a . . . (opposite pole) person?' (Pause.) If the child doesn't say either, 'Perhaps he's not a . . . person or a . . . person?' This model is then removed and placed out of sight and the examiner records the judgement on a prepared sheet. Then the procedure is repeated with next model, and so on, until they have all been categorized. The models are then replaced on the table and a similar procedure is adopted for the next construct, and so on for all the constructs in turn.

Considering the case of a class group of adolescent boys and girls, let us imagine that a grid has been devised to assess their construing in the area of visual aesthetics. The elements consist of eight reproductions of paintings, on cards measuring 8 inches by 6 inches, hung on a board at the front of the classroom, and each labelled with a letter from A to H. The constructs have been obtained, from adolescents from the same school of comparable age and academic grouping, by the method of triadic comparison on the elements involved in this task. Only those constructs which have been given by a large proportion of the sample are to be used in this task. Let us imagine that there are seven of these, to which will be added another supplied by the examiner: 'Good art/not good art'. Each subject has before him or her a stencilled booklet containing each of the constructs at the top of a separate page, and under each construct, the words, each on a separate line, 'Most', 'Next', 'Next', etc. The constructs begin with a buffer one: 'This painting would be likely to cost a lot of money/this painting probably wouldn't cost much'. (The reason for this buffer construct would be to familiarize the subjects with the elements.) The following constructs are those given by the sample previously tested, followed by the 'Good art/bad art' one.

The procedure is then introduced to the group in the following way. 'This is a procedure known as repertory grid technique. It can tell us something about the ways in which people see things. In this case, I am interested in how each of you sees paintings. No two people ever see paintings in exactly the same way and, anyway, there is not a right or wrong way of seeing them; it is a matter of opinion. The task I am now going to ask you to do involves making judgements about these eight reproductions up here on the board. The form in which I want you to do this is to put them in order on certain things, which are listed in your booklets. Look at the first page of your booklet. You see it says "This painting would be likely to cost a lot of money/not much". Your task is to decide, as well as you can, which of those paintings would be most likely to cost a lot of money, and then write the letter on it at the top of the page, where it says "Most". You then go on to the one you think would be the next most likely to cost a lot of money, and so on till you get to the last, which would be the one which would probably cost the least. Then turn over the page and do the same thing for the thing that is stated on the next page, and so on for all the pages. It is important not to look back once you have finished a page, as all your judgements have to be independent of each other. Work at your own pace and take as long as you like. If there's anything you don't understand please put your hand up. After you've finished the test, let me know if you'd like to hear more about this procedure and what it's supposed to show.'

These imaginary testing situations may give some idea of the very different kinds of requirement needed for introducing different types of grid to different ages of subject. Nothing has been said about how the results obtained from these two sorts of grid might be analysed; considerations of analysis and interpretation will be deferred till a later section.

Choosing the elements

Just as would be the case with adult subjects, the kinds of element which are likely to be suited to any particular grid for a child will depend on the area which the technique is designed to assess. Within the multiplicity of such possible elements, however, the age of the child to be assessed has some implications for what is likely to be suitable. In general, it seems fair to say that the younger the child, the lower the level of abstraction involved in grid elements ought to be. Whereas most older children are able to cope easily with verbally defined entities, pre-school and young school-age children are likely to need more concrete objects on which to carry out their categorizations. This makes sense in terms of views of the young child as operating in terms of physical objects and real actions, rather than in terms of symbolic entities and possibilities.

Elements likely to be suitable for use with young children include real objects, models and pictorial or photographic representations of objects, people or situations. In view of the fact that children of this age more readily understand judgements which are translated into actions, and not merely verbally expressed, it seems wise to devise as elements objects which can be physically moved about without difficulty, so that the child's judgements can be visibly expressed in this way. It also seems likely that with a sorting task as complex as rank ordering, young children would be unable to manage if the whole set of elements were displayed throughout the ranking procedure.

Taking a dividing line at about eight years, many children above this age will be able to cope with material of a less concrete kind. Elements may therefore be represented verbally, in the form of names of people, social roles or situations, for example. The first type of element has been particularly popular with investigators interested in children's constructs about people. Thus, Little (1967) used grids involving as elements the names of people known to his subjects, who were children aged from ten to eighteen years, while Brierley (1967) gave grids of this type to a group of whom the youngest was aged seven years. Even this does not represent the lowest age of child subject who has been asked to construe this type of element, since Allison (1972) actually used names of people with four-year-old children. However, his study was essentially an exploratory one, and no measure was obtained to check on the meaningfulness of this task with his youngest subjects. Judgement must therefore await further investigation, but, meantime, it would seem wiser to restrict this type of element to considerably older children.

Although it is probable that most children of about eight years and older will be able to categorize elements presented in verbal terms, there are obviously some subjects, even in this age range, for whom more concretely defined elements will be more suitable. The large category of children who have reading difficulties would be a case in point, as would those children who, while able to read, dislike having to do so. It is likely that the CGC psychologist, concerned to assess children with personal difficulties, will frequently meet this type of subject. In such cases, people, roles, activities or situations will need to be translated into more immediate terms, as would be the case with younger children.

Whether the elements used in grids for children consist of physical or verbal definitions, it is desirable to make sure that they do, in fact, refer to familiar and meaningful aspects of the child's experience. Ideally, the elements should come from the child himself, as people, situations or behaviours spontaneously mentioned by him in conversation. Alternatively, the psychologist can fill in gaps in the range of possible elements by asking him to supply these for constructs he has expressed; for example, a child might say that her friend is 'funny' and the psychologist might ask, 'Who else do you know who is funny? . . . and who else? . . . and can you think of someone who isn't funny?, etc. In some testing situations, however, it is not possible to elicit elements from the subject. This is likely to be so where grids are group-administered or where the psychologist is particularly interested in the child's construing of specific people or situations. In these cases, where elements are provided for the child to construe, every attempt should be made to check on the personal relevance of these to the particular subjects being tested. One way of allowing personal relevance to determine which out of a number of predetermined elements will be used in any particular case is a technique employed by Ravenette (1968) with children referred to a CGC. Ravenette uses, as grid elements, pictured situations taken from a projective technique and showing children alone, with other children, with family figures, and so on. The subject is asked to choose eight pictures from among these, representing those in which he can most easily imagine himself.

One general precaution which needs to be mentioned relates to the question of the different ranges of convenience to which different elements may belong. As with the previous problem, this is most likely to arise where interpersonal construing is being assessed. It is probable that children, to a much greater degree than adults, have relatively restricted ranges of convenience for constructions about people, being prepared, for example, to use certain constructs for boys and other, different ones for girls, or, again, to construe home and family figures in terms of particular dimensions which would not apply to people within the school context. That this can be so is borne out by two studies. Ravenette (1964), in an analysis of constructs derived from the essays of secondary school children (as part of a larger grid study), found that, though there was a wide range of constructs used in reference to peers, the number given for adults was small. Allison (1972) also found, with a wider age range of children, a tendency to tailor constructs to the type of social object the child is considering. His findings showed, for example, that for the boys in his sample, constructs referring to behaviour as distinct from appearance or psychological qualities, were used much more frequently for teachers than for family members, and for family members more frequently than for friends. Both these studies do, therefore, illustrate the fact that children's constructs about people may have restricted ranges of application and that care should be taken to ensure that a child is not asked to apply a construct to the sort of element he would not normally use it on.

Choosing the constructs

Having outlined some of the general principles which seem important for the selection of elements to be used in grids being composed for child subjects, let us turn to the other half of grids — the constructs. Kelly himself and, more recently, Bannister and Mair (1968) have emphasized that the distinction between the elements and the constructs in a grid is an arbitrary one, made purely for the purpose of determining how concepts are to be presented in the grid task and not representing any real distinction. The fact that what is selected as the elements and what, as the constructs of any particular grid, is based on matters of convenience and ease of handling, rather than upon any genuine conceptual distinction, means that the same general principles applying to the selection of elements also apply to the selection of constructs for any grid. So, for example, the necessity for ensuring that the material chosen for presentation as the constructs is meaningful to the child parallels its necessity in regard to the material presented as elements, while the importance of checking that the elements are within the range of convenience of the constructs obviously has implications for the choice of both parts of the material equally.

Eliciting. Constructs, like elements, can be chosen by one or two methods: by eliciting them from the study directly or by supplying them for the subject to use. Elicitation was, of course, the method employed by Kelly and is obviously truer to the principles underlying grid procedure. Essentially, it consists of sampling, by various techniques, the dimensions of meaning actually employed by the particular subject being assessed, within the area of construing that the investigator is concerned to assess. The advantage of such a method is, of course, that reference axes produced spontaneously by the subject are more likely to be meaningful to him when it comes to using them in the sorting task than reference axes defined by the investigator. All the same, elicitation from children has its own problems, which necessitate care in the procedures used. Kelly's original method of eliciting constructs by successive triadic comparisons has been used by several investigators working with child subjects, and it is obviously both feasible and appropriate for some children and for some purposes. In studies of construing of people among children of different ages, both Brierley (1967) and Little (1967) chose this procedure for eliciting constructs from their subjects. For both studies, the elements consisted of the names, on cards, of people known personally to the subject; thus, the situation was closely similar to the original one described by Kelly in his role construct repertory test.

While both Brierley and Little obtained results which seemed to make some psychological sense from grids employing constructs elicited in this way, it is possible that these results were to some extent an artifact of the method used. The simultaneous comparison of three people and the verbalization of some aspect differentiating them may be a very difficult psychological exercise for children as young as seven years, who formed part of Brierley's sample, and even for children of ten years, tested by both Brierley and Little. It is possible that, in this situation, young children are not capable of drawing upon the relatively abstract and perhaps infrequently verbalized constructs which they may possess, but, instead, may express more superficial, more readily available constructs. If this were so, it might partly explain the findings which both these investigators obtained, of a general progression, with age, from concrete, physicalistic constructs to abstract, psychological ones. From this point of view, the adolescent children investigated in both studies might more easily draw upon their repertoire of psychological constructs within this kind of eliciting situation than younger children, who might nevertheless possess the same kind of construct at a less accessible level.

A good deal of evidence does, in fact, exist that in freer and less structured situations than the triadic elicitation context, children provide rather different constructs and, in the area of person-construing, more constructs of a psychological type. Brierley herself, in the study just mentioned, administered a sentence completion test as well as the grid to the two older groups in her sample — consisting of children aged ten and thirteen years respectively. She found that, in contrast to the constructs elicited for the grid, the children's responses to this test consisted of psychological constructs to the extent of more than 75 per cent for both age groups. The study, cited above, done by Ravenette (1964) suggests a similar conclusion. Ravenette found that the triadic elicitation procedure, used with children attending a Child Guidance Clinic, produced, to an overwhelming extent, constructs of the type which he calls 'role' — 'older—younger' and 'boy—girl' being typical. Trying out a rather different method of eliciting constructs with a sample of non-clinic children of comparable age (junior school), he asked the children to write short essays about boys and girls and men and women, whom they liked and disliked.

In this context, very different constructs emerged, having in general personal rather than role connotations. Ravenette then went on to use the constructs obtained in this way as supplied constructs in grids given to a new sample of same-age children, obtaining results that appeared to be meaningful, in terms of reliability of construct usage and relationships between constructs. Indirect as this evidence is, it does suggest, first, that children aged eleven years and under may have constructs of a psychological type within their repertoire, which may not emerge in the triadic elicitation context, and, second, that constructs of this kind are likely to be meaningful to children of this age when presented as categories to be applied to elements in a grid. On this last point, a study by the writer (Salmon, 1967) is relevant. Here, boys aged between 7½ and 9½ were asked to apply, to photographs of boys, supplied constructs such as 'Probably does as he's told/probably gets into trouble with grown-ups' and 'The sort of boy I'd like to be like/the sort of boy I wouldn't like to be like'. The results, showing significant relationships for associations between these 'psychological' constructs and other independent measures of cognate aspects, suggest that such dimensions are meaningful to children as young as this.

In view of this kind of evidence, it seems likely that the original method of construct elicitation, consisting of triadic comparison of elements, may do less than justice to the repertoire of constructs which may be possessed by pre-school and junior school children, and possibly also by secondary school children who are rather inarticulate or who find difficulty in such a relatively complicated exercise. In such cases, less structured and more natural methods of eliciting constructs are needed.

One modification of the triadic method which was designed to make the child's task easier has been devised by Allison (1972). This involves dyadic rather than triadic comparison of elements. For most children younger than secondary school age, however, more informal techniques still are appropriate. The essay approach devised by Ravenette represents the way of tapping the child's operating distinctions within the area concerned; if this is the area of interpersonal construing, focusing the task on liked and disliked people increases the likelihood of evaluative constructs emerging. But writing an essay is too difficult a task for many children and too burdensome a task for still others, introducing those negative attitudes that were discussed earlier in relation to paper-and-pencil tests. This technique, like Allison's method of dyadic comparison, is probably better suited to children of at least nine years, and who do not have educational difficulties.

For pre-school and younger junior school children, the best way of eliciting constructs is normally conversation. Asking the child about some aspect of his experience, encouraging him to talk freely and questioning him about what he means by certain terms cannot fail to produce constructs from the child and is, also, a familiar, natural and, normally, enjoyable activity for the child. Given sufficient sensitivity on the part of the investigator, a situation of conversation with a young child about the people he knows, the things he likes and dislikes, what he does at school or at home, and so on, will provide plenty of information about the dimensions of meaning with which he invests these areas of his subjective experience. An essential part of the conversational procedure for eliciting constructs is, however, the full exploration of the meanings being expressed by the child. Such questions as 'Tell me a bit more about that', 'What do you mean by . . . ?' or 'And how would you know if a thing was . . . ?' will help to establish the real meaning of a distinction made by a child who might have used a word very differently from the way an adult would have used it.

There are some children, however, for whom conversational techniques are not congenial or easy. With a very shy child, or with a child who has difficulty in expressing himself in words, some other way is needed for enabling him to demonstrate his constructions of his world. In such cases, one method which has been used with some success by the writer consists of inviting the child to group elements together, on the usual basis of 'putting those together which belong together', and then, having produced groups, to try to put into a word or phrase the underlying basis of the groupings. This grouping procedure is then repeated with a new set of groups, and so on, till the child cannot think of any more groupings. Like conversational elicitation techniques, this procedure is apt to be a bit untidy, in that the child may produce a number of different groups in any one sorting, and his expression of the basis for these groupings may imply that he was using several different constructs simultaneously. It may also prove difficult for him to give a neat or clear expression of the basis underlying his groupings, so that the investigator may be left with rather clumsy constructs to put in his grid. Nevertheless, as a way of providing some raw material from which the constructs to be ultimately used in the grid can be defined, this largely non-verbal approach seems to have its uses with some children.

Supplying. In order to make comparisons between children in the way in which they construe aspects of their experience or in order to explore a particular area of a child's construction system, many investigators have found it necessary to supply constructs, rather than eliciting them from their subjects. Since supplied constructs ensure direct comparison across groups of subjects and since they enable assessment of specified aspects of an individual's view, it is easy to understand the decision to supply constructs in terms of convenience. Nevertheless, the supplying of dimensions does depart from a major principle of repertory grid technique, which was, after all, based on the idea that each subject should provide his own categories or meaning. In this writer's view, such a departure need not invalidate the use of grid technique, providing that certain necessary precautions are taken and given that the investigator remembers that the constructs actually used in the categorization will be the subject's own, as he equates them with the verbal definitions provided for him.

While the elicitation of constructs directly from the child who is to be given a repertory grid does not avoid the necessity for careful checks on the meaning of the constructs and their applicability to the elements to be used, this necessity is, of course, doubly important when it comes to providing the constructs which the child is to use. The first point to consider is where the constructs should come from. Many investigators have chosen to provide dimensions of meaning from within their own repertoire, drawing upon this for constructs which are seen as relevant to the situation of the particular subject involved. Thus, if a child has been referred for assessment because of seeming difficulty in accepting a new sibling, the psychologist might provide him with a construct such as 'Feels jealous of the baby/is glad about the baby', for example. In general, this sort of procedure seems legitimate provided that the psychologist takes great care to ensure that the dimension is one that makes sense to the child and that it is worded in a way that would be natural for him. It is possible to test the meaningfulness of the dimensions to be used by asking the child directly about this, in questions such as 'Do you know what I mean when I say . . . ?', 'Do you know any people/things, etc., that are . . . ?', and so on. If the child seems doubtful about meanings or cannot illustrate them by providing examples, it is likely that the dimension chosen is an inappropriate one for him and should be omitted. (Checking on the appropriateness of the wording can be done by asking the child, 'Do you sometimes say that?', 'What would YOU say when you meant that?' 'Or How would YOU put it, if you were talking to someone about that?'. Since adults use a rather different vocabulary from children, dimensions derived from the investigator's repertoire will often require translation into terms which seem natural for a child subject.)

A safer and probably more acceptable procedure theoretically is one which derives the dimensions to be used from a psychologically comparable population to the one to which the subject belongs. This entails the kinds of elicitation procedure described in the previous section being applied to children other than the child to be tested. For example, if the investigator wishes to assess how a particular child construes the school situation, he might elicit the dimensions to be used by conversations with other children in the same school. This sampling of constructs about school would serve to determine what kinds of dimensions are common currency among the group of which the child is a member. Besides drawing the constructs from people who are likely to be more similar, psychologically, to the subject than the investigator himself, this method of selecting supplied constructs has the additional advantage that there are likely to be fewer semantic problems than with the previous selection method. Certain wording problems may still arise, however, particularly with regard to ambiguities. There can obviously be no rule for avoiding ambiguity in wording the supplied constructs; all that can be said is that the psychologist deciding on the wording of the dimensions to be used should be constantly alive to the possibility of verbal confusions and should be prepared to reword the constructs if this seems likely.

One special type of construct which it is often wise to supply, whether the remaining constructs are supplied or elicited, is the buffer construct. If constructs have been elicited in ways that do not involve judgement of the elements, or if they are to be supplied, the child will be looking at the set of elements for the first time when he comes to make the categorizations involved in the grid. Although the instructions given to him are likely to include a request to examine all the elements before he makes any judgement, there is no way of ensuring that he does so, and children sometimes spontaneously remark that they would have made a different judgement if they had noticed a particular element earlier. An initial buffer construct, preferably one which calls for a simple kind of judgement, serves to familiarize the child with the element he is going to categorize, without wasting the judgements he might otherwise make on a construct in which the investigator was genuinely interested.

A further consideration regarding the choice of supplied constructs relates to what Kelly called their bipolarity. A fundamental assumption of personal construct theory is that all judgements implicitly involve contrast. By categorizing an acquaintance as interesting, we are at the same time rejecting the idea that he is a bore, with all that being a bore may entail for us. The fact that we are not necessarily consciously aware of this implicit judgement does not alter the fact that we are making it; every judgement inevitably contains its opposite. In devising supplied constructs for grids, however, many investigators have failed to allow for their essential bipolarity. The use of one pole only in defining the dimension supplied may seem perfectly reasonable, on the rationale that words have commonly agreed opposites which therefore do not need to be explicitly mentioned. Yet people do not always function like dictionaries in the way that they use their categorizations. The contrasts which both adults and children express when their own constructs are being elicited are idiosyncratic and often surprising. A failure by the investigator to define both ends of his supplied constructs, therefore, means that the child will provide his own opposite pole — and this may transform the construct into something very different from what the tester had in mind. Similarly, comparison of a group of subjects who used the same one-pole supplied construct becomes more dubious, since the commonality of its meaning is likely to have been reduced by different implicit poles for the various subjects, in effect making the construct a different one for each of them. That children do not necessarily attribute the 'correct' or conventionally agreed opposites to the verbal definitions they are given in grids, is illustrated by a study of Wooster's (1970b).

Finally, it is necessary to return to the question of devising constructs referring to persons. It was argued above that the use of apparently quite simple constructs such as 'Like me/not like me' or 'Like my mother/not like my mother' has certain difficulties, and should probably be restricted to children of at least seven years. Where the self-construct is involved, there is some evidence that constructs referring to ideal self are more relevant to the child's behaviour than are those defining his actual self. One such study was my own Ph.D. project (Salmon, 1967), which showed ideal self to have more relevance to conforming behaviour than did actual self. This finding suggests that ideal self, representing evaluative judgements, incorporates the child's intentions, and for this reason is more relevant to his current and future behaviour than actual self. The latter, as construed by children, who are nothing if not forward-looking, is more likely to represent a survey of past behaviour and may not carry any implications for the future, being merely descriptive.

In practice, many grids given to children are likely to be a compromise between supplied and elicited constructs; an investigator may wish to assess the sort of reference axes used naturally by the child to make sense of his experience, while also making sure that certain particular dimensions of meaning are provided for the child to use. The grid will therefore include both. There are some advantages in this kind of mixture of constructs. The constructs that the investigator has chosen to supply may be relatively peripheral in the child's construing system or may, indeed, have no meaning for him. If this is the case, it will be evident from the relationships between the two kinds of construct, since any meaningful structure will be restricted to the elicited dimensions. A grid consisting entirely of supplied constructs would not show whether the lack of structure was due to the irrelevance of the dimensions provided or to the child's inability to make any sense of the area of experience involved.

The sorting task

In considering what are the most suitable kinds of categorization for children being asked to do grids, the major questions are the form which such categorizations should take and the manner in which the child should express them. On the first question, the general principles involved in categorizing elements on constructs have been carefully defined by Bannister and Mair (1968). Such principles obviously apply equally to child and adult subjects. For example, a categorization which obliges the subject to distribute the elements equally between the two poles of a construct will do violence to the way he would normally conceptualize things if the construct is a lop-sided one. Similarly, the relationships emerging from grids involving different sorting tasks – ranking and rating, for example – are not directly comparable, since different kinds of conceptualization are entailed in them.

The ideal form of categorization for a child doing a grid is one which models the way in which he would naturally use the construct. Since the way young children construe things is likely to be rather different from the way older children do, a standard format in categorization for subjects of all ages is inappropriate. By and large, the younger the child, the simpler should be the sorting task he is asked to do. In view of Piaget's revelations as to the difficulties which pre-operational children have in making comparative judgements, it seems wise to avoid asking very young child subjects to rank-order elements. Wooster's (1968) success in obtaining meaningful results from a rank-ordering task with five-year-olds may appear to contradict this generalization, but it seems probable that some of his anomalous findings were due to the conceptual difficulty which this task must have involved for such young subjects. Probably the conceptually easiest, and the most natural, way of using a construct to categorize elements is to judge each element in turn as belonging to the positive pole, the negative pole or to neither. This latter category can mean various things; it can represent an intermediate position between the two poles of the construct, it can express uncertainty on the part of the child as to which pole it belongs to or it can indicate that the element is, in Kelly's terms, outside the range of convenience of the construct. Which of these possibilities is the case will usually emerge while the child is doing the grid, since if he does not say why he is placing the element in this category, one can ask him. But if for some reason it is not clear, subsequent analysis may be helpful. It may be, for example, that certain elements have been frequently allocated to this 'don't know' category; this is an important piece of information, since it suggests that the child has some difficulty in making sense of these elements.

In line with the attempt to make the sorting task model the child's natural construing, it is important to avoid restricting his free use of the three categories.

The child should be told that he is entirely free to place as many or as few elements as he likes in each of the categories and that he need not use any category if there are no elements that seem to fit in. A forced distribution, though tidier and easier to analyse, is likely to obscure the idiosyncratic ways in which many children make discriminations. The lop-sidedness of particular constructs, whereby events are frequently construed under one pole while the other pole is seldom or never applied, is an extremely important aspect of them, and it can only emerge within a grid which allows the subject freedom to distribute the elements unequally. On an intuitive basis, it seems likely that children have more lop-sided constructs than adults, since in the process of acquiring new axes of reference, one pole may be 'learned' more quickly than the other. Certainly, young children often happily extend the meaning of a particular term far more widely than an adult would be prepared to do, and this global usage may imply an unfamiliarity with applying the contrasting pole.

Although young children are likely to need a conceptually simple categorizing task in applying constructs to elements, more complex sorting procedures become possible when the child involved is about seven years or more. At this age, rank ordering elements on a continuum, rather than a straightforward 'Yes/No/Don't know' judgement, is normally within the child's capacity. Nevertheless, the limits which a child's relatively simpler modes of construing set are likely to be narrower than those applying to adults. The number of elements which can be simultaneously grasped for the purpose of ranking will be smaller. Even though meaningful results were obtained with ten-year-olds from grids involving the rank ordering of ten elements (in my own Ph.D. study), in practice it is probably advisable to restrict the number of elements to be ranked to eight. A further modification of the ranking procedure to fit the needs of child subjects is one which was introduced by Ravenette (1968). This consists of asking the child to select the elements, in turn, for the two poles of the construct. Thus, for example, the child might be asked to choose the person who was most kind, then the person who was most teasing, then the person, from the remainder, who was most kind, and so on. The purpose of this procedure is to ensure that the child keeps in mind the dimensions on which he is being asked to categorize the elements, which, as outlined previously, is as much defined by the implicit as by the explicit pole. Whereas adults are probably well able to maintain awareness of the complete construct they are using, younger subjects may have difficulty in remembering it; this alternative application of the construct's two poles will prevent such forgetting.

A third form of categorization, which is probably intermediate between dichotomous judgements and ranking, is the use of various kinds of rating. Children over about six years can usually manage this task quite easily, particularly if it is presented in the form of physical ordering of the elements, as will be described presently. Here again, the restrictions on the frequency with which the various ratings are to be given should be minimal, with the child being free to distribute the elements in any way he wants. The rating categories should be defined by words, such as 'very', 'a little bit', etc., rather than by numbers. It is probably as well to limit the number of rating categories more strictly than would be necessary for adult subjects; seven would certainly be too many for most children under about twelve, and five, or even three, are probably the most that younger children could use in a meaningful way. As with dichotomous judging procedures, there should be a 'don't know' category, since, again, it is important to identify uncertainty in the child's construing system.

When it comes to the devising of methods whereby the child is asked to indicate his judgement in the categorization tasks, considerable modifications from Kelly's original form of the grid will be needed. A general principle is that the younger the child, the more the procedure will need to demand an oral or a physical response from him rather than a clerical one.

Taking each of the three types of categorization in turn, the dichotomous judgement of elements lends itself to both verbal expression of judgements and spatial indications of these, equally well. The verbal form of this kind of task has already been outlined in an earlier section, where the imaginary situation of a five-year-old child construing models of people was described. It will be remembered that the task entailed the child saying 'Yes' or 'No', or 'I don't know' to questions from the tester about the pole to which the element belonged. Elements were physically removed from the child's sight once they had been judged, to avoid confusing the child by their continued presence. An alternative method, which works well with shy children who would prefer not to have to talk to the investigator, is to ask the child to put the elements into three piles, representing the three categories of judgement. With children who can read, the places on the table for the three groupings can be marked by three cards on which the two poles and 'don't know' have been written. Since children often forget which pile is which, it is a good idea to check from time to time that they have not become confused over the identity of the groups.

Rank ordering also lends itself to simpler modes of expression than the conventional clerical recording of judgements by the subject. For children under about nine, and for children who dislike writing or are likely to become confused by clerical tabulation, a preferable method is the spatial allocation of the elements according to their rank order. It is helpful, as with the previous procedure, to mark the table in some way so as to indicate which end represents which pole. The child is then simply asked to place the elements spatially between the two end points, so as to show where they belong. An advantage of this procedure is that it enables the child to show 'tied ranks' and unequal intervals between elements — this last feature being something which mere allocation of numerical ranks obscures. A further modification of rank ordering which proves suitable for some children, and is easier than physical placement where the elements are cumbersome and unwieldy, is to give some mark to each element, which may be a letter, a number or any symbol, and to ask the child to draw the mark on a sheet of paper on which a line has been drawn representing the space between the two poles of the construct. For most children over about nine, clerical recording of judgements is possible. Some children like their judging to be a private procedure, rather than being done in the full view of an adult. Here, it is more appropriate to ask the child to express his categorizations in writing. Similarly, if grids are group-administered, it is likely to be more convenient to require the child to record his judgements in this way. When children are asked to record their own rank orders, care should be taken to ensure that the recording task is made as simple as possible, and does not give rise to confusion on their part. The method of recording ranks which is normally used with adult subjects needs some modification to make it suitable for a child. Whereas an adult can cope with the recording of numbers indicating ranks, under the titles of the elements, most children find this complicated and are likely to need the more direct task of entering the symbol for each element under the appropriate rank. Similarly, though an adult subject will easily understand rank orders as expressed by numbers, for a child, the words 'most', 'then' or 'next', and 'least' or 'most' (opposite pole) are more readily comprehended. These modifications do, of course, need to be incorporated in the separate pages or booklets that the child will use.

The modifications needed for fitting the rating procedure to child subjects are essentially the same as those already described. Ratings can easily be shown in terms of spatial groupings which should ideally be identified by cards showing where each rating category belongs. Again, it is possible to record ratings by the method of entering the symbol for each element on a visual representation of the construct, in the form of large squares for each rating category.

From this account of some of the ways in which the sorting task entailed in grid procedure can be adapted to fit the needs of children, it will be obvious that this assessment technique is unusually flexible and can usually, therefore, unlike most measuring procedures, be presented in a form which is tailored to the age and personal needs of the subject.

Analysis and interpretation

On the question of the ways in which grids completed by children should be analysed, nothing specific needs to be said, since the same principles obtain here as operate for grids done by adults. It is in the construction of grids, rather than in the methods for analysing them, that special modifications are likely to be needed. Apart from the methods mentioned elsewhere in this book the reader may consult methods proposed by Bannister and Mair (1968). In theory, every kind of analysis, ranging from simple inspection of the allocation of the elements on a particular construct to complete principal component analysis, is possible in obtaining information from the grids of children. So far, however, most of the psychologists who have used grids with child subjects have either looked, in their analysis, at specific relationships between individual pairs of constructs or have employed relatively simple measures of the overall pattern, such as McWhitty's Cluster Analysis, or Hierarchical Linkage Analysis.

Although the childishness of the subject seems to have no particular implications for the ways in which grids should be analysed, it does make some difference to the kinds of interpretation that are likely to be appropriate and legitimate. Here, an attempt will be made to suggest certain general principles implicit in the theory underlying grids. Comments, in terms of these principles, will be made on studies that have used repertory grid technique with children.

It was argued earlier in this chapter that grid technique is better suited, on both practical and theoretical grounds, to certain kinds of research investigation than to others. Within the limits of its applicability, some particular interpretative themes seem likely to recur where child subjects are involved. At the risk of oversimplifying the purposes to which the technique has been and will be put, these themes can perhaps be categorized under four general headings. The first has to do with the content of the children's construct system and, in particular, with the ways in which dimensions of meaning change as the child grows older. Here, repertory grid technique appears uniquely useful, in so far as individually differing contents, derived from different children, can nevertheless be compared in terms of some kind of content analysis. Several investigators have applied themselves to this kind of question, and their work will presently be discussed in relation to the kinds of content analysis which seem appropriate to the general principles underlying grid technique. The second general type of interpretative question which is likely to arise from grid studies of children is one of cognitive skill or efficiency, as translated into grid indices. Structural rather than content measures will probably represent the focus of this sort of study. As yet, few psychologists have been concerned with this theme, but the work of Wooster makes a large contribution to it. Thirdly, many studies are likely to be designed so as to enable some interpretation to be made of how the child's environment, particularly his interpersonal environment, affects his construction of himself. Several investigators have tried to answer this kind of question, which is, of course, fraught with the methodological problems associated with measuring self-construction noted above, as well as certain theoretical problems relating to the construing process. Finally, grid studies with children lend themselves to the exploration of mutual and shared construing, in dyadic and other relationships, in which the kinds of interpretation made are likely to be in terms of mutual influence. Relevant though such questions are to Kelly's commonality and sociality corrolaries, very little work has as yet been done in this area. However, an attempt will be made to suggest how this kind of question might be approached and the kinds of interpretation which might be made.

Interpretation of content

Before discussing ways in which grid data might be interpreted to yield information about the content and changes in content in children's construing, existing work, together with the kinds of content analysis it has used, will be outlined. The three studies relevant here have been broadly similar, in that all three focused upon children's constructions of people and all three made interpretations about a broad shift with age, in terms of the kinds of dimensions used by children.

In a study published in 1967, Brierley categorized the elicited constructs of seven-, ten- and thirteen-year-old children into physicalistic/appearance, social role and personality trait constructs. Analysing her data in terms of sex and age, she found that both variables contributed to the variance in her construct categories. Girls were more inclined to use personality trait constructs than boys, but over and above this difference there was a clear progression for both sexes as they got older away from constructs referring to physical appearance and social role, and towards constructs concerned with personality.

Little, in a series of studies, has looked at roughly similar kinds of change with a slightly different age group. In one investigation (Little, 1967), the elicited constructs of children aged from ten to eighteen years were categorized under three headings — similar, though not identical, to Brierley's. Like Brierley, Little found significant effects of both age and sex in changes in the types of construct elicited. Both sexes used predominantly physicalistic constructs in early adolescence, whereas in later adolescence role and psychological constructs predominated. In contrast to Brierley's findings, however, age did not produce significant progression towards purely psychological construsing; the number of psychological constructs, but not their overall proportion, increased with age. With regard to the effects of sex, Little found girls to be not more but less 'psychologically' minded than boys, in so far as, at the pre-adolescent stage, they were more inclined than boys to use physicalistic constructs. In two further studies, Little reports partial confirmation of these findings (Little and Payne, 1968; Little and Tomlinson, 1968).

The third study of this type is one by Allison (1972). Allison gave a form of grid to a small sample of children aged between four and thirteen years. Constructs were classified under four headings: behavioural, appearance, role and psychological. Allison analysed his results by age, sex and type of element being construed, and found all three variables to exert a significant effect. Thus, for boys, appearance constructs were found to predominate at all ages, though not to the same extent for all age groups. This type of construct varied according to the type of element (teachers, family or friends), as did behavioural and psychological constructs, though not role constructs. With regard to the effect of age on use of psychological constructs — the question considered by both Brierley and Little — Allison found a general increase, but this was not, as just noted, independent of the type of element involved. For girls, unlike boys, no single type of construct was found to predominate at all ages. In contrast to the trend for boys, the use of psychological constructs by girls was found to rise and then fall with age. As with boys, interactions were found between age, type of construct and type of element.

The complicated results of the three studies outlined here do not enable any clear trends to be discerned in the ways in which children's constructions about people change with age. The contradictions within these findings, however, may be in part a function of the different categorization systems used by the three investigators. It seems worth examining some of these differences and considering whether an alternative approach to classification might be appropriate.

One difference in the mode of classifying constructs involved in these studies will be mentioned only in passing, since it involves a point which has already been made about the range of convenience which particular elements may present. In the three studies described, only Allison took the precaution of examining the type of construct in terms of the type of element from which it was elicited. In view of the differences which may be entailed for children in construing different sorts of person, this distinction seems a sensible one. The discrepancy between Allison's findings and some of those obtained by the other two investigators may partly be due to the fact that his construct categorization had this distinction built into it, whereas neither of theirs did so.

A different issue concerns the content of any categorization of constructs about persons. Despite their superficial similarity, all three classification systems involved in these studies are clearly different, and particular dimensions would certainly have been differently categorized by the three investigators. For example, Little's system divides up constructs referring to interest into either role or psychological categories, according to the degree of specificity. Allison includes, under the heading of appearance, constructs referring to location of residence and having children — dimensions which would be classified as physicalistic or role by the other two systems. To the writer, it seems likely that such confusions arise from the attempt to utilize an *a priori* system of any kind which, on the one hand, draws a broad distinction between physicalistic and psychological constructs about people and, on the other, rests on semantic analysis alone. These two points will be considered in turn.

The first point is that of the general progression, as a basis for categorization, from constructs referring to the physical properties of persons, at one end, to constructs referring to their psychological characteristics, at the other, with intermediate dimensions referring to social role or status. Persuasive though this idea may seem, it must be asked whether this is necessarily the most meaningful or developmentally useful view. Its validity rests on the assumption that the three broad kinds of construct embodied in the categorization represent a progression from simple to complex. Such a progression has yet to be demonstrated, and it is likely that the situation is really rather more complicated. For example, references to the physical properties of persons may contain implicit constructions about ways of behaving. In discussing adults' use of stereotyping, Willig (personal communication, 1973) makes the point that physical constructs may serve to bring into focus associated personality constructs. Whether some of the 'physicalistic' constructs obtained within the studies considered here had psychological implications buried in them cannot be known, although this is one of the things which might have emerged from a different sort of analysis, as will be discussed presently. But certainly some of the constructs classified as psychological in these studies, such as 'nasty', were probably less complex than the kind of observation which an adult may make (usually in a significant tone) that an acquaintance drives a red sports car or that another went to Eton. A priori, a reference to physical characteristics cannot be said to be conceptually simpler than an explicit reference to psychological characteristics.

A possibly more fruitful analysis of development within the area of person-construing would be in terms of a progression in the level of inferentiality. A number of studies have suggested that there is a progression, in the constructs which children use about people, towards increasingly refined and abstract dimensions. In one such study, for instance, Watts (1944) analysed the adjectives provided by children between seven and eleven years on a sentence completion task, and found that relatively crude and global distinctions, such as 'nice', gradually gave way to subtle and refined ones, such as 'sympathetic'. This illustrates the fact that even very young children make evaluative distinctions between people; as Watts puts it, a young child divides up the world of persons into those he likes and those he doesn't like, and only later starts to use more complicated dimensions. Rather than viewing developing interpersonal construing as the gradual acquisition of psychological constructs, it seems more appropriate to assume that even young children have such constructs and that development represents an increase in their complexity.

In all three studies discussed here, the method of analysis rested entirely upon a classification of the verbal labels provided by the child. Where no attempt is made to assess meanings in terms of interrelationships between dimensions, analysis being purely semantic, the validity of the resulting classification must rest entirely on the accuracy of the investigator's guess as to what the child meant by a particular verbal label. The difficulties of making such inferences, where adults are concerned, are notorious; and they seem likely to be increased by the fact that the subject is a child who has probably not fully mastered adult vocabulary. This problem is also liable to emerge where the subjects involved come from different backgrounds from each other and from a different background to that of the investigator. The verbal repertoire which is common currency in a child's home may sound simple or crude to a psychologist, but may in fact embody a rich network of distinctions about the ways in which people behave and feel, on the part of the child. The opposite kind of situation is equally likely. For these reasons, it is surely unsafe for an investigator to rely, for his understanding of a child's construction, on the meaning which particular words have for him.

The limiting of the analysis of the meanings of constructs to the verbal labels alone is, in fact, particularly inappropriate and unnecessary where repertory grid technique is involved. The kind of information which grids are designed to yield represents meaning as defined by the relationships between categorizations, rather than any meaning conveyed directly by those categorizations. It is essentially in terms of the association, in usage, of the subject's dimensions of meaning that the grid offers its particular kind of understanding. In the studies described here, no recourse was had to any analysis of construct interrelationships for a justification of the ways in which particular constructs were classified; it is possible that different allocations of constructs might have been made if this had been done and also possible that different kinds of classifying system might have emerged as more appropriate. If a categorization system based on complexity, or level of inferentiality, rather than physicalistic—psychological content were to be used, as suggested here, this could certainly not be derived from a simple inspection of verbal labels. Some kind of analysis of structure, revealing underlying components of meaning, would be needed, and ideally this should be supplemented by an implication grid of some sort, in order to establish relative superordinacy. As this chapter is concerned with straightforward grid technique only, such forms are beyond its scope; the reader is referred to Bannister and Mair (1968).

One final point concerns the degree to which it is appropriate, within the context of the theoretical assumptions underlying grid technique, to try to define a universal pattern of ontogenetic change in interpersonal construing — or, for that matter, any other area of construing. Kelly's individuality corollary expresses the notion of individual uniqueness on construction systems, and just as content will differ from one person to another, so the directions of changes in construing, over time, are likely to be different across different children. While it may be that certain overall trends, in terms, for example, of increased complexity, may be generally characteristic of developing construing systems, the detailed changes are likely to relate to the particular personal influences on construing which the child meets — notably the construction systems of those he meets. From this point of view, one would not expect to be able to demonstrate any precise progression of change in modes of construing which would characterize all children everywhere, a fact which further argues against the desirability of a construct-classifying system based on specific content, rather than broadly structural features. One of the investigators discussed here does, in fact, himself stress the individually variable patterns among his subjects, and his remarks seem highly pertinent here (Allison, 1972, p. 6):

It is obvious that at some point in the future some shrewd statistical analysis will be necessary to reduce these data to general trends. On the other hand, the data are encouraging in that they seem to present a complex picture of what is, presumably, a most complex phenomenon. It would have been rather alarming had we found there to be just one or two simple patterns, since this is certainly not the case with adult construing. Possibly one needs to extract 'types' of construers on some structural basis, or content analysis, and then to follow these through in a longitudinal study.

Interpretations about cognitive efficiency

Although most people who have used grids with children have not been concerned with questions about the general efficiency, from an adult's point of view, of the child's construing, such questions do seem to lend themselves to analysis within the terms of this assessment technique. In theory, this applies as much to the area of interpersonal construing as to the construction of the physical world. The paradigm can be adopted of requiring a child to predict the constructs of another person, or their actual usage, as in the 'insight' investigations sometimes used with adult subjects (e.g. Adams-Webber, 1969). In practice, however, this kind of investigation is likely to be carried out within the context of a general study of the child's personal relationships, rather than arising from an intrinsic interest in his mastery of the 'right' way of seeing things. Therefore, though recognizing that the distinction is not an absolute one but a matter of convenience, only studies of construction of the physical world, rather than those concerned with construing the world of persons, will be considered here.

A further difference between the areas of construction relating to the world of people and that of objects is that there is a much higher degree of agreement between people generally as to the right way to construe the latter. This means that it makes more sense to ask the question of how far a child has mastered the construction of the field used by the adults around him, in the case of the physical world, than in that of the idiosyncratically understood world of people's behaviour. When it comes to assessing such mastery by a particular child, or group of children, several approaches are possible, depending on the complexity of the criterion chosen. The simplest kind of criterion involves comparison with an adult consensus of the child's allocation of objects in terms of some dimension. At one level up from this, particular correlations between dimensions, resulting from a child's allocations on these dimensions, can be compared with those resulting from the adults in the consensus group. Finally, the total structure of a child's usage of dimensions can be compared with that of the criterion group. Of these approaches, only the first two have apparently been used so far, and for many investigatory purposes these seem likely to be sufficient. In both cases, the work involved is that of Wooster, who has been concerned in his studies to explore the relation between the child's grasp of socially agreed constructs about the physical world, and age and IQ variables. Again, it seems appropriate here to give a brief account of his work.

In the study which has already been outlined to illustrate a methodological approach, Wooster (1968) asked five-year-old children to rank-order eight plastic tubes on ten constructs referring to quantitative dimensions of objects. As already mentioned, these constructs were unipolar, and the ten included five pairs of opposites. They consisted of the following: biggest, shortest, highest, smallest, tallest, largest, lightest, longest, littlest, heaviest. The criterion used here was the first one mentioned above; Wooster used rank-order correlations to compare each child's orderings, on each construct in turn, with the way he himself ranked them. Taking as his criterion a 5 per cent level of significance for the intercorrelations thus obtained, Wooster found that most of his subjects used most of the ten quantitative terms correctly. They were not, for example, distracted from relevant aspects of the elements by the different colours of these. Some dimensions in particular were well understood by a very high proportion of the children. 'Biggest', 'littlest', 'highest', 'longest' and 'smallest' were correctly understood by over 90 per cent of the sample.

Within the context of a generally adult-like construction of quantitative aspects, it is perhaps the deviations which also occur that are most interesting psychologically; and here, Wooster's work makes a further contribution. In the study just outlined, three constructs were found to be used by the children in ways that were rather different from the criterion. These were 'tallest', 'largest' and 'lightest', the last construct being understood correctly by fewer than 40 per cent of the subjects. Further analysis showed that several children failed to appreciate the opposition of the concepts 'biggest' and 'smallest'. In a later study (Wooster, 1970), findings revealed that many children confuse dimensions of length and height.

The overall implications of Wooster's findings seem to be that, even by the early age of five years, most children have acquired a good grasp of the quantitative and relational terms which adults use to make sense of the physical world. Where young children seem to diverge from conventional adult understanding, this is likely to be due to their failure to master the implicit opposite of certain dimensions – presumably having their own idiosyncratic opposite pole, though Wooster's work does not help us to know what sort of pole this is. These findings also suggest that dimensions of both size and weight present certain difficulties to young children. Overall size may be equated with vertical size: a finding which has a direct bearing, it seems, on Piaget's conservation experiments. Some young children may be able to differentiate between height and length when the stimulus material offers variations in both dimensions, but may confuse the two where it does not. This seems to imply that quantitative constructs go through a stage where they need to be illustrated in the external world before they can be correctly used by the child.

Apart from the criticism, which already has been expressed, that Wooster fails to provide opposite poles for the constructs which he provides for his subjects, not to elicit from them the opposite poles which, in fact, they use in his testing situations, the sort of approach embodied in these experiments seems to serve as a model for the investigation of this kind of question via grid technique. There are, of course, many ways in which such work could be extended, some of which can be suggested here. The context within which this general kind of question is likely to be meaningful is that of education. To some extent, this can be defined as the enabling of children to acquire consensually agreed meanings. However, the level of abstraction which is involved in this shared content becomes progressively higher as the child progresses through school. At first, it is likely to involve the child mastering a set of linguistic or mathematical symbols; here, grid measurement of the type used by Wooster enabling direct comparison of element allocation with a criterion allocation, will be sufficient. Later on, the child is expected to grasp more abstract content, as, for example, when he is taught the principles of literary criticism so that he can go on to apply these himself to a piece of writing. Granted that in areas such as this considerably more individual variation in approach is allowed to those involved in studying them, even these subjects have a substantial body of consensually agreed interpretation — else public examinations would be impossible! In devising grid measures to assess mastery of areas like these, a more sophisticated assessment is needed than in areas where a lower level of abstraction is involved. It is here that measures of overall structure, derived from principal component analysis, for example, would be relevant.

The difficulties which are likely to arise for those investigators who are interested in exploring cognitive mastery from this point of view relate to obtaining criteria of socially agreed meanings. The higher the level of abstraction involved, the greater the difficulty is likely to be. At the lowest level, such as the level investigated by Wooster, the psychologist's own judgement can usually be taken as the criterion. However, as the abstraction level rises and there is more leeway for individual judgement, care must be taken to ensure that the criterion is representative and that it avoids elements where there is insufficient interjudge agreement. It is possible to overcome this difficulty where the index to be used is one of element allocation by calculating Kendall's coefficient of concordance on the ranks, or ratings, of a representative group of 'judges'. Elements where there is insufficient agreement, according to this index, can then be discarded and others tried until a sufficient number of well-agreed items remain. This technique can also be used to discard dimensions on which there is too little consensus. The most difficult problems are likely to be presented by criteria which rest on the degree of agreement between the subject and the criterion group, in terms of construct interrelationships or total structure. Here, some technique of analysis is needed, such as Slater's DELTA program, which enables the comparison across grids of measures of relationship.

Finally, it might be useful to extend the study of children's thinking, in terms of grid measures, to the wider areas of intelligence and educatability. Although the concepts of IQ and educational aptitude are of a very different order to those involved in construct theory, it may be that the areas to which they refer could be better understood in terms of grid-type measures. It can be argued that the ability to do intelligence tests and to understand orthodox educational procedures depends on having a network of constructs, within the particular areas involved, with the same verbal labels, the same sorts of interrelationship and the same order of superordinacy as those held by the people who use them to devise such procedures. This means that a certain degree of commonality, of both structure and content, needs to obtain between those who devise tests or administer educational procedures and those who are the subjects of the tests and procedures. What this, in turn, suggests is that it might be more fruitful, in the long run, to investigate the content of a particular child's construction of an educationally relevant area than to put him through the mill of intelligence, aptitude and attainment tests. The argument for such an approach lies not only in the more thorough investigation of the child's view of the area concerned but also in its potential for revealing existing relationships, so that an educational approach can build upon the child's logic.

Influences on the child's self-construction

The question of how the child's environment affects the way that he conceptualizes himself is a very broad one, which could clearly be approached in many different ways. The investigators who have been concerned so far with this general issue have all adopted rather different orientations. Before discussing the sorts of problem which might arise in making interpretations about grid data designed to shed light on this area, it seems appropriate to give a brief account of some investigations which have explored it.

If the conditions of children's lives are atypical in some way, this might be expected to affect the ways that they see themselves. Such an argument underlies two studies carried out by Wooster. In one study (Wooster, 1970a), he was concerned with the effect of personal limitations imposed by low intelligence. Wooster found, as hypothesized, a significant difference between ESN boys and boys of normal intelligence, the latter having more stable and more highly related self-constructs. Commenting on this finding, he suggests that the lack of clear conceptual categories for understanding himself is likely to impair the child's social capacity, since he lacks the fine distinctions needed in many interpersonal situations. In a further study done with Harris (Wooster and Harris, 1972), Wooster examined the effects on the self-conceptualizations of children of high geographical mobility. As predicted, highly mobile boys had much poorer self-definition than geographically stable boys. Wooster and Harris suggest that this conceptual impairment is likely to be due to the way of life which high geographical mobility entails. In other words, the child may be left 'bewildered and unable to cope with the task of making judgements about himself or others. His sources of information are too many and too often changed, and because of this he may fail to develop skill in self-assessment'.

A different approach to the influences on the child's developing construction of himself is in terms of the effects of significant others. The interested reader is referred here to the writer's exploration of group-orientation in pre-adolescent boys (Salmon, 1967), or to part of this, separately published (Salmon, 1969).

The third sort of approach which has been adopted so far to the general question of influences on the way children construe themselves is that of the individual case study. The pioneer of this approach has been Ravenette. In a series of unpublished papers, Ravenette has illustrated the use of repertory grid technique in the exploration of the outlooks of children referred to a child guidance clinic. It is clearly not possible here to summarize findings from this series of individual case studies, but it seems fair to say that Ravenette's examples provide a convincing demonstration of the usefulness of this technique in elucidating themes in the way an individual child sees himself in relation to others and to his life situation.

Some of the problems relating to the assessment of grids of children's self-constructions have already been mentioned and need not be repeated here. Discussion can therefore be restricted to questions about the general choice of grid material and the kinds of interpretations of process which are likely to be appropriate. An important point for all studies of self-construing in children concerns the decision whether to supply constructs or to elicit them from the child. As in all studies which involve more than one child, it is often convenient to have at least some supplied constructs, in order to enable comparison of content. Yet where the area to be explored is as central and as personal as the child's own private view of himself, the exclusive prescribing of the dimensions of meaning to be used is perhaps minimally justified. While the writer's own study, described above, certainly merits the criticism that no such safeguard was included in it, this point perhaps applies still more to studies like those of Wooster. Where the concern is with structure rather than with content, there seems to be no good reason for supplying dimensions rather than obtaining them from the subjects. Thus, the impaired clarity and lack of definition found by Wooster in his intellectually deficient and socially deprived groups of children could presumably have been demonstrated as clearly where the content of self-construing was individually different across his subjects. Additionally, since it has been shown in a number of studies that the network of construct relationships is stronger in personally selected than in prescribed dimensions, there is an obligation for those investigators interested in degree of structure to give this the best possible chance of emerging. When it comes to individual case studies, this stricture has less force, since a knowledge of the people and circumstances in a particular child's life enables the constructs to be individually tailored to him; even so, the eliciting of his own constructions as well seems wise, since no psychologist can be sure that he has rightly inferred all the crucial meanings for a child merely from a consideration of his circumstances.

Finally, it is in studies concerned with how children conceptualize themselves that considerations of the construing process, as envisaged by Kelly, should be paramount. The ideal paradigm for such studies is one that enables examinations of the ways in which successive events alter the construction of self, rather than the usual design in terms of 'individual differences'. If grid studies are to enlarge our understanding of *how* children come to see themselves in certain terms, they should involve the possibility of examining changes in self-construction in relation to ongoing events. This means that more than the demonstration of group differences is required. Findings that certain environmental conditions or personal character-istics are associated with particular ways of construing the self in children do not show how the effects occurred, though they may suggest this. What is needed is a design which enables the detailed tracing through of events in a child's life and the concomitant changes in the way in which he views himself. Of all test situations, the individual case study seems to offer the best possibility for such work. The psychologist himself is frequently also the child's therapist, and therefore is in an unusually good position to know the kinds of salient event that the child is experiencing. Even if his role is purely advisory, he is likely to be able to keep in touch with such events through the psychiatrist and PSW concerned with the child and his family. From this point of view, it seems a pity that Ravenette, in his studies of individual CGC cases, has restricted his exploration to the 'presenting problems', rather than following up the child's changing view in relation to the events he meets in his life. Ultimately, the understanding of the child's changing construction of himself, however, is likely to rest on the analysis of the influence of his construing of other construct systems, and it is with this area that the final section of this chapter is concerned.

Mutual and shared aspects of construing

On this final area in which repertory grid technique might be brought to bear, very little, if any, work seems as yet to have been done. Discussion must therefore be limited to considering the possible fruitfulness of such an approach, together with the kind of grid instrument which might be devised for it.

It was argued in the previous section that the assessment of the influence of other people in the child's life must eventually lead to the assessment of their own construct systems. To some extent, the measuring of other systems against which to compare the child's construing was entailed in some of the ways, already discussed, in which the child's mastery of educationally relevant content might be measured. There, however, the direction of influence is typically one-way, since education is directed towards enabling the child to acquire publicly agreed networks of meaning. In other contexts, the exchanges of meaning and the direction of influence are mutual; the child's construction of events affects and alters the construing of other people. This is particularly likely to be the case in the child's relationships with peers and siblings, and, of course, in his prolonged and intimate relationship with parents, particularly his mother. In all these relationships, both individuals must have some understanding of the other's subjective world, however rudimentary, in order for the relationship to function. Since a child's construing is likely to change rapidly and extensively as he encounters new events, this imposes the need for changes in the other person's construing of him, in order to accommodate the new constructions upon which he is going to act. The view of interpersonal relationships as based on each person's construction of the other's constructions is the one put forward by Kelly in his sociality corollary, just as the view of certain themes being shared in the construct systems of those involved in relationships is expressed by his commonality corollary.

If the approach indicated here is in line with the theoretical system on which repertory grid technique is based, the technique itself is uniquely well suited to its assessment. Within the context of the close personal relationships of a child, the dimensions of meaning are likely to be both individually different and constantly changing. A measuring instrument which, like the grid, can incorporate new axes of reference as the need for them arises is therefore ideal. This may perhaps become clearer if the general ways in which grids might be adapted to assessing a particular relationship — between a child and his mother — are roughly sketched out.

The exploration of any mother–child relationship would entail devising grid measures which incorporated salient events and situations for the dyad. The focus would be upon each member's self-construction, his construction of the other, and his construction of the other's construction of himself and other people and situations. Such measures would be repeated over time to enable the assessment of mutual influence and change. It is likely that these measures could not be given to children until they were well past babyhood, for practical reasons, but the mother's changing construing of her child and of herself in relation to him would lend itself to this sort of assessment from the earliest stages of relationship. Once the child became able to be assessed in this way, much information could be derived from a comparison of his own and his mother's grids. Thus, it would be possible to assess, not only how each person saw himself and the other, and how well he understood the other, but also how far each was assuming unwarranted similarity or dissimilarity. Obviously, increasingly complex grid measures could be used as the child grew older and as familiarity with the procedures became greater.

Although this sort of study has not yet been done, it is possible to outline one form of grid which would meet the requirements of part of this approach to exploration. As part of the study by the writer of the group-orientation of junior school boys (Salmon, 1967) measures were designed to assess the children's level of understanding of the evaluative positions of adults, on the one hand, and peers, on the other. These grids, which seemed to work well as measures of insight, could be easily adapted to apply to the assessment of the degree to which a child understood specified aspects of his mother's construing, and, similarly, to assess how far she understood aspects of his.

The first grid was aimed at measuring how far each boy understood the evaluative attitudes of teachers. It was therefore initially given to a criterion group of teachers, to establish agreed evaluations and to exclude items where insufficient agreement obtained. It was then given to the boys themselves, to assess their accuracy in guessing at teacher's evaluations. The elements used in its final form were of behaviours in which boys aged eight might engage; they included 'having a dirty neck', 'telling a lie to help out another boy' and 'bullying smaller boys'. The construct the criterion group of teachers was asked to use, to rank-order the elements, was the degree of personal disapproval which they would feel towards such behaviours. The construct on which the boys were asked to rank the elements was 'things most teachers think are bad/things most teachers don't think are so bad'. The measure of insight simply consisted of the correlation between each boy's rank order and the criterion, group, ranking. A similar grid was used to assess the boy's understanding of their peers' evaluative preferences.

Since the purpose of describing these grids is to suggest methods of assessing some aspects of the mother—child relationship, rather than to give the details of the study in which they were used, all that need be said here is that the measures of insight derived from them were found to be significantly associated with measures of adult or peer group-orientation, as predicted. It is also worth commenting on their status in general intellectual terms, since it might be thought that this kind of understanding is simply an aspect of general intellectual competence. That this is not the case is supported by the findings that the two kinds of insight were not significantly related to each other, and neither was significantly related to intelligence. It seems, therefore, that measures derived from this kind of methodology do relate to the quality of the child's relationship with members of the group concerned. From this point of view, the approach seems promising for the assessment of mutual understanding in relationships between mothers and their children. While the writer intends to explore such a usage of the technique in this context, it must, however, be said again that its usefulness as yet remains conjectural rather than proven.

References

Adams-Webber, J. (1969). 'Cognitive complexity and sociality'. *Brit. J. Soc. Clin. Psychol.*, **8**, 211—216.

Allison, B. (1972). *The Development of Personal Construct Systems — A Preliminary Study*. Unpublished Manuscript, Memorial University, St. John's, Newfoundland, Canada.

Bannister, D., and Mair, J. M. M. (1968). *The Evaluation of Personal Constructs*, Academic Press, London.

Brierley D. W. (1967). *The Use of Personality Constructs by Children of Three Different Ages*. Unpublished Ph.D. Thesis, University of London.

Little, B. R. (1967). *Age and Sex Differences in the Use of Psychological, Role and Physicalistic Constructs*. Unpublished Manuscript, Oxford University.

Little, B. R., and Payne, K. A. (1968). *Paternal Person—Thing Orientation as a*

Factor Affecting Children's Construct Usage. Unpublished Manuscript, Oxford University.

Little, B. R., and Tomlinson, P. (1968). *The Content and Complexity of Constructs Elicited by Primary School Children.* Unpublished Manuscript, Oxford University.

Ravenette, A. T. (1964). *Some Attempts at Developing the Use of the Repertory Grid in a Child Guidance Clinic.* Address to Symposium convened by N. Warren, Brunel College. London Borough of Newham.

Ravenette, A. T. (1968). *The Situations Grid: A Further Development in Grid Technique with Children.* Unpublished Manuscript, London Borough of Newham.

Salmon, P. (1967). *The Social Values and Conformity Behaviour of Primary Schoolboys, in Relation to Maternal Attitude.* Unpublished Ph.D. Thesis, University of London.

Salmon, P. (1969). 'Differential conforming as a developmental process'. *Brit. J. soc. clin. Psychol.,* 8, 22—31.

Watts, A. F. (1944). *The Language and Mental Development of Children,* D. C. Heath, Boston.

Wooster, A. D. (1968). 'Testing the ability to respond to verbal instructions'. *Brit. J. Disorders of Communication,* 3(2), 156—160.

Wooster, A. D. (1970a). 'Formation of stable and discrete concepts of personality by normal and mentally retarded boys'. *J. ment. Subnormality,* 16(1), 24—28.

Wooster, A. D. (1970b). 'The pragmatic meaning of relational terms'. *Primary Mathematics,* 8(3), 137—145.

Wooster, A. D., and Harris, G. (1972). 'Concepts of self and others in highly mobile service boys'. *Educational Research,* 12, 46—52.

3

USING GRID TECHNIQUE WITH THE MENTALLY HANDICAPPED

Elizabeth Spindler Barton, Terry Walton, Dorothy Rowe

Summary

Many of the patients in hospitals for the mentally retarded are there because they also suffer from social disabilities or personality disorders, or present behaviour problems. But most methods of assessing personality traits are not suitable for patients who are mentally retarded. The possibility of using grid technique is examined.

It is found that adolescents or adults with an IQ of 50 or over can usually be persuaded to complete a grid, given a little ingenuity and coaxing. For example, if the patient cannot read, the psychologist needs to be inventive in his display of the elements. Advice is given on eliciting and supplying constructs and elements, and on using ranking or grading. The kinds of construct commonly used are described. Results from patients' grids are compared with other aspects of their behaviour in a series of short case studies. Grid technique is found to have advantages over most of the commonly used methods of personality assessment for patients who are mentally retarded. They accept it readily. It requires little or no literacy or sustained concentration, it avoids using unintelligible or inappropriate terms, and it provides reliable and valid pictures of their construct systems. At a time when the policy is to discharge patients if possible, it can be adapted to provide relevant information for planning programmes to train them for discharge. (P.S.)

Introduction

Mental handicap is usually accepted as an itelligence quotient (IQ) of below 80—85 on a standard test and the range of subnormality is divided in terms of standard deviations (s.d.) below normal. Assuming a standard deviation of 15, this results in the following classification:

IQ	70—85	minus 1 s.d.	borderline intelligence
IQ	55—69	minus 2 s.d.	mild retardation
IQ	40—54	minus 3 s.d.	moderate retardation
IQ	25—39	minus 4 s.d.	severe retardation
IQ	below 25	minus 5 s.d.	profound retardation

While the trend is to keep in hospital patients of the severe and profoundly retarded categories, there are still many in-patients who are moderately, mildly or even borderline retarded. Amongst the mild and borderline groups, hospitalization commonly results from social disability, personality disorder or behaviour problems. Many such problems arise from the subnormal's misjudgement and inability to appreciate relative values (Gunzberg, 1970) and (over the profound level of retardation) IQ alone is not a particularly good predictor of adjustment — either in or out of hospital. It is with patients whose hospitalization is not the result of mental handicap alone that personality assessment techniques could be of considerable use. Many 'personality tests' have been attempted with retarded patients. Both the Rorschach and the Thematic Apperception Test (TAT) have been quite extensively used; Sarason (1949) in his book on the psychological problems of mental deficiency devotes a chapter to projective techniques (although in many early studies, the Rorschach was used to assess intelligence or brain damage rather than personality). Rorschach (1942) himself suggested that inkblots would 'be of value in depicting the influence of the patient's emotional life in inhibiting or expediting intellectual functions, and in demonstrating inherent but perhaps unrealized capacities in the personality of the subject'. Sarason and Sarason (1946) are rather more circumspect in their evaluation; differences in extreme groups of behavioural pattern were associated with different Rorschach responses and the number of human movement or whole reponses was not highly correlated with intelligence, but the number of 'minus or poor forms' was correlated (negatively). Any difficulties associated with the application of the Rorschach to subjects of normal intelligence also, of course, apply with the mentally handicapped. Further, much of the earlier work on projective techniques in subnormality hospitals may well have been carried out on quite a different population from that found today, as the average IQ of patients in hospitals for the subnormal is becoming progressively lower.

Sternlicht and Silverg (1965), using mildly retarded patients, obtained TAT stories which were merely short lists of objects in the pictures. Their experience must be a common one with those who have attempted the TAT with subnormals. Masserman and Balken first attempted to use the TAT with the subnormal in 1938 and concluded that the stories obtained showed 'a characteristic naivety of material and dearth of imagery'. Most who have used the TAT with the subnormal have had similar results, although it can sometimes yield interesting material.

Intelligence tests

There have also been attempts to assess the subnormal personality using various draw-a-man type techniques, but these have largely been found to lack validity. The possibility of assessing personality from the results of different intellectual sub-tests (on, for example, the WAIS or WISC), as is sometimes done with those of normal intelligence, is considerably diminished, if not reduced to zero, by the sub-test scatter produced by the intellectual deficiency alone.

Questionnaires

Pencil-and-paper type tests are, as a rule, beyond the capability and/or motivation of the handicapped person; moreover, normal intelligence is usually presumed by the test authors. An exception is the Eysenck—Withers EPI for the IQ range 50—80.

The present authors have, however, found this to be of limited value and difficult to administer, except with those who are fairly sophisticated verbally and are literate. Many patients cannot cope with this kind of test format or even understand the questions, which are often inapplicable; also, many patients are unused to introspective thinking about their feelings or their behaviour.

Many difficulties have been reported on the use of paper-and-pencil type questionnaires with the subnormal, among these being illiteracy, distractibility, poor verbal comprehension and concrete responding (Burg and Barrett, 1965; Gallagher, 1959).

Learning theory approaches

Hogg (1971) queries whether tests suitable in form for normals can be justifiably used with the subnormal and goes on to suggest techniques carried out should yield information relevant to remediation. This view is also held by Gardner (1971), who feels strongly that many tests and procedures are quite inappropriate both to the subject and to any decision regarding misbehaviour that might be made. Furthermore, many evaluation procedures have insufficient predictive validity when used with the subnormal and have questionable value as a result of the subnormal's limited language skills and limitations in self-perception. The mentally hadicapped have a limited ability to report their own or another's feelings and this can create considerable problems in such tests as the TAT. Gardner also describes faulty assumptions about test data generally, inappropriate statistics and little relationship between the data and the decision required.

It is suggested that one way of avoiding some of the difficulties outlined by Gardner is by a learning theory approach to personality assessment. Hogg (1971) discusses the possibilities in some detail while warning that such an approach can only be 'as adequate as the theoretical acceptability of operations through which learning and performance can be assessed in the general field of learning studies', and feels that heed should be taken of the well-worked-out methodology of some of the learning experiments.

One of the most interesting of the learning theory approaches is that based on reward-seeking and punishment-avoiding attributes. Many studies have been carried out on individual differences (among those of normal intelligence) towards achievement, often using the TAT. In 1957, Atkinson suggested that individual differences in motivation could be related to whether people were mainly concerned with achieving success or with avoiding failure, and subsequent experiments suggested that people playing risk-games do show a preference for one mode of response.

McManis, Bell and Pike (1969) had similar findings with retarded people using various discrimination and bar-pressing tasks. They carried out a series of experiments to try to establish the reliability and validity of these constructs. Under reward and punishment conditions, they consistently found an orientation with regard to preference and persistence, but results on the accuracy of the subjects' performances were equivocal. McManis and Bell (1968) suggest their findings might well have implications for the work setting, insofar as greater persistence should be achieved if the reinforcement contingencies are matched to the subjects' reward-seeking or punishment-avoiding orientation. Looking at some of the above theories from a slightly wider angle, Hogg, Evans and Preddy (1971) constructed a questionnaire to assess inhibitory versus excitatory characteristics with particular reference to differences in the process of internal inhibition. These characteristics are particularly important insofar as learning is concerned, and a study was carried out relating the performance of retarded children in a generalization experiment to their assessment on this questionnaire. The assessment was related to the second factor extracted from an analysis of the questionnaire and was in terms of response inhibition, or 'behaviour characterized by restraint'; the first factor was one of stimulus inhibition, i.e. the 'inhibition of extraneous stimuli, an attention process'. Hogg, Evans and Preddy found the questionnaire results were able to reliably differentiate the children's performances on the learning task and they concluded that, while theoretical problems are large, their findings have considerable practical significance. These results are of great importance to those involved in assessment of the handicapped, but one of the problems of using this technique routinely would appear to be the need for hardware.

Other techniques

Following counselling experience, Kirk (1953) deduced that the retarded often lose jobs not because of inability but as a result of problems of social adjustment or personality factors, and he felt that the individual needed to accept his own disability. Following this, Collins, Burger and Doherty (1970) hypothesized that mild or borderline retarded adolescents would have a more negative self-concept than normal adolescents, and they somehow managed to assess this using the Tennessee Self-concept Scale (100 self-report items yielding scores on fourteen scales, e.g. self-criticism, identity, self-satisfaction, and so on). They reported significant differences, in the expected direction, on the self-criticism, identity, social self and moral-ethical self scales but not on the self-satisfaction, behaviour, physical or personal self scales. The authors, however, do not report how they managed to carry out this test with their subnormal subjects.

It has been found that the Bene—Anthony Family Relations Test can sometimes be carried out by patients of quite low intelligence. The patients' problems, however, often lie outside the province of family relations and, in fact, many patients have never had a family or family life.

Repertory grid techniques

The Bannister—Fransella repertory grid technique for the assessment of thought disorder is inapplicable to the subnormal person. Bannister and Fransella (1966) give an IQ of 80 as being the lower limit for this test and, of course, the purpose of the technique is to assess a dysfunction unusual in the subnormal. The fact that the Bannister grid technique cannot be used with the mentally hadicapped does not, of course, exclude other grid techniques. Information from a construct analysis might be valuable in assessing patients with only mild degrees of retardation but with personality/behaviour problems. The future of patients who are not severely or profoundly retarded is determined largely by social skills and personality. Check lists (e.g. Gunzberg's Progress Assessment Chart for handicapped adults) provide a picture of social skills; the grid technique could do likewise for problems of personality, personal adjustment and stability. Intelligence and social quotients can be quite high, but personality problems may prevent a patient from functioning outside the hospital or even in certain hospital departments, and so examination of the patients' world in terms of their constructs and elements may prove a useful technique.

The aim of the work reported in this chapter was to examine the possibility of using the grid technique with the mentally handicapped. It was hoped to show that subnormals *do* develop construct systems, although often simple and sometimes unworkable, and to see if the grids could suggest the area where specific modification could be carried out. In summary, grid analysis could be of considerable value in trying to assess some of the difficulties of the mentally handicapped, particularly as the alternative methods (with the exception of the learning techniques which largely cover a different sort of problem and different sort of patient) have been shown to have considerable limitations, and many, if not most, are quite inapplicable.

The subjects

Repertory grids were obtained from twenty-four in-patients and two out-patients in a hospital of 700 beds for the subnormal. It would have been useful to grid more out-patients, but in this particular hospital an immediate report/conclusion was usually required for out-patients (emergency and court cases). The patients who were able to do a repertory grid were of both sexes and from both long-stay and acute wards. Most had been referred for personality disorders or behaviour problems, e.g. sexual misbehaviour, obsessionality, unpredictable aggression, instability, tense domestic situations, inability to perceive others' rights, and so on.

Age

The average age of the patients was twenty-nine years and the range from fifteen to fifty-five years. Whether a grid could be completed by a subnormal person of less than fifteen years is not known, as most if not all of our patients under the age of fifteen years fall into the severe and profound retardation categories and would by reason of lack of intelligence alone be unable to complete a grid. The upper age range could, however, be readily extended beyond fifty-five years, although patients of greater age were not usually referred because at this age less consideration is given to the possibilities of hostel placement or other change.

Intelligence

The IQs of the twenty-six patients ranged from 39 to 95 with a mean of 66 (measured on the Wechsler Adult Intelligence Scale in all but two cases, where the Stanford—Binet was used). As a general rule, an IQ of 50 may be taken as the lower limit at which a grid can be completed, unless a patient is verbally quite able and has lived in an environment encouraging verbal expression, in which case it might be worthwhile trying a grid on a patient of lower intelligence. With those whose IQ was 50+, given a little ingenuity and coaxing, it has not been found difficult to carry out repertory grid testing. The patient with an IQ of 39 (which was a reliable estimate) was rather exceptional in being able to describe his feelings. Although an IQ of 95 is not generally classed as subnormal by psychologists, there are in hospitals such patients who were long ago classified subnormal on grounds of social inadequacy.

Length of hospital stay

Length of hospital stay was not found to be a limiting factor in the use of the grid technique. Our patients varied from one who had never been in hospital to one who had been admitted twenty-five years previously at the age of six. The average length of hospital stay was seven years.

Reading age

A patient's inability to read was not a deciding factor as to whether the grid could be used, but rather it demanded that the psychologist be inventive in his display of elements. Reading age varied from zero to normal amongst the patients reported on in the study.

Social abilities

Social abilities (as measured on the Vineland Social Maturity Scale or similar check-lists) ranged from a social quotient of 45 to near normal, and these were usually similar to intelligence quotients. No particular social ability appeared to be linked to 'grid ability'.

In conclusion, therefore, if a patient has an IQ of 50 or more, regardless of his age, sex, reading ability or institutionalization, he should be able to cooperate with a repertory grid.

Method

Deciding when to do a grid

The decision to use the grid technique was made when it was thought it might clarify a personality or behaviour problem, or suggest a remedial treatment. In addition, grids were carried out to elucidate the construct system from which a patient was operating in the hope that more accurate predictions could be made about his behaviour either in a present or future situation. Some patients completed grids with overlapping elements which gave interesting insights into ward communities and also into the similarity between constructs held by long-term patients.

Eliciting constructs

The triad method of eliciting constructs (i.e. 'In what way does element C differ from A and B?') is of limited use to the retarded, who find this sort of thinking quite difficult, as exemplified by their common failure on similarities (WAIS) and on similarities and differences (Binet). It is better to elicit constructs by 'talking around' the elements during the first interview, noting down which constructs are used spontaneously and being careful not to reinterpret or suggest constructs. Mentally handicapped people may use a word or phrase they have often heard and have no idea of its meaning; it is therefore necessary to check whether they are using constructs without attaching any meaning to them (e.g. on a long-stay ward a number of patients will have been stereotyped by the staff, 'she's a clown' or 'he's as mean as muck', and some patients will pick up these expressions and use them themselves without any understanding, the phrase having become associated with a particular name). Also, the mentally hadicapped often use very concrete descriptions; for example, when asked about a friend they may report on appearance rather than personality (people of normal intelligence sometimes do this too, of course, as it requires less thought and is, in a way, safer). The handicapped often take the easy way out. Further, many do not even feel the need to answer at all, and they can be very expert at playing the role of the subnormal which may have served them very well in the past. Most retarded patients have to be pushed, but this should be done in a non-threatening way.

The sort of questions found to be of value in eliciting constructs are: 'Who is your best friend/do you dislike?', 'What sort of person is he?', 'Why do you like/dislike him?' and 'How does he behave?'. Answers to these questions can then be followed up, e.g. 'When you say he is kind, what do you mean?' or 'Why do you think he is kind?'. It is not easy to know exactly how much to push, but perhaps a rough guide is to keep going as long as the patient is relaxed and interested and to stop when he starts repeating himself. In this way, most of the constructs which the patient habitually uses can be elicited.

Supplying constructs

Sometimes a construct may not be elicited but felt to be of great relevance. This is particularly the case of constructs dealing with anger or fear, both of which may be important but which may not spring readily to the patient's mind (particularly fear). One cannot, however, simply supply anger or fear or other constructs to the subnormal patient without making quite sure that they have some meaning for him. It is preferable to lead him to describe the particular emotion in his own terms, e.g. by using a slightly circular discussion: 'What makes you feel frightened?', 'Thunder', 'How do you feel when you hear thunder?'.

Construct form

A number of our patients have found it easier and more meaningful to use constructs such as 'makes me feel annoyed' rather than 'irritating'. Expressing the constructs in terms of the patient's own feeling in this way requires less 'abstract' thought than making a judgement about another person's behaviour. This is particularly the case with patients in the lower IQ levels.

Discarding constructs

It sometimes happens that, having used a construct apparently quite meaningfully in conversation, when asked to rank or rate on it the patient looks confused and asks what the construct means. This is usually the result of his repeating a phrase he has heard others use, and it is probably best to simply discard such a construct.

Choosing elements

Obviously those elements are chosen which are of major importance to the patient at the time and are particularly relevant to the behaviour under assessment. If a patient has been in hospital for some time and is rarely, if ever, visited, the elements will consist largely of other patients and the hospital staff. It is well to be wary of including people whom the patient thinks are important to you, rather than those who are important to him. For example, a number of our patients did not consider other patients on the ward to be of any interest whatsoever — staff, like gods, come first. This same effect can lead to difficulties in ranking, as will be discussed later.

Another point to bear in mind when selecting elements is that they need not necessarily be people; this is illustrated by the following examples. A male patient was very solitary and wandered alone around the grounds most of the day — accompanied, however, by his dog. The dog was occasionally smuggled up to bed and so it was obviously important to include the dog amongst that patient's elements. Another patient was referred for tranvestite behaviour; he was asked to use as elements items of male and female clothing. A female patient was a withdrawn obsessional person who carried her belongings about with her. The importance of these to her was determined by including her belongings in her grid elements. As other people had no meaning to her, it would not have been useful to examine her construct system by asking her to rank people.

If background information about the patient is obtained from his everyday situations and/or an objective period of observation of him is made, it is usually possible to judge if elements are appropriate and relevant.

Presentation of the elements

If the patient is able to read there is no problem. Further, many patients who cannot score on a formal reading scale can recognize their own and other names when printed in large capitals on a small file card. These can be supplemented by symbols or drawings. If the patient can recognize no letters at all, the elements can be presented solely by drawings or symbols. So far, we have found no patient who required a drawing on every card. If in doubt, one can check by asking the patient to say the name out loud as he picks each card up. It is sometimes necessary to spend 5 minutes teaching the patient to recognize the elements, but this can be quickly and easily done. A severely spastic patient can 'eye point' the relevant card if they are spaced out and it can then be moved into place by the tester. Most of the symbols we have used have been characteristic physical features of the particular element concerned, e.g. moustache, beard, spectacles, bow tie, fatness, the car, white coat, wheelchair, etc. We have successfully used up to fifteen elements with some of the brighter patients, but even those in the lower ranges were able to cope with eight or nine elements.

Ideal self

This is not an easy element for the mentally hadicapped to use, but it can be meaningful if the patient does not interpret it as a complete ideal and rank it first on all the 'good' constructs and last on all the 'bad' ones. It can be particularly interesting with the more intelligent patient, particularly the psychopathic one. The most straightforward technique is to present the element of 'ideal self' *after* the other elements are ranked on each construct. It can be presented with a question of the type 'Would you really like to be more or less . . . than Mr. Bloggs?' (picking some median point), and by this method find the right rank or rating.

Ranking and rating techniques

The usual method is to present the patient with the elements (printed, drawn or otherwise symbolized) on small file cards. These are placed in front of him on the table and laid out in a group such that he can see each one, but not in a line which might suggest a ranking or rating to him. (It is often difficult to convince the patient that there is not a 'right answer', and many of them will be looking for clues to it.) He is then asked to rank or rate the elements on the first construct, e.g. if the construct is 'tells tales', one would say something like: 'Which of these people tells the *most* tales; who is the biggest tale-teller?'. When this card is removed from the group, it is placed in a line position away from the remaining cards but near enough for the patient to be able to see it. The patient is then asked something like: 'Now out of all *these* people who tells the most tales?'. Many mentally handicapped people are very passive and may need prompting for every ranking. After a while, they might cease ranking and say 'none of these ever tells tales very much'. At first one can try with 'who sometimes tells tales', and if this gets no response then 'who *never* tells tales', being sure to emphasize the 'never' as some patients are slow to switch from the positive aspect of a construct to the negative. Most subnormal patients find it easier to rank than rate as long as tied ranks are permitted. Sometimes, the patient indicates that a particular construct is applicable to only a few of the elements, e.g. 'very generous to me'. It is quite in order for him to simply rank those he thinks are relevant and then leave the rest with a tied rank position. Sometimes, it is worthwhile to check and see if he can rank some of the remainder on the negative aspect of the construct.

Some patients cannot rank at all; they find it very difficult to either observe or think about more than one thing at once. With these patients, we have found it necessary to use a 'more than/less than' technique: after the patient has picked out his first element on a construct, we choose another element at random and say 'Is Fred more of a tale-teller than Bert, or less?' or 'Who tells more tales, Fred or Bert?'. This is very slow, particularly on the last element, but it enables one to get a fairly reliable rating or ranking from quite a dull patient. If the patient cannot do this, he can sometimes group the elements crudely into two or three groups: high (medium) low. Obviously the more difficulty a patient has, the more careful one has to be to prevent haphazard or random placing. One must also watch out for 'position' habits, e.g. institutionalized patients tend to rank staff first because they are more important. A related difficulty is the refusal of some patients to rank staff on 'bad' constructs. In order to get around this difficulty, it is necessary to establish the reason for refusal, which in itself can be very illuminating about a patient's problems. Many patients simply need reassuring that the tester will be discreet and that it is not bad, disgraceful or impolite to so rate staff. It is usually the chronically institutionalized who find this difficult, as they still remember the 'old days' when charge nurses and sisters were lords and ladies and the medical superintendent was the 'supreme being'. (Unfortunately, not only patients hold this misbelief.) If a patient refuses to rank staff on 'bad' constructs because he really believes they do not apply, then he is, of course, allowed to rank the staff as not possessing these constructs.

If the patient finds he can neither rank nor group nor connect his elements and constructs in any way, it is necessary to check that the elements and constructs are really meaningful to him. If they are meaningful and the patient is really motivated to try but simply cannot comprehend the task, there is no alternative but to abandon the attempt. However, the effort will not have been completely without benefit because some idea will have been gained of the sorts of construct that that patient uses. If the patient is not cooperating with the task, the problem might well be one of motivation. In this case, there is no reason why attention and cooperation should not be reinforced with an appropriate reinforcer, being careful to check that a particular ranking is not being reinforced. Many patients tire of concentrated effort after a while, in which case a short tea-break or adjournment till the following day is advisable.

A general point about the patient's attitude

It should not be supposed that because the mentally handicapped patient is initially unresponsive, fatuous or silent but pleasantly smiling, that he might not use many more elements or constructs and be able to rank them than he will admit to. Many subnormal patients, although admittedly of below average intelligence, have been conditioned to act as if they are much more handicapped. 'Playing dumb' is an almost unbeatable defence and it can enable one to avoid jobs and responsibilities, as one patient commented: 'When you're bright you're fort (*sic*) about here, I don't want to be finked (*sic*) about so I act daft'. If 'acting daft' is suspected, it is useful to observe whether the staff members most closely concerned tend to complain about the behaviour of brighter patients, while saying about the duller ones: 'Oh, he's lovely, you have to do everything for him but he's no trouble'. The patient's behaviour will almost certainly reflect this attitude. Threatening or frustrating the patient must, however, also be avoided. While a retarded person might take more time than normal to decide on a rank, if he sits unmoving, staring at the element cards for more than a couple of minutes, it is unlikely to be the grid he is concentrating on. If such lack of motion is the result of lack of motivation, then one must motivate; if it is the result of confusion, then the task should be presented more simply.

Results

Analysis of the grid

The grids, having been obtained as described in the method, were computed in the usual manner. Most of the grids elicited were computed using the INGRID program and the resulting data were examined according to the procedure recommended. The system found to be most appropriate and convenient with our population was as follows;

    (a) A graph was made showing the loading of the elements and constructs on the first two components; if the first two components took up less than

70—80 per cent of the variance, a table of the loadings (both positive and negative) on the first three components was drawn up.

(b) The correlations were examined in order to assess those constructs which were significantly correlated (this can be compared with the graph and table as a check). Of particular interest were unusual or incompatible correlations.

(c) The position of self in relation to the constructs and to the other elements is important, as well as the distance between elements.

(d) The variance was examined to see if it was evenly spread and to see the amount taken up by the first three components.

The INGRID 72 program gives the correlations between elements and constructs, and this tabled printout can be scanned for significant correlations.

General data

The findings described in this chapter relate to a group of twenty-six patients seen at a hospital for the mentally handicapped. Twenty-four had IQs between 48—85, i.e. between 1 and 3 standard deviations below normal. In the group classified as borderline there were seven patients, in the mild group fourteen patients and in the moderately handicapped group three patients; there was also one patient of normal intelligence and one severely retarded. IQ was not correlated with the number of constructs or elements elicited, nor with the amount of variance taken out by either the first or all three components. Nor was IQ correlated with age, but, as one might expect, those of higher intelligence had spent less time in hospital.

The average grid size was 10 x 10, the range of constructs was from six to nineteen, and the range of elements from seven to fifteen. The smallest grid was based on six constructs and eight elements and the largest on nineteen constructs and eleven elements. IQ was not related to the number of elements or constructs used. The average amount of variance extracted by the first three components was 85.5 per cent (range 56—98 per cent) and by the first two was 76 per cent. The literature suggests that when normal versus neurotic people are compared, more variance is taken up by the first two components for the neurotic than for the normal group. Ryle and Breen (1972) compared normal and neurotic grids and found the first two components took out significantly more variance in the neurotic group (65 per cent as opposed to 59 per cent). The 76 per cent variance shown on our grids suggests that either neurosis is one of a number of characteristics which will restrict construct systems or it is some feature of neurosis (e.g. rigidity) which also occurs with low intelligence that increases the variance taken out by the first two components. The first component accounted for a mean of 58 per cent of the variance, the second took out on average 18 per cent and the third 9 per cent, although the range was quite wide (component 1, 37—88%; component 2, 6—28%; component 3, 2—18%).

Range of constructs

Anger. Altogether 257 constructs were employed, of which sixty-five (27 per cent) were used only once. It is interesting that 92 per cent (twenty-three) of the patients produced 'bad-tempered' or 'loses temper easily', contrasting with only 38 per cent (ten) using 'friendly', the second most common. Of course, many of the patients with IQs of 55+ who remain in hospital are classified as having a personality or behaviour disorder, in which immaturity and poor control of emotions — particularly anger — are common features, which may explain the high percentage using 'bad-tempered'. Unfortunately, it was not possible to compare these data with base rates for the normal occurrence of various constructs, and so whether or not 'bad-tempered' is more often used by 'disturbed' patients is something to be examined at a later date. Our present sample is too biased toward the disturbed patient to be able to extract such data from within the group. 'Bad-tempered' could be a construct often used by subnormal patients because it is an emotion which is easily seen and is therefore more obvious to them than, for example, sorrow or sympathy.

Concrete constructs. Visibility of a construct was obviously important to our patients, particularly for the less able ones: Jan, who is moderately retarded, used 'brings presents' as a positive construct, while Jon judged his positive feelings by whether or not a person was 'good to play football with'. Where possible, constructs which were merely physical descriptions were excluded. Concrete constructs do not equip a person well for life either outside or inside an institution: while it might be appropriate initially in hospital to classify one's visitors 'nice' or 'nasty' as to whether or not they have brought a present (the correlation was 0.85 between 'nice' and 'brings presents' for Jan), such a construct will soon lead to unreasonable expectations and disappointment. In Jan's case, it also led to frustration, as she applied the construct to herself, too, and was unable to fulfil it as often as she wished. During the interviews Jan spent much time detailing all the presents she had received and given; she was preoccupied with presents and the construct system shown by the grid clarifies this (component 1 — 55 per cent of the variance — was largely 'bad-tempered' versus 'nice' and 'brings presents'). It is hoped that Jan will learn that 'present-bringing' is not a very good predictor on a long-term basis. Looking at her history, it is possible to speculate on the development of this construct, as from an early age Jan has been in different hospitals many times and the main role her family has played has been that of present-bearing visitors.

Other 'popular' constructs. Over half the patients used 'helpful' or 'kind' as an important construct. Such constructs might be expected from grids including medical and nursing staff among their elements. 'Helpful' and 'kind' are also valuable constructs to the mentally handicapped, who often need help and need to know whom to ask for it. The next most common construct was 'orders people about' or 'pushes people around', and was used by nearly a third of the patients. This is not surprising in view of the authoritarianism which inevitably lingers in institutions for long-stay patients. When this construct was linked with staff, it was generally correlated more highly with 'positive' constructs such as 'good' than when it was attached to other patients.

Inappropriate constructs. A number of patients used constructs which, while being of value within the hospital, would prove quite inappropriate in a normal work setting. This was the sort of construct we looked for in a pre-discharge patient or in one who had failed in the community. A good example of such a construct was 'has a bit of fun' or 'you can have a laugh with this person' being used as having a high correlation with 'good', 'nice' or 'sympathetic'. Quite a few patients also used this construct as having a highly significant negative correlation with a 'bad' construct, which could lead to difficult and inappropriate decisions. For example, Jan negatively correlated 'has a bit of fun with you' and 'says nasty things' ($r = 0.71$). As 'has a bit of fun with' was also one of Jan's predictors of an affectionate kind person, she was much more upset by someone saying 'nasty things' than she need be. Paula correlated 'makes you laugh' (+0.91) with 'makes you happy'; both constructs were negatively correlated at the 0.8 level with 'can't be bothered with me'. The part which 'makes you laugh' played in her system was (while appropriate within the hospital) too important for successful prediction of interpersonal relationships and communication outside the hospital. It was felt that although, in hospital, affection and sympathy is often expressed between staff/patient and patient/patient by 'joshing them along' or 'joking all the time, such behaviour might very well be quite inappropriate outside a hospital, particularly, say, on a first day at work. The foreman or supervisors might very well consider 'have a bit of fun with' to be not such a positive characteristic.

Other constructs. The other constructs employed by the patients covered a wide range. Although 25 per cent of patients employed 'afraid of' or 'frightened of', such a percentage would probably be below that of a psychiatric group; neurosis and, also, psychosis are not common conditions in a hospital for the subnormal. Seven patients (25 per cent) used 'natters' or 'gets onto you', a behaviour which is important in close community living, 21 per cent used 'nice', 'anxious' and 'understands me', and 17 per cent 'gets on your nerves', 'likes/loves me' and 'generous'. Only three out of twenty-six used 'clever' or 'intelligent' as a construct. This was rather unexpected because the patients often comment on each other as 'low-grade', 'thickie', etc., although few patients thought of as 'low-grade' gave a grid or featured as elements in other grids. When such patients were included, it was largely because of their bad-temper or other irritating qualities, rather than their level of intelligence. Thus, many patients appear to understand that there are different levels of intelligence around them but they do not include this concept in their system. 'Successful' was also a rare construct; in fact, it was employed by only one patient, envied by many, who earned £30 p.w. as a dustman!

Language

The range of feelings expressed by the patients was wide and complex, although the language by which feelings were described was often simple, and the emotions 'cruder' and more self-related than might be the case with normal people. Some examples would be 'makes me mad' or 'gets onto you' instead of 'irritating', 'lets me go out' instead of 'non-authoritarian', and 'feel all worked up' instead of 'gets anxious'. Other examples are: 'got mucky ways', 'does lots for you', 'runs you about a bit', 'blames people for things they've not done' or, as Chester defined his elements, 'pests', 'buggers', 'lazy', or 'innocent'.

Patient/staff dichotomy

Four patients showed a clear patient/staff dichotomy in their ranking, seeing the former as all 'good', the latter as all 'bad', though few went as far as Fred, who refused even to rank the staff on negative constructs. This presumably results from institutionalization and is, to a limited extent, adaptive in hospital where sanctions are largely controlled by staff; it would not, however, be as adaptive outside hospital where people are not so easily classifiable. Such a finding is, therefore, of particular importance with pre-discharge patients. It will be interesting to see whether a construct system involving such a dichotomy is predictive of success or failure after discharge — success may perhaps be predicted if the dichotomy reflects the political fashions of the time!

Distance between elements

Trends were examined in the distances between elements. Such data may be very interesting, particularly with reference to self. For example, the distances between self and other elements in Ivan's grid were all very close to 1.0; this was also shown in the grid table drawn up for his three components:

Component 1 (66% variance)	+ horrible, bad-tempered, orders (boss, police, disliked sib)
	− nice, happy to be with (Mam, Dad, liked sib)
Component 2 (17% variance)	+ makes me calm, excited, work hard
	− self, subnormal friends

It can be seen from this that Ivan is relating himself neither to his other elements nor to his major constructs. He sees himself as being 'outside' his first 'nice/nasty' component; guilt, order and the urge to work are all imposed on him by other people, with whom he does not relate himself. His fairly large first component shows a simple black and white classification, but he cannot place himself or his subnormal friend in this picture. Ivan, who is mildly retarded, lives outside hospital most of the time but finds it difficult to get on with people. Recently when he became depressed he also showed depersonalization and poverty of thought. The problem of relating to people is reflected in the distance between elements. The grid suggests that a possible reason is Ivan's inability to place or describe himself and he chooses as his only companion a person about whom he can also say little. It cannot be easy to operate a construct system in which self has little meaning. Ivan requires role-training and self-assertion plus conditioning to inquire habitually into and classify his own thoughts and actions.

Effects of intelligence and institutionalization on grids

It is difficult to get a clear picture of the effect of intelligence or institutionalization on a grid without specifically designing an experiment to test this, although in our experience grid findings do not appear to be greatly affected by below-average intelligence. Further investigations are to be carried out.

Element position

When a graph is drawn of the loadings of the elements and constructs on the first two components, sometimes one or two elements lie close to the central point, having low loadings on both components. In this case, if the loading is also low on the third component, it is clear that the subject is not saying much about that particular element. Identification of the element should enable one to decide why the subject is not committing himself; either he is not prepared to say much about the particular element (which would, of course, need following up) or he might simply not know the element very well. This has happened a number of times with our patients, who included in their elements a person they did not know but felt to be important — not quite understanding that a person could be important without being important to them.

Effect of wards and subgroups of patients

The patients asked to do a grid came from two main groups of patient (residing on three wards within the hospital): (a) a pre-discharge group of males, all reasonably competent but lacking the full control, maturity and good work habits necessary for discharge, and (b) a male and female group of more disturbed 'psychopathic' patients. The grids yielded by the groups can only be roughly compared as direct and detailed comparison is not possible because the patients were seen as individuals, there being no basic experimental comparison design. However, a few observations are worth following up, particularly the possibility of predicting a patient's success or failure on discharge. On the whole, the pre-discharge patients had less inappropriate correlations and more basically useful and reliable systems. These patients also had a more realistic concept of their ideal self and therefore more chance of realizing it than did those who saw their ideal selves in terms of the unobtainable and often imagined qualities of the omnipotent staff. It is perhaps worth noting that the pre-discharge ward was run on less authoritarian lines, with the staff attempting to build relationships with the patients other than that of guardian or custodian. It would be interesting to follow up patients discharged from this ward compared with patients discharged from other wards to see if a realistic 'ideal self' is correlated with success.

The patients on the 'psychopathic' wards produced more constructs related to anger and violence ('loses temper', 'pushes people around', 'hits me', etc.) than those on the pre-discharge ward (30 per cent as opposed to 16 per cent of constructs elicited respectively). This is not unexpected, however, as it is this sort of behaviour which leads to a patient being admitted or transferred to a 'psychopathic' ward.

Intelligence

As has already been stated, over an IQ of 50 or thereabouts, intelligence does not apparently affect whether or not a person can do a grid. Nor, in our study, was it linked with the number of elements, constructs or amount of variance taken up by the three components. The *quantities*, therefore, are not affected. However, the constructs used by the less able patients were simpler, more concrete and less subtle than those used by the brighter patients, as might be expected from their verbal ability. Inappropriate constructs, or those of little value, were linked more to the emotional adjustment or behaviour than to intelligence level.

Interpretation

The interpretation of grids with the mentally handicapped is best described by giving a number of typical examples, as, beyond suggesting a simple procedure to follow and mentioning things to look out for, no fixed procedures can be suggested. Generally, a grid is given with a specific question in mind, e.g. 'Could this patient be transferred to a less firmly controlled ward?', 'Does this patient have particular difficulties with members of the opposite/same sex?' or 'What is the basis for such difficulties?'.

Case studies

Ivan

Ivan (24 years; IQ 56) had been discharged on a number of occasions but was unable to settle down at home. He was confused and irritable and also had had some delusional ideation during a depressive phase. The main complaint was of attention-seeking behaviours. The grid suggested that a basic problem was one of role: not knowing what his role was and being unable to examine himself in his own terms. In the grid, the element 'self' was not really examined; it had little loading on his first component which took out 66 per cent of the variance. This component could roughly be labelled 'nice/nasty'. Guilt, orders and motivation to work were all correlated with this first component, and were thus supplied to Ivan by other people rather than internally. Ivan's family were at the 'permissive and nice' end of component 1, his boss and the police at the other end. Ivan could not identify himself or his subnormal friend, Ben, in the schemata.

It was suggested that Ivan be helped to internalize control, motivation, etc., by being shown that firmness and hard work could be combined with affection, sympathy and enjoyment by putting him with this sort of a boss.

Don

Don (17 years; IQ 71) appeared quiet and submissive but took advantage of inexperienced staff. When admitted, assessment and social reports showed him to be very impulsive with no control over his desires and an inability to think beyond them. Further, some reports of his behaviour were rather bizarre. Don was unable to talk about himself, being a reticent non-verbal person with little concentration. The grid can be a useful instrument in this situation as it does not require the sustained concentration necessary, for example, for the TAT; the ranking decisions can be carried out one at a time and each only requires a moment's thought.

On Don's grid component 1, taking out 63 per cent of the variance, was 'good-tempered and loves me/bad-tempered, does not love me'. Component 2 (22 per cent of the variance) was 'authoritative/non-authoritative'. Self and two out of seven elements were not loaded onto either of the components. Mother and female nurses were good but not authoritative. Fellow patients were rated highly on 'bad-tempered, does not love me'. The grid shows Don's simple but rather shallow classification and prediction system. It does not include himself; he makes no predictions about his own behaviour. Women are rated much more highly than men on component 1 ('good, loves me') but, interestingly, are not rated lower on authoritativeness. This suggests that his advances toward female staff are based more on a prediction that they will love him than on an assumption that they will be less authoritarian.

Ben

Ben (33 years; IQ 69) was competent in many areas. He was literate, with good work skills and was very creative and imaginative. The problem that kept him in hospital was his homosexual and paedophiliac behaviour. The grid was given to see if there had been any change in his orientation and also to judge his present attitude towards children — particularly potential victims. Ben's grid involved fifteen constructs and thirteen elements. The constructs were:

Loses temper easily	Frightening	Kind
Guilty conscience	Jealous	Happy
Troubled with nerves	A nuisance	Mean
Comes straight to the point	Strict	Bad
Fancy going to bed with	Tale-telling	Lonely

'Fancy going to bed with' was correlated positively with two other constructs, 'guilty conscience' ($r = 0.79$) and 'mean' ($r = 0.76$), presumably demonstrating the effect of his previous sexual experience. There is a theme of guilt which runs through much of the grid. It is correlated +0.75 or more with 'mean', 'jealous', 'fancy going to bed with', 'nuisance' and 'tale-telling'. Ben ranked the children (a boy and a girl) and all his male and female friends high on 'bed with', suggesting there is still no discrimination between sex or age as regards sexual interest; however, he does associate such interest with guilt. This is connected with a common problem in institutions for the mentally handicapped: is any sexual interest/activity to be permitted, and in what direction. Ben is a rather tense, desparately eager to please person and a possible underlying reason could be guessed at by the high correlation between self and lonely. Parents and family are idealized good figures and Ben has little contact with them. Hospital staff are kind, but firm, and there is little contact there also.

Amy

Amy (24 years; IQ 76) was referred with a view to revision of a compulsory detention order and possibly discharge. The main difficulty at home had been a Bill Sykes set-up involving her mother and boyfriend. Although Amy professed dislike for her mother who 'curses hell let loose', she had modelled herself on her. The completed grid when graphed showed that Amy now saw herself as being very different from her mother and boyfriend. Ideal self and the 'lady doctor' were close together at the positive end of the first component, with mother and boyfriend at the negative end. Amy placed herself well toward the positive end. The first component could be labelled 'truthful, understanding, calm vs. jealous, mad, hits out'. The grid suggests that Amy has now a more appropriate model (in terms of the behaviours involved) and is aiming herself toward it. It was suggested that she be allowed increased freedom and responsibility.

Marty and Poppy

Marty (35 years; IQ 55) and Poppy (24 years; IQ 66) both showed violent and attention-seeking behaviour and often competed in their attention-seeking. They had, however, very different backgrounds. Poppy had been in children's homes and hospitals for many years, whereas Marty had been an only and rather spoilt child and had not been in hospital long. Both rated each other highly negatively on their grids: Marty said Poppy was 'onto me' and 'tells tales', whereas Poppy said Marty was 'bad, with mucky ways'. Both, however, also recognized some of their own failings in the other girl: Marty classed both herself and Poppy at the negative end of component 1 ('kind, generous/unkind, mean') but placed them at opposite ends of component 2 ('truthful/tale-teller'). This was useful insofar as one could use this knowledge to help point out the effect of various behaviours, particularly where they might be tempted to excuse such behaviour in themselves but not in another.

The grids were similar, with large amounts of the variance taken up by component 1 and the other components showing little power at all. Events were seen in terms of black and white, a person or an element being either good or bad with no other decisions possible. This was seen clearly in the behaviour of both girls who, if criticized even slightly, immediately classified the criticizer as bad, not loving them and nasty in every way. Such a pattern admitting of no shades of grey, where predictions are largely made on the basis of one component, is one which a few of our patients have shown and — tentatively — appears to be a pessimistic prognosticator for discharge.

May

The case of May (45 years; IQ 62) illustrates the use of a slightly different type of grid. May had been ten years in hospital, had acquired good social skills and was thought to be a reasonable candidate for transfer from the ward for disturbed patients to the pre-discharge ward, as her previous violent behaviour had long since ceased.

May, however, appeared to resist any change. In addition, there were reported a number of obsessional behaviours. It was thought that a grid might show what the different ward situations and the obsessional behaviours meant to her, as she was unable to discuss this outright. The elements that were chosen were the different environments she had been in, the new ward and the places where some of her obsessional behaviour had been observed:

Her old home
The mental hospital from which she was admitted
Her present ward
The new ward
Occupational therapy department where she spent her day
In the village with another patient

In the village alone
In the bathroom with others there, washing her hair
In the bathroom alone, washing hair
Washing up
Folding clothes up into her locker at night
In bed

The constructs were: 'In this situation I feel . . . all worked up, anxious, safe, at home, frightened, sad and miserable, calm and quiet, happy, like I can't do anything right'.

The first component took out 53 per cent of the variance and could be labelled 'safe, happy/frightened, sad'. Those elements closely associated with the positive end of the scale were 'bed', 'folding clothes', 'washing up' and, surprisingly, 'the new ward'. This suggests those things she does obsessionally have an axiety-relieving component; the new ward and bed, however, are also seen as safe. So, despite her protests about change, May's attitude to the new ward is a very positive one and it was suggested that she could move straight away. Also both the village situations were seen as fearful and so accompanied trips to the village of increasing length and with increasing responsibility were instituted.

The second component, though small (17 per cent), was important as it was largely composed of fear of not being able to do anything right, which compares with the observed obsessional traits. Analysis of the construct correlations also showed a high correlation ($r = +0.8$) between 'safe' and 'at home', showing that May does not feel safe in a new place. Any move outside the hospital should, therefore, be preceded by visits to accustom her to it. The grid therefore was able to clarify a number of points which were not clear in the rather confused interviews which May had given.

Val

Val (20 years; IQ 85) had spent much time in isolation because of violent behaviour and absconding. Shortly after the grid was completed (in an attempt to suggest important areas to work on in psychotherapy), Val became so disturbed she was transferred to a long-stay hospital for the criminally insane. The behaviours which led to the transfer were strong serious attempts to kill both herself and others. The grid shows that Val sees herself and her mother as disliked, disloyal, aggressive and withdrawn. Others see her even more in this light. Ideal self would be 'sane, sincere and intelligent'. Her despair, depression and feelings of suicide follow from her recognition of the near impossibility of ever achieving such an ideal. In fact, shortly before she was transferred Val wrote a short essay on euthanasia, suggesting that it should be considered for the mentally subnormal.

Jon

Jon, aged 25, borderline retarded, had spent his whole life in institutions. He had all the skills necessary to make him an ideal candidate for discharge to a hostel at least. However, he resisted all attempts to get him outside the hospital, even refusing to go to the local working men's club with the other patients (free drink), to go out shopping or on trips and holidays. His grid, when analysed, showed a very tight patient/staff dichotomy, all the former being 'bad' and the latter 'good'. Moreover, 88 per cent of the variance was taken up by the first component (basically 'good' versus 'bad'). It was proposed that this, while adaptive to a limited extent within the hospital, was resulting in confusion outside and that Jon's resistance to going out was an avoidance response to an anxiety-provoking situation. Treatment consisted of gaining Jon's confidence and then taking him out on a series of graded excursions — initially taking him for a drink and building up to taking him shopping and persuading him to do the buying himself. It was hoped that by increasing his social contacts in this way his construct system would become more adaptive and increasing social success would desensitize his fear. When Jon's social confidence improves, a further grid will be carried out to see if it reflects the change in his behaviour.

It is interesting to note that one of the criteria which Ryle and Breen (1972) found distinguished significantly between patients and normals was a large amount of variance taken up by the first two components.

Ron

Ron, aged 39, is borderline retarded. He has a job, earns a good wage and usually lives in a hostel. However, he has outbursts of temper and aggression which necessitate admission to hospital, although once there his behaviour is good. A grid was completed in an attept to elucidate Ron's behaviour problem.

When alanlysed, the grid showed all the hospital staff to have high positive loadings on the first component ('good-tempered, friendly, trusting, doesn't make me feel afraid'), while his workmates had correspondingly high negative loadings on this component. Moreover, the person in charge of the hostel had a high positive loading on component 2 ('annoying, doesn't let you have your own way'). Outside the hospital, Ron was confronted with people of whom he was afraid and whom he saw as bad-tempered and not trusting him; in the hostel was a warden he found annoying and authoritarian. On the other hand, he saw the hospital as providing much more congenial surroundings and it was suggested that the temper and aggression were both reactions to and attempts to escape from the hostel and job.

Peter

Peter (19 years; IQ 63) was referred following alleged episodes of fetishistic behaviour; the fetish was said to be clothes, and particularly his mother's clothes. Peter was asked to rank several items of his own and other people's clothing, together with one or two prized possessions, on a number of constructs which described the feelings that that item could give: e.g. 'makes me feel happy' (elicited), 'makes me feel guilty' (supplied), 'means an awful lot to me' (elicited), 'makes me want to play with myself' (supplied), 'makes me feel bad' (supplied) and 'like to have it on me' (supplied). The resulting grid was analysed on the INGRID 72 program. The relations between constructs and elements showed two major groups. In group one, female clothing had negative correlations (most of them significant) with all the constructs; thus Peter denies that these items have any effect on him. Group two was comprised of Peter's own clothes, football gear and football, all of which had significant positive correlations with the feelings described by the constructs. The clothes fetish is seen by the positive correlations between 'wearing it', 'makes me want to play with myself' and 'feeling bad'. The grid suggests that the fetishism included Peter's own clothes and football gear; whether or not female clothes are included is difficult to say as Peter may well have felt it socially desirable to rank these low, although he did *not* take the opportunity of not ranking on the construct at all or denying that it had any relevance to the elements.

Conclusions

In conclusion, it may be said that we have found it possible to obtain reliable and valid pictures of our patients' construct systems using the repertory grid technique. With the mentally retarded, this technique has advantages over most commonly used and readily available 'personality' assessment techniques, insofar as it requires little or no literacy, sustained concentration and does not use concepts which may be not understood and/or inappropriate. It is also an attractive technique and one which, in our experience, is not found threatening.

There is currently a strong and desirable move to discharge as many mentally handicapped as possible (in the moderate, mild and borderline ranges) to suitable hostels or sheltered lodgings. In order to devise programs to train these patients for discharge, it is necessary to know their level of intellectual functioning and, more important, social functioning; it is also necessary to understand their attitudes to themselves and others, the basis from which decisions are made and actions stem. The repertory grid can therefore play a part as a basic instrument in the pre-program assessment of the mentally handicapped person.

References

Atkinson, J. W. (1957). 'Motivational determinants of risk-taking behaviour'. *Psychological Review*, 64, 359–372.

Bannister, D., and Fransella, F. (1966). *Manual of the Grid Test of Schizophrenic Thought Disorder*, The National Foundation of Educational Research, Slough, Bucks.

Burg, B. W., and Barrett, A. M. (1965). 'Interest testing with the mentally retarded: a bi-sensory approach'. *American J. Mental Deficiency*, 69, 548–552.

Collins, H. A., Burger, G. H., and Doherty, D. (1970). 'Self-concept of E.M.R. and non-retarded adolescents'. *American J. Mental Deficiency*, 75, 285–289.

Gallagher, J. J. (1959). 'Measurement of personality development in preadolescent mentally retarded children'. *American J. Mental Deficiency*, 64, 296–301.

Gardner, W. I. (1971). *Behaviour Modification in Mental Retardation*, Aldine-Atherton, New York.

Gunzberg, H. C. (1970). 'Subnormal adults'. In P. J. Mittler (Ed.), *The Psychological Assessment of Mental and Physical Handicaps*, Methuen, London.

Hogg, J. (1971). 'Personality assessment of the subnormal as the study of learning processes'. Paper presented to Ciba Foundation and Institute for Research into Mental Retardation. Study Group No. 5 on *Psychological Assessment of the Mentally Handicapped.* Ciba Foundation, London, December 13th, 14th and 15th, 1971. To be published by J. and A. Churchill, London, in P. J. Mittler (Ed,).

Hogg, J., Evans, P. L. C., and Preddy, D. (1971). 'Inhibitory aspects of learning and behaviour in the S.S.N. and E.S.N'. In *Learning Deficits in the Severely Subnormal*. Mimeographed report of the Symposium delivered to the Annual Conference of the B.P.S., Exeter, April, 1971.

Kirk, S. (1953). 'The mentally retarded'. In *Counselling for Psychological Acceptance of Disability* (U.S. Dept. of Health, Education and Welfare O.V.R. Rehab. Serv. Series No. 2601), A.P.A., Cleveland, Ohio.

McManis, D. L., and Bell, D. R. (1968). 'Retardate reward-seeking or punishment-avoiding under three types of incentives'. *American J. Mental Deficiency*, 72, 844—850.

McManis, D. L., Bell, D. R., and Pike, E. O. (1969). 'Performance of reward-seeking and punishment-avoiding retardates under reward and punishment'. *American J. Mental Deficiency*, 73, 906—911.

Masserman, J. H., and Balken, E. R. (1938). 'The clinical application of phantasy studies'. *J. Psychol.*, 6, 81—88.

Rorschach, H. (1942). *Psychodiagnostics*, Grune and Stratton, New York.

Ryle, A., and Breen, D. (1972). 'Some differences in the personal constructs of neurotic and normal subjects'. *Brit. J. Psychiat.*, 120, 483—489.

Sarason, S. B. (1949). *Psychological Problems in Mental Deficiency*, Harper, New York, pp. 222—262.

Sarason, S. B., and Sarason, E. K. (1946). 'The discriminatory value of a test pattern in a high grade familial defective'. *J. clin. Psychol.*, 2, 38—49.

Slater, P. (1967). *Notes on INGRID 67*, Grid Research Unit, St. George's Hospital Medical School, London.

Sternlicht, M., and Silverg, F. F. (1965). 'The relationship between fantasy aggression and overt hostility in mental retardates'. *American J. Mental Deficiency*, 70, 486—488.

4

SOME CLINICAL APPLICATIONS
OF GRID TECHNIQUE

A. Ryle

Summary

Descriptions are given of grids of different kinds which have proved particularly suitable for studying states of mind of patients suffering from neurotic disorders, and for recording changes in their states during the course of treatment. Among these is the dyad grid which takes relationships between people as elements: for instance, 'my boss to me', 'myself to my wife', 'my wife to my son', and vice versa, might be construed in such terms as 'dependent on', 'loving towards' or 'angry with'. Methods of examining and interpreting the results from such grids are described and evidence on their diagnostic value is reported. (P.S.)

The need for access to a patient's views of himself and others

The aim of psychological testing in the clinical setting is to provide an economical source of information of diagnostic value and to allow measurement of the degree of disorder present and of change. Testing procedures vary widely in their form and intention. One important dimension of difference is between the objective and projective type of test, a difference which has been described a little cynically as being between those tests in which the client guesses the meaning of the tester's questions and those in which the tester guesses the meaning of the client's answers. Another important distinction is between the nomothetic and idiographic approaches, the former relating measures to general laws based on studies of populations and the latter investigating individual cases and experiences.

Grid technique does not belong at either end of these two dimensions. Its approach is both projective and idiographic in that a large part of the subject's test performance is his own, with minimal structuring by the tester and with no necessary reference to normative values, yet the results of testing do not depend upon any form of subjective interpretation to make them of value and, while being uniquely the individual subject's product, they may, in some respects at least, be interpreted by reference to population norms.

In this chapter, attention will be directed to the use of the technique to gain access to the subject's view of himself and others. This use of the method is most relevant to the study of patients with personality or neurotic disorders, where symptoms and behaviour are so largely a function of problems of relationships, and to the study of changes in self-concept and relationship patterns, whether as a result of treatment or of other experiences. This focus is a reflection of my own use of the technique with student patients in a psychotherapeutically oriented university health service. The technique, however, is applicable to less articulate patients of lower IQ.

Development and variations in grid technique

Grids used in clinics are generally ones in which elicited elements are rated or ranked against elicited constructs; and this form of the grid, for many purposes, is the one most productive of useful data. Allowing the patient to provide the elements and constructs demonstrates the focus and range of his attention and facilitates the investigation of his personal psychophathology. However, for certain purposes, variations of this customary technique are of value and the exact form of testing used needs in every case to be devised around the nature of the questions being asked. In the following section, a number of variations in grid construction and technique will be described. In the subsequent section, the psychological interpretation of grid data will be considered and illustrated.

Multiple selves

Additional information about a subject's construing of himself can be acquired if different versions of the self are included in the test as elements. The inclusion of the ideal self (yourself as you would like to be) is the commonest example of this technique. The ideal self indicates, from the self—ideal self distance, the degree of self-dissatisfaction and, related to this, the amount of motivation for change. The location of the ideal self in relations to the self on the two-component graph derived from the principal component analysis indicates the direction of change desired by the subject. Another form of multiple self is to have, as elements, the self as perceived by others; e.g., yourself as your wife sees you or yourself as your employer sees you. In a study of three drug addicts (R. R. Ryle, personal communication), both these variations on the self were employed, the self being included as the real self, the self on drugs, the self you fear you may become, the self you would like to be and the self your boy- or girlfriend would like you to be . In two of the three cases, the self on drugs was nearer the ideal self and the self that the girl- or boyfriend would like you to be, i.e. the drug reduced the dissonance between the self and the desired self. In the third case, the self on drugs was further from the desired self and nearer the feared self. Information of this sort can clearly be of value in assessing the chances of successful treatment.

Group studies

For some purposes it may be of value to be able to compare how an individual's construct system resembles or differs from those of others with whom he is associated. In such cases, at least some degree of standardization of the grid may be desirable; e.g. by supplying some or all of the constructs and some or all of the role titles of the elements. Grids used in this way can still be of value in describing the individual case, but they may also help to define differences between groups. In the validation study reported below, controls and patients were compared on semi-standardized grids of this sort. In another study, of the change in social work students during training, the values of certain distances and construct correlations in individuals could be defined in terms of difference from the group mean. An even more structured form of testing was applied to a population in which parental and sex-role identification was being investigated (Ryle and Lunghi, 1972). In this study, all the elements were people fitting supplied role titles and all the constructs were supplied. These constructs were grouped by the investigators into those considered to refer to instrumental and those considered to refer to expressive qualities. Element relationships were considered in these two clusters separately, as well as in the whole construct space. In this way, an individual could be characterized, for example, as having a high loading on instrumentality and a low loading on expressiveness; or two elements could be seen as being relatively similar overall or, for example, as being similar in terms of instrumentality but relatively different in terms of expressiveness.

The relationship as element — the dyad grid

People are customarily taken as elements and rated against constructs in terms of general characteristics; e.g., as being more or less 'mean', or more or less 'kind'. It is clear, however, that peoples' characteristics differ in their different relationships, often to a marked degree. To enable the subject to record such differences, the dyad grid was developed (Ryle and Lunghi, 1970). In this form of test, the elements are the relationship of one person to another rather than the persons themselves; thus, rather than rating 'self', 'wife', 'mother' and 'father' on constructs like 'dependent', 'suffocating' and 'angry', the subject would rate elements like 'yourself to your mother', 'yourself to your wife' or 'your mother to your father' (or vice versa) on constructs of the form 'dependent upon', 'suffocated by' and 'angry with'. Commonly, the majority of dyadic relationships in a dyad grid will be those in which the 'self' is one member and, indeed, it may consist only of such pairs.

Dyad grids are analysed on the standard INGRID program; each relationship will generate two elements, e.g. 'self to mother' and 'mother to self', and in plotting the two-component graph this can be indicated conveniently by joining the reciprocal elements by a dyad line.

The dyad form of grid is of particular value where relationships are the main focus of interest, as, for example, in the investigation of couples or in the investigation of role relationships (Ryle and Breen, 1972b and 1972c).

The occasion as element — records of process and change

If the same element is rated on the same constructs on a number of occasions, each occasion can be regarded as an element and the resulting grid provides a record of change through time. An important application of this method is to the study of the process of change during therapy. A patient's view of himself and of his problems through the course of therapy can be derived from a series of self-descriptions, each description being taken as an element as described by Slater (1970). The recording by the psychotherapist of a series of psychotherapeutic sessions in terms of the patient's behaviour and the therapist's feelings and the themes and issues dealt with in the session can similarly provide an ongoing account of the process of therapy. The combination of these two techniques would seem to be of potential value in research into the psychotherapeutic process.

Grid measures of change

Changes in an individual's construct relationships and in the dispersion of elements within his construct space can be recorded by serial repertory grid testing. Where identical tests are used the DELTA program provides measures of change and locates the points of greatest and least change. Where different elements are rated on the same constructs, the COIN program provides evidence of construct change. The main application of repeated grid testing of this kind is to the measurement of the effects of exposure to procedures designed to produce change, notably psychotherapy or other treatments, and teaching. In studies of this sort, the aims of the proposed intervention may be stated at the outset, formulated in grid terms. In this way, the desirable change can be defined taking account both of the individual's particular problems and initial situation and in terms of the declared aims of the intervention. An example of individual prediction in the case of psychotherapy has been published (Ryle and Lunghi, 1969). In a study of the effect of social work training, the dyad grid was used, and in this latter study predictions were made both of individual change in the light of their first grid testing and also of group changes in the light of the aims of the course (Ryle and Breen, 1974). These latter predictions included some referring to features of the construct space; it was predicted that the mean variation around construct means and the total variation accounted for by the first component would diminish through time, representing an increasing complexity of the subjects' construing of their professional relationships. These predictions were fulfilled.

Grid measures of empathy

To understand another is to know how he experiences the world, and one way of measuring how far this understanding has been achieved is to predict how another has completed a repertory grid. In clinical work, this has been applied to two situations: one to test the ability of therapists to predict their patients' grid responses (Rowe, 1971; Ryle and Lunghi, 1971), the other to test the ability of couples to predict each other's grids (Ryle and Breen, 1972b). In both these approaches, the DELTA program allows one to identify the areas of maximum misperception. This information can be used to clarify the nature of the therapist—patient or husband—wife interaction.

Psychological meaning of repertory grid test results

The repertory grid, at its simplest, can be regarded as a summary of the subject's conscious view of himself and of significant others. At a rather more subtle level, it can be seen as a definition of the possibilities or options open to the subject. Still more subtly, and indirectly, grid results may provide some data indicating the operation of unconscious processes. These three types of interpretation of grid data will be considered in turn.

Views of the self and others

The two-component graph provides an immediate shorthand view of the subject's constructs of himself and others. The location of the self in this representation of the construct space may show, for example, that the subject sees himself as 'strong' and 'intelligent' or as 'weak-willed' and 'cold', or characterized in some other way. The relation between self and ideal self indicates the degree and nature of self-dissatisfaction. The position of the self in relation to possible identification models may also be of interest; e.g., the self in relation to parents as identification models or, in the case of a student, self in relation to tutors or to academically successful peers.

Options

If the two-component graph is regarded as a map, then the subject's potential for change can be seen to be determined either by the possibility of redrawing the map, i.e. by altering construct and element relations, or by moving through the map, i.e. by reassessing the self in terms of the same construct structure. If the grid is being studied with a view to identifying the possibilities and implications of change, this map analogy may be a useful one and sometimes may serve to identify dilemmas which the individual is unable to resolve. For example, a female student in academic difficulty may produce a grid in which the self, to be academically successful, must move further from that part of the grid representing femininity, showing that the cost of academic success in her terms is the denial of femininity, or vice versa. The possible solutions open to her, therefore, are denial of aspects of the self, or reconstruction. In some cases, movement within the construct space without changing construct relations may offer a possible resolution to the difficulties. For example, a man who sees himself poised between a father who is seen as 'strong' but 'unkind' and a mother who is seen as 'weak' but 'loving' might be able to move into an area where strength and warmth were combined; the likelihood of being able to do this would probably be increased if a potential identification figure was located in the appropriate area of his construct space.

Grid evidence of unconscious mental processes

Interpretation of grid data in terms of psychodynamic formulation is more controversial than the approaches described above, which rest essentially upon common-sense. Applying psychodynamic insights to grid data is worthwhile in two ways. On the one hand, one may be doing no more than an exercise in translation, for many grid features can be seen as representing alternative formulations of psychodynamically described phenomena. Thus, certain construct correlations may indicate the presence of fantasy; e.g. high correlations between 'cruel' and 'potent' and low correlations between 'masculine' and 'kind' might represent the operation of what in psychoanalytic terms would be called 'castration anxiety'. The concepts of repetition-compulsion and of resistance can be seen as manifestations of the relative inertia or stability of construct systems. Transference can be understood in terms of the location of the therapist in the subject's construct space.

The second sort of application of psychodynamic formulations to grid data is more indirect and, for some purposes, may require special grid techniques.

Ambivalence, for example, can be detected if key elements are rated under two conditions; e.g. in the dyad grid study of couples, the couples were asked to rate their own relationships under two conditions — 'going well' and 'going badly'. In disturbed couples, the 'going badly' condition was shown to be accompanied by perceptions of the self becoming more childlike and the other becoming less parentlike (Ryle and Breen, 1972b). Relatively simple grid structures (indicated by the fact that the first and second components account for a relatively large proportion of total variance) and high mean construct variation (indicating a tendency towards extreme rating) are both indications of simplification and stereotyping and may be related to splitting mechanisms. In interpreting a grid it is, I believe, justifiable to examine the space on the two-component graph polar to that occupied by the self and significant others, on the assumption that this space, or elements located in this space, may stand for denied or split-off aspects of the elements under consideration. Repression or denial may be indicated by the subject's selection of constructs (e.g. avoidance of constructs referring to sexual feelings or negative emotions) or by the low total variance accounted for by such constructs. Finally, in the dyad grid, the relative positions and directions of the dyad lines for the relationships self—parent, self—spouse and mother—father may be interpreted as giving evidence of successful or unsuccessful sex-role identification and resolution of oedipal issues.

In summary, it is argued in this section that grid evidence is as open to interpretation as any other evidence produced by patients. The tester who is prepared to utilize psychoanalytic concepts of development and defence may extract from the grid, in some cases, evidence not accessible to the eye prepared to receive only more direct signals. Some support for this argument is provided by the validation studies described below.

Validation studies

To test how far interpretations of grid data along the above lines was a valid procedure, two experiments were carried out. In the first (Ryle and Breen, 1971), data from the repertory grid testing of eight patients and eight controls were presented blind for rank-ordering according to the probability that the subject was a patient. The ranking was carried out using the kind of evidence which has been indicated above; a very satisfactory sort was obtained, numbers 1 to 6, 8 and 10 being the grids of patients. This study, therefore, demonstrated some degree of reliability in indentification of neurotic features in the grid. It should, however, be noted that the eight patients were people who had already presented for treatment; it might not be so easy to identify in a non-consulting sample those who might subsequently become patients, as the act of consultation may, in some way, modify self-constructs. The kind of data used in this rank-ordering procedure may be illustrated by the cases described in the Appendix of the paper referred to above. The clinical summaries were provided by the doctors looking after the patients. The grid data are as recorded before access to the clinical records, except that the grammar and style is improved. Case records are modified in detail to preserve their anonymity.

Four illustrative cases are described: case 1 (the highest ranked patient), case 7 (the highest ranked non-patient), case 10 (the lowest ranked patient) and case 16 (the lowest ranked non-patient).

Case 1. Female

Grid data. The first principal component distinguishes 'weak' from 'strong' and the second 'aggressive' from 'passive'. Construct correlations of 'warm' and 'strong' are positive and there is a high degree of identification of the subject with 'parents'. The 'ideal self' was not rated. Element distribution shows the subject and her 'family members' huddled at the extreme 'weak' end of the first component and all but one of the other elements are at the opposite pole. It is concluded that this is a patient; she sees all virtue and resources to be lacking in the family, which suggests a depressive, simplified (split) view of the world.

Clinical data. Patient. She consulted because of social isolation and academic difficulty due to inability to attend seminars and tutorials. She avoids relationships because her feelings are so ambivalent and she is prone to vent anger on inanimate objects. There have been episodes of self-injury. The problem is seen as one of schizoid withdrawal.

Case 7. Female

Grid data. There is a high 'self—ideal self' separation and the distance of 'self' from 'mother' is one of the highest of the series. The 'self' is far closer to 'father' suggesting cross-sex identification. In the elements distribution, 'self' is the 'strongest' and 'mother' nearly the 'weakest' of all elements, but 'ideal self' is located near 'mother'. The construct 'likely to need psychiatric help' has a low loading on both first and second components, suggesting that this is not a relevant construct. It seems probable that this girl may succeed as a student at a cost of conflict over femininity which might lead to psychiatric presentation at some stage. There is a possibility of homosexuality.

Clinical data. Control series. Medical records, however, recorded a consultation a year after testing, for menstrual irregularity, depression and work difficulty.

Case 10. Male

Grid data. There is a small 'self—ideal self' separation and the distance from 'parents' is median for the series. The element distribution on the first two components shows that 'parents' are polarized, 'father' being seen as 'cold' and 'likely to succeed academically', whereas 'mother' is seen as a 'warm' and 'strong' personality. The 'self' is nearer 'mother' than 'father', and 'ideal self' nearer still. This suggests the possibility of sex-role problems, though, as identification is with 'mother' seen as 'warm' and 'strong', this may not be so. The fact that academic values are seen as opposed to creative ones may lead to work difficulties.

Clinical data. Patient. The presenting complaint was a severe tic with no other symptoms of emotional distress. He seems to use the tic to gain attention, especially from his mother. He shows considerable drive and need to gain approval by being on top. It seems especially important to him to placate his father. Contrary to this need, however, he has a quite unrealistic ambition to become a painter. There is probably an underlying oedipal difficulty in this case.

Case 16. Female

Grid data. There is a high degree of identification with 'mother' and the 'self—ideal self' separation is median for the series. There are positive correlations between the constructs 'warm personality' and 'weak' and between 'cold' and 'likely to succeed academically'. The first component distinguishes 'warm' from 'cold' and the second distinguishes 'needs psychiatric help' from 'intelligent'. 'Mother' is seen as 'warm' and 'father' as 'cold', and both are seen as 'weak' and 'needing psychiatric help', while 'self' is seen as 'strong' and 'intelligent'. While she is likely to be an effective student and unlikely to become a patient, the fact that 'ideal self' is nearer 'mother' shows an awareness of some deficiency in herself of the softer attributes. Her view of her parents could represent the one-dimensional attitudes of someone emerging from adolescence. If she can move towards her ideal she should manage well enough.

Clinical data. Control series. There has been one consultation for migraine.

In the second experiment (Ryle and Breen, 1972a), a selection of grid measures were taken from the grids of thirty-three patients and fifty-four controls, all of them students. The grids were of standard form, with sixteen elements in each, including in all cases 'self—ideal self' and both 'parents', and with sixteen constructs, of which seven were supplied. Differences between patients and controls in the scores on twenty-three selected measures were investigated and, as a second measure of neurotic disturbance, these same selected grid scores were correlated with the summed scores from five of the scales of the Middlesex Hospital Questionnaire (Crown and Crisp, 1966). (The H-scale, which is scored higher by normals than by patients in this age group, was excluded.) A number of the predicted differences between patients and controls, or of the predicted associations of the twenty-three grid measures with M.H.Q. scores, were confirmed at significant levels. Results were as follows.

(a) Comparison of patients with controls

Nine predictions were confirmed at the 10 per cent. level or better (using two-tailed t-tests) as follows:

1. Patients showed greater 'self—ideal self' distance.
2. Patients of both sexes showed greater 'self—father' distance than controls (significant for sexes combined and for males alone).
3. Patients showed significantly lower values for 'self—mother' minus 'self—father' distances.
4. The mean distance of 'self' from 'mother' and 'father' was higher for patients than controls.
5. Patients showed more extreme loadings for 'self' on the first two principal components than did controls.
6. The total variance accounted for by the first two principal components combined was greater in patients than in controls.
7. Patients had more elements at a distance of one or over than did controls.

Two differences were in the opposite direction to prediction at significant levels.

1. Patients chose significantly *fewer* elements of the same sex than controls.

2. The mean construct correlations between 'likely to succeed academically' and 'a cold person' was significantly *lower* in patients compared to controls.

(b) Relation of grid measures to M.H.Q. scores

The summed scores on the five M.H.Q. scales (excluding the H-scale) were correlated with the grid variables, the results being given in Table 4.1.

The majority of the significant associations of the combined M.H.Q. scores are with variables which were also significantly related to patient status. In addition, distance of self from mother (variable 3), a high correlation between warmth and

TABLE 4.1   Correlations of grid measures with scores on the M.H.Q

Variable		Combined score on M.H.Q. scales 1—5
1.	Number of same sex elements	−0.049
2.	Self—ideal self distance	0.369***
3.	Self—mother distances	
	whole sample	0.335***
	males	0.332*
	females	0.356
4.	Self—father distances	
	whole sample	0.286**
	males	0.423***
	females	0.235
5.	Self—mother distances minus self—father distance	
	whole sample	0.018
	males	−0.090
	females	0.072
6.	Mean of self—mother and self—father distances	0.389***
	Extremity of loading on first component of	
7.	Self	0.380***
8.	Ideal Self	0.027
9.	Mother	0.222
10.	Father	0.132
	Extremity of loading on second component of	
11.	Self	0.369***
12.	Ideal self	0.231
13.	Mother	0.110
14.	Father	0.191
	Construct correlations	
15.	Warm and strong	−0.155
16.	Warm and passive	0.324***
17.	Likely to succeed and cold	−0.145
18.	Warm and likely to need help	0.260*
19.	Weak and likely to need help	−0.142
20.	Size of first component	0.203
21.	Size of first two components combined	0.222
22.	Mean construct variation	0.315***
23.	Number of elements with distance of more than one from self	0.368***

*$p < 0.05$ **$p < 0.02$ ***$p < 0.01$

passivity (variable 16), a high correlation between warmth and the likelihood of needing psychiatric help (variable 18) and a high mean construct variation (variable 22) were related to high M.H.Q. scores.

On the basis of this experiment, therefore, the beginning of a repertory grid portrait of the neurotic patient emerges. The neurotic, as characterized through grid data, sees himself as unlike others in general and unlike his parents in particular (based upon element distances), he is dissatisfied with himself (large self—ideal self discrepancy), he tends to operate with extreme judgements and a relatively simple construct system (evidenced by extremity of loadings of self on the principal component, by the size of the principal component and by a high mean construct variation), and he shows some assumptions which differ from those of normals, e.g. that warmth and passivity are highly associated (derived from construct correlations).

It should be noted that both these validation studies were carried out on a student population, and clearly it would be desirable to replicate them in other groups. A similar attempt to validate the interpretation of the dyad grid is in progress. The studies of couples, referred to above, provide some evidence that this method can distinguish normal from neurotic relationships.

References

Crown, S., and Crisp, A. H. (1966). 'A short clinical diagnostic self-rating scale for psychoneurotic patients'. *Brit. J. Psychiat.*, **112**, 917.

Rowe, D. (1971). 'An examination of a psychiatrist's predictions of a patient's constructs'. *Brit. J. Psychiat.*, **118**, 231—234.

Ryle, A., and Breen, D. (1971). 'The recognition of psychopathology on the repertory grid'. *Brit. J. Psychiat.*, **119**, 319—321.

Ryle, A., and Breen, D. (1972a). 'Some differences in the personal constructs of neurotic and normal subjects'. *Brit. J. Psychiat.*, **120**, 483—489.

Ryle, A., and Breen, D. (1972b). 'A comparison of adjusted and maladjusted couples using the double dyad grid'. *Brit. J. med. Psychol.*, **45**, 375.

Ryle, A., and Breen, D. (1972c). 'The use of the double dyad grid in the clinical setting'. *Brit. J. med. Psychol.*, **45**, 383.

Ryle, A., and Breen, D. (1974). 'Change in the course of social work training: A repertory grid study'. *Brit. J. med. Psychol.*, **47**, 139.

Ryle, A., and Lunghi, M. (1969). 'The measurement of relevant change after psychotherapy: use of repertory grid testing'. *Brit. J. Psychiat.*, **115**, 528.

Ryle, A., and Lunghi, M. (1970). 'The dyad grid: a modification of repertory grid technique'. *Brit. J. Psychiat.*, **117**, 538.

Ryle, A., and Lunghi, M. (1971). 'A therapist's prediction of a patient's dyad grid'. *Brit. J. Psychiat.*, **118**, 546.

Ryle, A., and Lunghi, M. (1972). 'Parental and sex role identification of students measured with a repertory grid technique'. *Brit. J. soc. clin. Psychol.*, **11**, 149.

Slater, P. (1970). 'Personal questionnaire data treated as forming a repertory grid'. *Brit. J. soc. clin. Psychol.*, **9**, 357—370.

5

THE MEASUREMENT OF SELF-IDENTITY

Hugh Norris, Fawezeya Makhlouf-Norris

Summary

The self-identity system is put forward as a hypothetical construction having the property of reducing uncertainty. A person's self-identity is seen as being integral with his behaviour. The choices he makes depend on his self-identity system and their outcomes validate or invalidate his self-conception. A repertory grid method is described for collecting and computing essentially subjective data in a standardized and quantitative form to obtain measurements of self-identity. Operational definitions are given for concepts such as self-isolation, self-alienation and social alienation, etc. The procedure is illustrated with examples of the self-identity indices of patients whose behaviour is constrained in the form of neurosis or drug-dependence and of less constrained normal subjects. (P.S.)

Different conceptions of the self

The concept of 'self' has recurred throughout philosophical and psychological writings as an important but problematic theme. Each of us is subjectively aware of the importance of his own identity; the prospect of loss of identity is scarcely less awful than that of death. Yet scientific studies have encountered great difficulty in defining or measuring self-identity. Indeed, there are schools of psychology which assume that the study of Man can afford to ignore his sense of identity, to treat it as an irrelevancy and an illusion. This chapter is based on the assumption that an understanding of self-indentity is *crucial* to the study of Man. A particular man's conception of his identity may be unrealistic, even delusional, but it is not irrelevant, either to him or to a scientific understanding of his behaviour. In this chapter, we will outline methods of quantifying aspects of self-identity and explore the implications of some simple and basic assumptions about its nature. We are particularly concerned with self-identity in the context of behavioural constraints, such as those which we classify as 'neurosis' or 'personality disorder'.

To explore the ramifications of incorporating a concept of self into the science of human behaviour, we can usually follow the well-established scientific practice of setting up a hypothetical construction of our concept which is explicitly attributed with certain properties. We can predict the consequences in behaviour of this hypothetical construction and compare our predictions with the results of empirical investigations. Such currently well-founded entities as the electron and the gene began their existence in our thinking as mere hypothetical constructions.

We propose to call this hypothetical construction the self-identity system, hereinafter S-I.S. We suppose that if the S-I.S. is found to be a useful conception it will be possible to examine it in a variety of different contexts and attribute to it a number of distinct properties. However, we propose at this stage to examine the S-I.S. in the context of a person identifying himself in terms of his personal social environment, i.e. of the people who are significant in his life. We would attribute initially only one property to the S-I.S., that of reducing self-uncertainty by defining the self relative to others.

We will assume that self-conception is not unitary and that there are at least three important components, which are listed below:

The actual self, being the representation of himself now
The social self, being the representation of other peoples' conception of him
The ideal self, being the representation of his aim or direction of desired movement.

We assume that the S-I.S. performs the function of reducing self-uncertainty by defining the relationships between the three self elements and the representation of the personal—social environment. Furthermore, a system which defines the relationship between a person and his social environment must have implications for behaviour. We conceive of the S-I.S. as being integral with behaviour in that the S-I.S. is developed as a summary of previous behaviour and its consequences, and the system itself determines the range of choices and the selection made in present and future behaviour.

Let us now turn to methods by which evidence can be obtained to support or reject the assumptions made about the existence of the S-I.S. and its relevance to behaviour. For methodological purposes, we will assume that the S-I.S. can be understood in spatial terms, that it is structured and that the structure can be specified in terms of points and dimensions in multi-dimensional space. On this basis, it is possible to collect data in terms of elements and constructs and compute their spatial relationships, using INGRID 72. Examples illustrating the results of such methods are taken from a large study of subjects who have sought help for neurotic and other problems and of normal subjects, i.e. people who have not sought psychological help.

Data and computing

The data presented below were elicited using a grid of twenty elements and sixteen elicited constructs. Seventeen of the elements were listed as a sample representative of the people who constitute each subject's personal—social environment, together with the three principal self elements. A list of element roles which was used as the basis of element elicitation for most of the examples is quoted in Table 5.1.

These suggested element roles were not imposed on every subject but were used to elicit the names of people significant in his life. When a particular role failed to elicit from the subject anyone he felt to be significant, other roles were suggested until an element of significance emerged. Notes were made on the relationship of each element to the subject, to establish whether the element was a component of the subject's present or past personal—social environment. Six element roles are constant throughout: the self elements, the parents and the sexual partner; the others vary between subjects.

TABLE 5.1

	Element roles
1	Mother or surrogate
2	Father or surrogate
3	Myself as I am
4	Myself as I would like to be
5	Myself as seen by others
6	Brother or surrogate
7	Sister or surrogate
8	Old friend of the same sex
9	Spouse or sexual partner
10	Liked teacher or person in authority
11	Disliked teacher or person in authority
12	Liked boss
13	Disliked boss
14	Person I like or feel comfortable with
15	Person I dislike or feel uncomfortable with
16	Successful person
17	Unsuccessful person
18	Religious person
19	Ethical person
20	Person I confide in

To obtain dimensions spanning the space occupied by the S-I.S., each subject's own constructs were elicited by the self-identification method (Kelly, 1955). Every elicitation triad was composed of the actual self and two other elements. The subject was asked to state in which way two elements were alike and thus different from the third. In this way, sixteen bipolar constructs were elicited (Makhlouf-Norris and Jones, 1971). The subject was then required to construe each element in terms of each construct using a seven-point rating scale. For each subject, ratings were entered into a matrix (twenty elements by sixteen constructs) and the matrix was analysed using the program INGRID 72.

We have suggested that the S-I.S. can be treated spatially by considering the elements as points and the constructs as dimensions. Spatial organization can be examined in terms of principal component analysis of element–construct space, which is described in the companion volume. Alternatively, one can look at construct organization in element space or element organization in construct space. A method of examining construct organization, yielding a classification of articulated, monolithic or segmented structures, has been published (Makhlouf-Norris, Jones and Norris, 1970; Makhlouf-Norris and Norris, 1973). A method of examining element relations in construct space is described below.

The INGRID program gives the distance between any pair of elements as a ratio of the expected distance between all pairs of elements in the grid. This measure has a minimum of 0, a mean of 1, and it seldom exceeds 2, although as a ratio it has no predetermined maximum. Thus, any pair of elements which are separated by a distance close to 0 are seen as being similar, with a distance close to 2 they are seen as being dissimilar, and with a distance close to 1 as being neither similar nor dissimilar but indifferent to each other.

We can use this measure to examine how a subject identifies himself as being similar to certain people or dissimilar to others. An axis can be drawn and the distances of all elements from the actual-self (E 3) plotted on it. We can say that the subject identifies himself as being similar to those elements at small distances and dissimilar to those at large distances. Elements at distances close to 1 do not contribute to his self-identification; he is neither like them nor unlike them. A useful procedure is to examine the identification of the actual self and of the ideal self simultaneously by setting up two axes, orthogonal to each other and intersecting at 1, and plotting the distance of each element from E 3 and E 4. It should be stressed that the use of orthogonal axes does not imply the assumption that the variables are orthogonal; they may well be correlated, either positively or negatively.

The self-identity plot

Table 5.2 gives the distance from the actual self and the ideal self of all other elements for a normal subject. Figure 5.1 shows these values plotted, as described above, forming a two-dimensional self-identity plot. Although three self elements were used in all grids, only two dimensions can conveniently be depicted on a plane. In this chapter, we concentrate on plots of the dimensions of similarity of the actual and ideal self elements, but similarity to the social self can be plotted in a similar way.

We see that the actual and the ideal self elements are separated by a distance close to 1. The actual self is similar to mother (E 1), sister (E 7), old friend (E 8), spouse (E 9), and liked teacher (E 10). It is equally clearly dissimilar to the disliked teacher (E 11), boss (E 13), a disliked person (E 15) and the successful person

TABLE 5.2   Distance of all elements from
the actual self (E 3) and ideal self (E 4)

E	Actual	Ideal
1	0.56	0.90
2	1.04	1.10
3	0	0.89
4	0.89	0
5	0.55	0.83
6	0.94	1.09
7	0.69	1.12
8	0.38	0.80
9	0.59	0.69
10	0.59	0.77
11	1.47	1.14
12	1.13	0.65
13	1.49	1.17
14	1.02	0.98
15	1.50	1.25
16	1.39	1.08
17	0.78	0.98
18	1.08	1.02
19	1.01	0.90
20	1.25	0.81

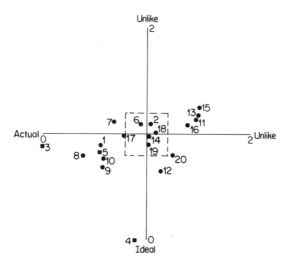

FIGURE 5.1

(E 16). The ideal self is somewhat similar to the spouse (E 9) and the liked boss (E 12) and is dissimilar to the disliked person (E 15). A central area between 0.8 and 1.2 on both dimensions is marked by dashed lines. Elements within these limits are close to the average of all element distances, and, being neither similar nor disimilar, can be said to be 'indifferent' to each other. The range of this central indifferent area of 0.8 to 1.2 was set rather arbitrarily in the first place.

If this plot serves as an index of the hypothetical S-I.S., and if the assumption that the S-I.S. serves to reduce uncertainty about the nature of the self is valid, then this plot will convey information which identifies the two self elements. It does appear to convey such information, in that the actual and ideal self elements are shown to be like certain non-self elements and unlike others, but how can we be sure that this apparent information really is informative? One reasonable way is to compare this plot with one obtained from data which we know does *not* convey information.

If we complete a grid matrix, not by asking a person to rate the people he knows on constructs but by consulting a table of random numbers and entering the numbers 1 to 7 randomly in the matrix, we can be sure that these data convey no information identifying the self or anything else. We can compute these data, using INGRID 72, and obtain distances between elements. Figure 5.2 shows the distances of all elements from elements 3 and 4 plotted as a two-dimensional plot, for such a random grid.

We see that almost all elements fall close to the average distance and within the central indifference area between 0.8 and 1.2 on both variables. None are particularly like or unlike E 3 or E 4, so the nature of E 3 and E 4 is not defined by similarity or dissimilarity to other elements.

Using Slater's GRANNY program (Slater, 1974), 100 grids of twenty elements by sixteen constructs were generated and analysed, and it was found that 92 per cent. of all element distances fell between 0.8 and 1.2. Thus, the initally arbitrarily

84

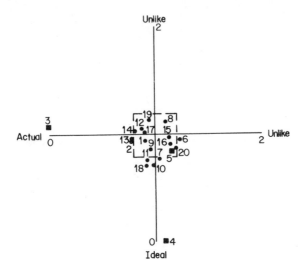

FIGURE 5.2

set limits of the indifferent area are found to contain 92 per cent. of all randomly determined element distances. One might adjust the limits of the indifferent area to contain, say, 95 per cent. of element distances from random grids, but it is not obvious what merit the value of 95 per cent. has over 92 per cent. Perhaps it is sufficient, for the present, to know that the central area, with the limits around 0.8 to 1.2, contains the overwhelming majority of randomly occurring element distances.

We can be sure that a grid composed of random numbers does not represent an S-I.S. If the grids obtained from people were indistinguishable from random grids, they would be consistent with the absence of an S-I.S. We see that the grid illustrated in Figure 5.1 is clearly distinguishable from a random grid, and, in fact, we have not observed any normal subject's grids which did not have the majority of element distances outside the central indifferent area of 0.8 to 1.2 from both self elements, nor any random grids which did not have the majority of element distances within this area — so there is no overlap between normal subject's and random grids. We can conclude, therefore, that normal subject's grids, when examined in terms of the two-dimensional self-identity plot, are not consistent with the absence of an S-I.S., insofar as random grid entries represent the absence of an S-I.S.

Definition by dissimilarity

The dimensions of similarity to the self elements are bipolar dimensions. Figure 5.1 illustrates a plot in which both the actual self and the ideal self are defined in bipolar fashion, in terms of the similarity and dissimilarity to non-self elements. Quite commonly, however, subjects defined one or another self element in a monopolar fashion, identifying only the similarity or the dissimilarity pole of the self dimension with other people. In subjects complaining of the behavioural constraints associated with neurosis, the definition of the self by the dissimilarity pole only is quite common.

(a) Actual self isolation. Figure 5.3 shows a two-dimensional plot in which no non-self element is similar to the actual self, so that only the dissimilarity pole of this dimension is defined in terms of other people. The ideal self dimension is defined in bipolar fashion. This subject is thus defining only what he is not and is failing to define what he is, and we may suppose him to be in a state of uncertainty as to what sort of person he is.

The distinction which Bruner (1974) makes between direct and indirect validation may serve to clarify the point. Bruner gives the example of a child who is trying to define for himself what is meant by the concept 'cat'. Each time an animal appears, the child says either 'This is a cat' or 'This is not a cat' and his parent tells him whether he is correct or not. If it so happens that the child sees only animals which are not cats, he will be able to validate his hypothesis about the nature of a cat only indirectly, because he will validate only his residual hypothesis of what a cat is not. Only when he identifies an animal that is a cat can he test his hypothesis directly. Thus, a person who shows actual self isolation is in the position of Bruner's child, when he is able to test his residual hypothesis. In this case, he knows in many ways what he is not, but he has failed to identify, in terms of other people, what he is.

Insofar as we take the elicited elements to be a sample of people representing the whole of his personal–social environment, then actual self isolation indicates that the subject sees himself as being unlike everybody he knows. We should note that this picture emerges not from the application of one construct but from the application of sixteen constructs. The emergence of this clear picture across sixteen constructs indicates a degree of consistency in which he is separating the actual self from other people, in terms of many constructs. Insofar as we take the sixteen

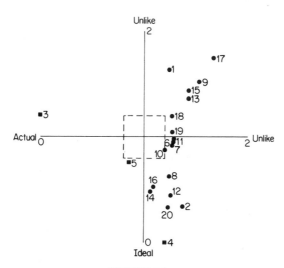

FIGURE 5.3

elicited constructs to be a sample representing his whole repertoire of constructs, we may conclude that he construes himself as being dissimilar to everyone in terms of the majority of all the attributes he uses.

A subject showing actual self isolation represents himself as being alone. In being separate from others in all other respects, he will not share thoughts, feelings or behaviour with others (see Kelly's communality corollary — Kelly, 1955). Thus he has no basis for personal—social interaction.

The plot illustrated in Figure 5.3 represents the S-I.S. of a man who was seen following a suicide attempt, who had no history of psychiatric disorder. After long service in the armed forces, he had been made redundant from two civilian jobs and had subsequently failed to obtain employment. His marriage had broken down in divorce. In the self identity plot it is interesting to note some of the elements which polarize the dimension of similarity to the ideal self. Close to the ideal is his father (E 2), and very different from the ideal are his mother (E 1) and his ex-wife (E 9). This two-dimensional plot gives a fair summary of the fact that this man represented himself as being alone in the world and estranged from those to whom he had in the past been close.

(b) Ideal self isolation. Figure 5.4 shows a two-dimensional plot in which no non-self element is similar to the ideal self. Element 20 is at a distance of 0.8 from the ideal self, so the plot complies with the definition of ideal self isolation which is given later in this chapter. The subject in this case is defining what he does not want to be in terms of others, and not what he wants to be. His ideal for himself is to be unlike most of the people who constitute his personal—social environment and to be like none of them. Thus, in Bruner's terms, he lacks direct validation of the nature of his ideal and it is identified only by what it is not.

The subject in this case was a young man who was admitted for psychiatric treatment following an unsuccessful suicide attempt. His condition was not

FIGURE 5.4

diagnosable in terms of the categories of psychiatric illness, but he declared the intention to commit suicide unless certain impossible conditions were met. In due course, he fulfilled that intention in a well-prepared fashion.

We have not found many examples of ideal self isolation. Some normal subjects show a tendency towards it, but examples of the kind illustrated all come from individuals operating within severe behavioural constraints.

(c) Social alienation (double isolation). Figure 5.5 shows a plot in which the features of actual self isolation and ideal self isolation are combined. Neither self element is defined in terms of its similarity to non-self elements. Thus, the individual is representing himself as not only being actually unlike all other people but also wanting to be unlike all other people.

The subject in this case was a severly depressed woman, who had been undergoing psychiatric treatment unsuccessfully for several years. We see that this is an example in which the social self is very important. The actual self is not clearly defined in terms of other elements, even at the dissimilarity pole, but the ideal self is strongly defined by dissimilarity to the mother (E 1) and to the social self (E 5).

Definition of self elements in terms of each other

In the example of Figure 5.1, the two self elements are separated by a distance close to 1, so being neither similar nor dissimilar they do not serve to define each other. Commonly, however, the actual and ideal self elements are not indifferent to each other and, depending on their degree of similarity, we can say that one is defined in terms of the other.

(a) Self alienation. Figure 5.6 shows an example in which the actual and the ideal self elements, being widely dissimilar, are mutually defined in opposition to each

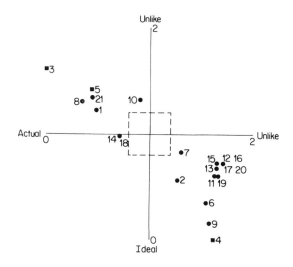

FIGURE 5.5

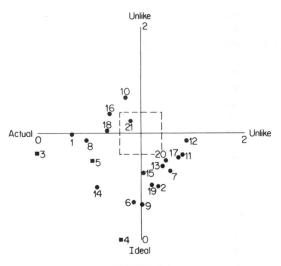

FIGURE 5.6

other. The dimensions of similarity to the two self elements are strongly negatively correlated. We can say that the two self elements are defined by one set of attributes and its reciprocal. Constructs are polarized by the opposing self elements and when the separation between the self elements is large most of the constructs are polarized along a single dimension. The subject of Figure 5.6 is a woman diagnosed as suffering from neurosis with both depressive and phobic aspects.

Self alienation is frequently combined with actual self isolation and has been observed in obsessional, depressed and anxious neurotics, and in alcoholics, but it has not so far been observed in individuals who were not seeking help.

Figure 5.7 shows the plot of an alcoholic who combines self alienation with actual self isolation. The subject is thus representing himself as being not only the opposite of what he wants to be but the opposite of everyone who constitutes his personal—social environment. Element 6, which we see is identical in location to the ideal self (E 4), is in this case 'myself in a year's time', so the subject is saying that 'In a year from now I will be exactly what I want to be', which is just the reciprocal of what he presently conceives himself to be.

(b) *Self convergence.* In Figure 5.8 there is great similarity between the actual and ideal self elements, so the two elements are practically identical. In this case, both elements are defined by the same attributes and the same pole of each construct is applied to both. Thus the dimensions of similarity to the two self elements are strongly positively correlated. A person who identifies himself in this way is stating that he, as he is, is just as he wants to be and that he has no desire for change in himself.

To achieve this degree of self-satisfaction, one might suppose that there are three alternatives:

Either the subject scales down the attributes of the ideal to those of the actual self

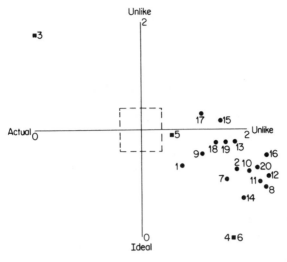

FIGURE 5.7

Or unrealistically scales up the attributes of the actual self to those of the
ideal self

Or, alternatively, some realistic achievement manifests the attainment of the
ideal, if only temporarily.

Self convergence of the degree shown in Figure 5.8 has not frequently been
observed, but it has occurred in normal subjects, in social deviates such as drug
addicts, and in cases of 'personality disorder'. The subject of Figure 5.8 is a heroin
addict who is also considered to be something of a psychopath. Taken at its face

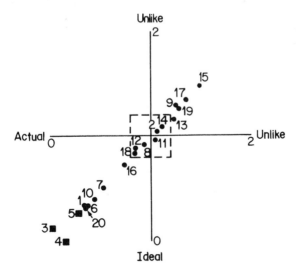

FIGURE 5.8

value, this plot seems to indicate that the subject has no willingness to consider any change in himself. If we are to choose between the three alternatives for attaining self convergence which are outlined above, we must take into account the behaviour and the life situations of this subject. In this case there was no obvious evidence of real achievement justifying such self-satisfaction, so we can rule out the third alternative and can conclude that the subject had succeeded only in either scaling down his ideal self to approximate to his actual self or scaling up his representation of his actual self to approximate to his ideal, and we cannot distinguish between these alternatives.

Changes in self-identity

Slater (1974) has pointed out that the conventional statistical methods for assessing the reliability of psychometric techniques do not apply to grids, because the assumptions concerned with sampling randomly from defined populations are not met. Rather than using the technical term 'reliability', it is preferable to speak non-technically of the stability of grid indices of self-identity. We invariably reapply each grid at between two and seven days of its original application to check on stability, and rarely find changes in the features outlined above. Some subjects have been reexamined repeatedly with the same grid over several months, and it has been the common finding that the indices change little unless some intervention occurs which results in substantial behavioural change.

The subject whose first grid is illustrated in Figure 5.6 was reexamined four weeks later, prior to starting treatment, and the plot is shown in Figure 5.9. We see that the two plots are substantially the same and differ only in detail. Subsequently, a course of psychological treatment started and she ceased to be phobic and depressed and started expanding her range of independence and competence. A grid applied six months after the first examination gave the results illustrated in Figure 5.10. We see that she is no longer self-alienated and that some non-self elements have moved closer to the self elements, e.g. her husband (E 9) and her brother-in-law (E 16).

In our experience, these methods seem to be both adequately stable and adequately sensitive to change to be useful for evaluating responses to treatment, when taken along with behavioural records.

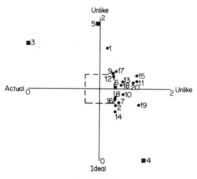

FIGURE 5.9

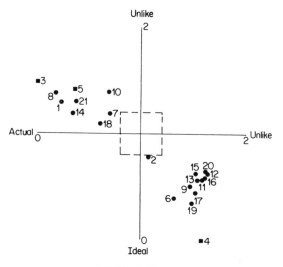

FIGURE 5.10

Operational definitions

Operational definitions for the features of self-identity plots which have been exemplified are given below.

(a) Actual self isolation. There are no non-self elements within a distance of 0.8 from the actual self.

(b) Ideal self isolation. There are non non-self elements within a distance of 0.8 from the ideal self.

(c) Social alienation. There are not more than two non-self elements within a distance of 0.8 from either the actual self or the ideal self.

(d) Self alienation. The actual self is separated from the ideal by a distance greater than 1.2, and not more than two non-self elements are closer to the ideal than is the actual self.

(e) Self convergence. The actual self is separated from the ideal by a distance less than 0.8, and not more than two non-self elements are closer to the ideal than is the actual self.

We would not like to see these defined features becoming another typology so that a patient could be labelled as 'a social alienate'. Instead, we put them forward as temporary aids to communication in the difficult area of self-identity measurement, in the hope that with advancing understanding and technology they will soon be supplanted by terms which convey both greater precision and greater insight into the relationship between an individual's conception of his own identity and his behaviour.

92

References

Bruner, J. S. (1974). *Beyond the Information Given*, Allen and Unwin, London. P. 150.

Kelly, G. A. (1955). *The Psychology of Personal Constructs*, W. W. Nordon, New York.

Makhlouf-Norris, Fawzeya, and Jones, H. G. (1971). 'Conceptual distance indices as measures of alienation in obsessional neurosis'. *Psychol. Med.*, 1, 381–387.

Makhlouf-Norris, Fawzeya, Jones, H. G., and Norris, H. (1970). 'Articulation of the conceptual structure in obsessional neurosis'. *Brit, J. soc. clin. Psychol.*, 9, 264–274.

Makhlouf-Norris, Fawzeya, and Norris, H. (1973). 'The obsessive compulsive syndrome as a neurotic device for the reduction of self-uncertainty'. *Brit. J. Psychiat.*, 122, 277–288.

Slater, P. (1974). *The Reliability and Significance of Grids*. St. George's Hospital Medical School.

6

A PERSONAL CONSTRUCT APPROACH
TO SUICIDAL BEHAVIOUR

A. Landfield

Summary

Suicide is interpreted in terms of personal construct theory: it is when a man's construct breaks down and he can no longer make sense of the world he lives in that he feels inclined to commit suicide. Grids of students, some of whom have made serious suicidal attempts, are examined in support of the argument and distinguishing features are pointed out. A case is presented in detail of a girl who completed a grid shortly before committing suicide. A special form of grid is used. As in Kelly's Rep Test, the elements are derived from roles, but constructs are elicited by presenting the elements in pairs and asking the informant to describe the difference between them, or, if they are alike, to pick out the least similar of the other elements and construe the contrast. Constructs are accepted which do not extend to all the elements and measurements are obtained from the number of cells in the grid which do not contain definite entries. (P.S.)

Some interpretations of suicidal behaviour

Suicidal behaviour appears in many contexts. Certain behaviour, such as fast driving or riding in airplanes, face-saving behaviour such as hara-kiri, acts of dying for one's religious or intellectual principles, the heroic death of a soldier or protecting parent, and taking one's life in the context of terminal illness, are more readily understood. However, certain acts of taking or attempting to take one's own life voluntarily and intentionally occur within a context of circumstances or conditions that would not justify such an act in the eyes of the community. The difficulties inherent in understanding this latter type of suicide have been thoughtfully surveyed by such authors as Berkowitz (1962), Dublin (1963), Schneidman and Farberow (1957) and Weiss (1959). Berkowitz states (p. 322): 'Suicide is a highly complex phenomenon, and there is relatively little agreement among authorities as to its cause. . . .' Dublin, former statistician of the Metropolitan Life Insurance Company states (p. iii): 'In spite of the many additional studies that have been made of the incidence of suicide and the impressive advances in psychiatry, the phenomenon is still as baffling as ever.'

Research on suicidal behaviour is an exceedingly difficult undertaking. First of all, it is an infrequent event which all too often comes to the attention of the investigator long after it has taken place. It also is an event which escapes direct research scrutiny since it is unethical to promote suicidal behaviour. Moreover, many known suicides are not labelled and many suicidal equivalents may not be recognized. Clinical statements about the suicidal do suggest hypotheses to be tested. Unfortunately, many may also be applied to persons who are seriously maladjusted but not necessarily suicidal. Then, too, the hypothesis that suicidals are psychotic or are distorting reality may preclude seriously considering the relationship between psychotic and non-psychotic suicidal behaviour. Moreover, there is confusion about whether an investigator is talking about a person who has been analysed in the context of his suicidal attempt or at some temporal distance from the act. There also is confusion about whether one is talking about a person who tries suicide but does not mean to do it and one who means to do it, i.e. confusion between threat and actual serious attempt. Finally, there is the confusion between attempt and accomplished fact.

Ansbacher (1969), in a recent paper, suggests that investigators would agree that suicide and suicidal attempts are forms of communication and therefore are interpersonal events. He also reviews the context within which Adler has discussed suicidal behaviour. Adler took the position that it should be understood as an interpersonal act; may be a vehicle of hostility towards others and a way of extorting appreciation from others; is a mistaken solution which may occur in states of temporary delusion; and may be a problem solution for people who are more normal and who are not deficient in social interest. Bakan (1966) asserts that the most profound research on suicidal behaviour points to an exaggeration of individualistic and mastery needs and a de-emphasis of social communication, living with others and living beyond one's self.

Suicidals have been described as depressed, hostile, individualistic, externally oriented and unsuccessful. However, most patients who are described in these ways do not make serious suicidal attempts. In other words, when we consider patients who are *not* suicidal, they too may suffer from depression, hostility and social failure. An inability to differentiate the suicidal from the non-suicidal patient does not mean that these variables, which are often associated with suicidal behaviour, are unimportant or have no relationship to suicidal behaviour. Our inability to differentiate does suggest that the variables associated with suicidal behaviour must be approached differently, and possibly other variables must be considered as well. Perhaps we need a different theoretical slant as much as we need more data.

The remainder of this paper focuses on a particular theory, the psychology of personal constructs, and an hypothesis derived from this theory which may highlight the nature of the suicidal event, an hypothesis which does not discount the observations of those theorists who perceive the suicidal as being alienated from his society.

Personal constructs

The central units of meaning with personal construct theory are defined by the contrasting ways of understanding life events employed by the individual as he tries to make sense of his experience. These central units of meaning, or personal constructs, are dimensions of understanding which may be defined by inclusion, exclusion and antithesis. Personal constructs, their contents and structures, understood as a system, are assumed to have profound implications for one's behaviour.

A personal construct approach to suicidal behaviour

A personal construct interpretation of suicidal behaviour points to an individual's anticipation of chaos and potential breakdown of the system he employs for encompassing, interpreting and relating to events which are primarily social in nature. The imminence of a breakdown in one's construct system is the *instigating context* of suicidal behaviour. The *purpose* of the behaviour is that the suicidal act may validate the person's life or may prevent further invalidation of his life (Kelly, 1961). Suicide is an assertion of meaningfulness. It is an assertion of the validity of a system by which one lives or dies. The suicidal act may pre-empt Man's journey into total chaos by preserving his ways of interpreting, valuing and living. He clings to his values by not exposing them to further invalidation. That suicidal behaviour may be found in the context of anticipating chaos is not such a divergent idea. However, to state that the intent of the behaviour is personally constructive and validating, when it is objectively so destructive, is more difficult to understand, but is nonetheless interesting.

The primary aim of the present paper, then, is to outline an exploratory study in which we have tested an hypothesis about the *instigating context* of serious suicidal attempts, i.e. *imminence of construct system breakdown*, an hypothesis derived from Kelly's (1955) discussion of the choice and organization corollaries.

Hypothesis derivation

Kelly states (p. 56): 'Each person characteristically evolves for his convenience in anticipating events, a construction system embracing ordinal relationships between constructs.' Commenting on this corollary, Kelly further states (p. 56): 'Different constructs sometimes lead to incompatible predictions, as everyone who has experienced personal conflict is painfully aware. Man, therefore, finds it necessary to develop ways of anticipating events which transcend contradictions.' In other words, *Man creates systems of meaning within which he may minimize confusion.* Restating this point, Man may employ higher-order generalizations or superordinate construction to resolve his conflicts. It is through the use of organization that problems are resolved. Shaw (Landfield, 1965) takes a similar position when he states that conflicts are resolved through the reconciling of opposites.

Kelly (1955) then states (p. 67) that '. . . the principle of elaborative choice also includes a person's tendency to move toward that which appears to make his *system* more *explicit* and *clearcut* . . . This may, in some instances, appear to call for constriction of one's field — even to the point of ultimate constriction suicide'.

Restating the above, Man makes sense of his personal world through organizing it. Organization provides a way of minimizing personal conflict. However, when a particular organization fails, one may begin to constrict his focus to that which can be more readily organized. When constriction becomes too great, suicidal behaviour may occur. This latter statement suggests that much loss of organization may lead to the awareness of the imminent breakdown in one's personal construct system.

The foregoing theoretical statements provide the context for an explicit hypothesis about the instigating context of suicidal behaviour. *Suicidal behaviour will be found in the context of disorganization and constriction of one's personal construct system.* Restated in a more elaborated form, one which encompasses the idea of change, suicidal behaviour will occur in the context of a decreasing ability to make sense of, interpret or react to one's personal world, most importantly, a personal world of people.

The Rep Test

The method of inquiry utilized in this investigation is a modification of Kelly's (1955) role construct repertory test, or Rep Test. In this particular form of the Rep Test, each subject is asked to record on a Response Sheet (see Figure 6.1) the first names of fifteen different acquaintances, fitting certain role types such as 'mother', 'father', 'close friend', 'a person with whom you feel uncomfortable', etc.

The next step in the procedure outlined by Kelly, but modified in our procedure, is to ask the subject to compare triads of acquaintances, in specified combinations, by stating how two of the three acquaintances in each triad are similar to each other and different from a third. This triad approach was modified by asking the subject to compare dyads of acquaintances rather than triads. Clinical experience with the triad approach suggested that a subject, when restricted to finding a similarity prior to stating a difference, occasionally is unable to respond. For example, the subject may perceive all three acquaintances as similar, yet he may think of someone outside the triad as being different. Feeling that data may be lost in the triad approach, we asked subjects to consider pairs of acquaintances, whether they are primarily different, giving contrasting descriptions, or primarily similar, and then locating another acquaintance who can be described as a contrast.

The Rep Test Response Sheet in Figure 6.1 shows two circles in each row opposite constructs. These two circles placed under acquaintances' names indicate which acquaintance dyads are to be initially construed in each row. For Example, in row one, 'mother' (element 1) and 'someone who dislikes me' (element 7) are compared. Following the establishment of a construct dimension, the thirteen acquaintances not differentiated in the development of this particular construct are also rated. For example, in Figure 6.1, after the subject established the first construct of 'religious superficially/stimulating', she rated each of the other thirteen acquaintances on this construct in the remaining cells of row one. A religiously superficial person was given the rating of '1'. A stimulating person was given the rating of '2'. If the terms 'religious superficially' and 'stimulating' were not applicable to a particular person, she placed an 'N' in the cell under that person's name in row one. Finally, if she felt that these terms were applicable to a particular person but was unable to decide which term was more applicable, she used the rating of '?'. After rating all acquaintances within the first construct dimension, she constructed fourteen more dimensions within which she rated all acquaintances. In the case of this particular subject, as well as in all other instances of Rep Test administration, instructions were first presented orally and then printed instructions were left with the subject and the task was completed without further assistance from the investigator.

Measures of constriction

The use of 'N' and '?' ratings, our second modification of the Rep Test, is suggested by Kelly (1955) in the following quotation (p. 271):

FIGURE 6.1   Rep Test response sheet

	1 Mother	2 Father	3 Brother	4 Sister	5 Boyfriend	6 Friend (female)	7 Dislikes me	8 Uncomfortable with	9 Want to know better	10 + Teacher	11 − Teacher	12 Unsuccessful	13 Successful	14 Happy	15 Unhappy	1	2
1	(1)	2	2	1	2	?	(1)	?	2	2	?	?	N	N	N	Religious superficially	Stimulating
2	2	(1)	2	2	?	?	?	?	1	1	?	2	(1)	?	2	Lots of drive	Weak-willed
3	2	1	(1)	2	1	?	2	2	1	1	(1)	2	1	1	1	Interested in others	Self-important
4	1	2	2	1	2	2	(1)	(1)	2	2	(1)	?	2	2	2	Self-important	Fun to be around
5	?	?	?	?	?	1	?	(1)	2	?	2	(1)	2	?	?	Drinks	Pseudo-sophisticated
6	2	2	2	(1)	2	(1)	1	1	?	2	?	?	?	2	2	Impatient	Comforting
7	1	1	1	1	1	1	2	2	(1)	1	2	?	1	1	(1)	Humorous	Dull
8	(1)	?	?	1	?	(1)	?	?	?	?	?	?	?	?	1	Like long hair music	(No response)
9	1	2	1	2	(1)	2	?	?	2	?	?	?	?	?	(1)	Dissatisfied	Outspoken
10	?	1	1	1	1	?	?	(1)	1	?	?	2	1	2	2	Independent	Quiet
11	?	1	(1)	(1)	1	2	2	1	1	(1)	2	1	1	1	2	Unselfconscious	Careful in appearance
12	2	1	1	1	1	1	?	1	1	1	?	?	(1)	1	2	Enjoy life	Unhappy
13	2	1	1	?	(1)	?	?	?	1	1	?	?	(1)	1	2	Sensitive to others	Withdrawn
14	1	1	1	1	1	?	?	?	(1)	1	?	(1)	1	1	?	Steady friends	(No response)
15	?	1	1	?	1	2	2	2	1	(1)	?	?	1	(1)	N	Interested in people and their problems	Self-centred

The assumption which is specific to the grid form of the test is that all the figures fall within the range of convenience of the constructs. . . . This may not be a good assumption in all cases; it may be that the client has left a void at a certain intersect simply because the construct does not seem to apply one way or the other.

Kelly (1955) further states (p. 562) that 'a construct's range of convenience comprises all those things to which the user would find its application useful'. Applying this definition to the Rep Test, one may refer to the utility of a personal construct dimension for encompassing acquaintances. Inability to widely apply a construct dimension to people is viewed by the present author as one type of constriction in the use of that construct. *Constriction in the application* of one's constructs on the Rep Test then may be measured by the total number of 'N' and '?' ratings on the 15 x 15 grid. Using such a grid, 195 non-applications are possible after one has formed constructs in relationship to his fifteen pairs of acquaintances.

Another type of constriction may also be inferred from the *content* of the construct descriptions. In this instance, one's descriptions of people are excessively *concrete*, i.e. descriptions which point to that which is more factual or superficial or that which suggests a lack of imaginative capacity. More specifically, the category of concrete content is comprised of any one of three sub-categories: factual descriptions, descriptions connoting low imagination and descriptions of external appearance. These post-coding categories (6, 9b, 13) are fully described by Landfield in a recent publication (1971) in which he states (p. 132) that concreteness is used increasingly more by therapy clients judged as least changed: 'In other words, clients judged to be least changed over the therapy period show increased constriction or impoverishment of the ways in which they view their fellow men.'

The following descriptions of acquaintances are examples of this content concreteness: always lived in the same town, brother, college educated, engaged, father, female, older, beautiful, fat, looks old, masculine, messy dresser, red hair, short, tall, ugly, concrete, doctrinaire, down to earth, matter of fact, reactionary and realistic. Assuming the use of fifteen constructs with their thirty-pole descriptions and scoring a pole only once for concreteness, the content constriction scoring range is 0 to 30.

These two measures of *constriction*, one in *application* and the other in *content*, are viewed as indices of system failure. A third measure of personal construct system failure is the low degree to which the individual's dimensions of social meaning or personal constructs are interrelated, i.e. *disorganization*. Construct interrelatedness will be determined by comparing grid row ratings or grid column ratings (Figure 6.1) which define people and concepts. After we have found which columns are related to other columns of ratings and which rows are related to other rows of ratings, a measure of construct relatedness or organization will be extracted which is called the FIC, or functionally independent construction score.

To derive the FIC score, one simply counts the number of 'grid inferred' dimensions and clusters of dimensions which are independent of one another. For example, assuming fifteen descriptive dimensions as defined by row patterns and, further, assuming that ten of these dimensions are unrelated to other dimensions (ten points), then, assuming that the remaining five dimensions are interrelated forming a cluster (one point), the total FIC score for concepts is eleven. Another

FIC score can be derived by noting the similarities and differences in the ways in which *People* are rated, i.e. column rating patterns. The range of scoring for both concept FIC scores and people FIC scores is 1 to 15. We refer to the concept organization score by the symbol FIC (c); the organization score for people is FIC (p). Since we focus on the total grid organization score, people plus concepts, the symbol becomes FIC (cp). The range of total scoring is 2 to 30. This FIC method is fully elaborated by Landfield (1971).

The single case

Theoretical structures, methods of investigation and statistical analyses remain lifeless abstractions until we apply them to a single human being. The Rep Test shown in Figure 6.1 was taken by one of our seriously suicidal subjects, SA 1, whom we will call Helen. Now Helen may be considered a predictive case since she was seen in an intake interview late one afternoon, she was given a Rep Test at that time and she made her serious attempt early the following morning. The intake interviewer recognized that she was seriously disturbed from the way she talked about 'feeling apart from other people' and 'lacking energy'. He urged her to consider several days in the Student Health Hospital for rest and a physical checkup, where she would have the opportunity to talk about her feelings at the same time. She refused to consider the alternative of hospitalization, but made the definitive statement that she would return to the clinic the following morning. That evening, Helen attended a movie which focused on the theme of prostitution. She returned to her room after the movie, wrote a suicide note and took what she thought would be a lethal dose of tranquillizers. She became very ill and sought relief from her physical pain. The clinician who interviewed her after the attempt and the clinical director of the hospital agreed that the attempt was a serious one.

Helen gave explicit instructions in her suicide note that she should be buried in her pleated skirt and with her high school jewellery. She indicated that she could not marry her fiance or any other boy. She was very attracted to many boys and felt that she no longer would be able to control her sexual urges. She felt like the prostitute in the movie. Apparently, the movie clarified the nature of her problem. In the interview which followed her unsuccessful attempt, she reiterated her fears of losing sexual control and felt unable to 'give anything' to her boyfriend. She then stated that she was 'unworthy to live', which might imply that she was 'worthy to die'. Furthermore, she stated that it was her clear intention to take her life, that failure to do so greatly upset her and that she would try again. Helen was considered too much of a psychiatric risk to continue her studies and receive treatment on an out-patient basis.

Helen's behaviour on the Rep Test fits our three formal expectations: (a) her disorganization score is elevated (FIC 21), (b) construct descriptions such as 'drinks', 'likes long hair music' and 'careful in appearance' suggest some concreteness in thinking, at least more than is found on the protocols of control subjects, and (c) her use of seventy-two '?' ratings suggests that she feels very uncertain about how to apply her constructs to other people, and we suspect to herself as well.

A personal construct analysis of Helen's descriptions of people involves the interesting assumption that her more important experiential and behavioural alternatives may be encompassed by her own language system. For example, Helen's construct 2, 'lots of drive/weak-willed', suggests that she may be capable of experiencing and behaving in both weak-willed and driving ways. Is it possible that Helen's sexual fears (loss of control) may be encompassed by this construct? Is her strong sexual urge an instance of high drive, high weakness, or both? She might have found it most difficult to define herself within this construct. It may be hypothesized that at the point of her suicidal attempt she was being strong rather than weak-willed. In this instance, her suicidal strength may be construed as an assertion of her belief that one should be sexually controlled. She was behaving responsibly and with dignity. Helen's medical history of numerous minor complaints, including fatigue, suggests that sickness might have been an attempt to control these urges. Her sickness was not just a way of *reacting to* her problems any more than her suicidal attempt was *just a reaction to* anxiety and depression. Helen's sickness and suicidal attempt were active ways of solving her problems. Was her attempt *just* a cry for help? We think not. Her clinic visit was the cry for help. At that time, Helen communicated the desperateness of her situation, one in which she was feeling alienated from others. Although this alienation from others was the verbalized distress, an underlying disengagement from her own system of values and thinking can be inferred from the Rep Test. Her social concepts are becoming fragmented and less useful, as shown by the disorganization and constriction scores. Her alienation from people is more than *just* guilt and withdrawal — it is a confusion about people and herself and a failure of the system by which she comprehends people, including herself.

An examination of Helen's construct 1, 'religious superficially/stimulating', suggests some preoccupation with religion as an important part of one's life. Her overuse of 'self-important' and 'self-centered' (constructs 3, 4 and 15), in contrast to descriptions of meaningful social interaction, suggest the possibility of a conflict between self and others which is based on feelings of superiority (or inferiority) of self. Constructs 9 and 10, 'dissatisfied/outspoken' and 'independent/quiet', suggest that satisfaction is related to being outspoken and dependence is related to being quiet. These relationships suggest that Helen would prefer being more aggressive. Suicide presumably is a more agressive act. A grid analysis shows that people are more interrelated than descriptions. The core of interrelated persons in Helen's life are all males — father, brother and boyfriend. Two small clusters of interrelated descriptions, constructs 3, 4 and 7, and 12 and 13, encompass the contents of 'egocentricity/socialization' and 'enjoyment, sensitivity to others/unhappiness, withdrawnness'.

Summarizing our clinical assessment of Helen's behaviour, the Rep Test suggests that her suicidal attempt occurred in the context of social construct system disorganization and constriction. Moreover, Helen's self—other conflict, potentiality for unhappiness and withdrawnness, a wish to be more aggressive and independent, the centrality of men in her life and the importance of self-control may be inferred from the test. Kelly's position that suicide is an assertion of the validity of one's life is supported by the Rep Test, but indirectly. Disorganization and constriction of one's social construct system provide the context for a reaffirmation of oneself. Information from the interview does suggest that she may have construed her suicidal act as responsible behaviour which was prompted by an anticipated 'loss of control' and consequent 'unworthiness'.

Procedures of primary study

Rep Tests were administered individually to the following six types of student group: a serious suicidal attempt group (SA 5), a gesture group (SG 6), an ideation group (SI 5), a long-term therapy group (LT 24), premature terminators from long-term assignment (PT 11) and a control group of better adjusted students (BA 10).

SA 5 is comprised of five students who made serious suicidal attempts. Experienced Mental Hygiene Clinic (M.H.C.) psychologists made the decision regarding suicidal status. SA 5 were hospitalized in the Student Health Hospital (S.H.H.) following suicidal attempts. They took more lethal doses of drugs or alcohol than the SG 6 group. Drugs included an assortment of aspirin, tranquillizers, patent medicine, etc. Four students sought help only at the point of acute sickness. M.H.C. staff inferred, from interview contact, that these students had wanted to end their lives. None of these students seemingly had tried to 'set up' their attempts to ensure rescue. Each student was asked to take a Rep Test within 48 hours of his attempt. One student was seen at the M.H.C. first and took the Rep Test 10 hours prior to the attempt.

SG 6 is comprised of six students who made less serious suicidal gestures. They were first seen in the S.H.H. and took drugs in smaller quantities than the students in the SA 5 group. M.H.C. staff inferred, from interview contact, that they had not wanted to end their lives. They either had contact with other students immediately after their gestures or had made certain that others would view the gesture. The Rep Test was administered within 48 hours after the gesture.

SI 5, the ideational group, is comprised of five students who talked about suicide. None had a history of suicidal attempt or gesture and their therapists did not feel that their suicidal talk would eventuate in gestures or attempts. The Rep Test was administered at the M.H.C.

LT 24 is comprised of twenty-four students who completed at least twelve sessions and thirteen weeks of therapy at the M.H.C. They had been assigned originally as longer-term and more difficult cases. Rep Tests were administered at intake. These LT 24 clients were subdivided by three experienced judges into twelve most and twelve least maladjusted (MM, LM) at intake, as judged from intake typescripts.

PT 11 is comprised of eleven students who terminated psychotherapy prior to seven interviews. They were assigned as longer-term cases and may be considered premature terminators. Rep Tests were administered at intake.

BA 10 is comprised of ten better adjusted students as judged by short (25-minute) interviews. Fourteen students volunteered to take part in a short interview and testing session. Four students were eliminated because of obvious adjustment problems. Only one student of the remaining ten had ever considered seeking counselling for personal problems and none anticipated any need for such help. The ten students were making at least a 'C' average in their coursework; all seemed to be making adequate interpersonal adjustments and there was no obvious evidence of psychosomatic problems. These students felt their own adjustment was at least average and the clinician agreed with their judgements. Rep Tests were administered after the interview.

In the context of Weiss' (1959) comment about the complexity of defining suicidal behaviour, we have summarized the nature of the five suicidal attempts and the six suicidal gestures.

Attempts

SA Client 1, female, 18, took an overdose of tranquillizers and contacted the S.H.H. three hours later. She also left a suicidal note. She was seen at the S.H.H. for numerous minor complaints prior to the attempt, but was never referred to the M.H.C. She stated that she meant to commit suicide and would try it again. She feared loss of control of her sexual impulses. Figure 6.1 shows her Rep Test.

SA Client 2, male, 21, ingested a quart of vodka, a pint of wine and a 'six-pack' of beer. He wanted to die and, except for some excellent emergency medical care, he would have died. The student felt that there was very little to live for and felt alienated from everyone. Seriousness of his physical condition delayed testing for nine days.

SA Client 3, male, 21, swallowed 120 aspirin tablets and thought that it would work. He had a history of wrist-cutting. The student called the S.H.H. only after becoming very nauseated. The clinical report stated that this boy was experiencing considerable sex-role confusion and his thinking seemed somewhat 'schizy'.

SA Client 4, female, 21, took an overdose of iron pills, patent diuretics, aspirin tablets and anything else she could find in the medicine chest. This attempt occured at the point of breakup with a 34-year-old man. She had threatened him with suicide previously. He had not responded to two previous threats. The psychologist felt that, at the point of taking the pills, she really wanted to die. When she was asked whether she would try something like this again, she responded in a most superficial way. The clinician felt she might try it again.

SA Client 5, male, 17, ingested 100 aspirin tablets. He took them impulsively and could not give any reasons why he had done so. The psychologist stated that this boy was suffering from 'the fallen star syndrome'. He had been very successful and popular prior to attending the University. Now he found it difficult to study, did not make friends and his importance was in sharp contrast to what it had been in high school. This case was considered the most marginal one of the five as to categorization as serious or gesture. Research data on this boy are not in the direction of our predictions.

Gestures

SG Client 1, male, 20, took twenty-five aspirin tablets. He admitted that he did it to gain sympathy; he did not think it was lethal. The fact that he called a friend immediately after ingestion of the aspirin would indicate that he was not seriously intent on suicide.

SG Client 2, male, 18, took forty aspirin tablets, after which he checked in at the S.H.H. He did not think that much would happen. Taking the tablets had something to do with 'making himself face his problems'. It was as though he were underlining the fact that he had problems and must do something about them. He pointed out that even though he had a high grade-point average of 4.0, he lacked social and athletic skills. He wanted to do something more constructively with his social life, but had to really face up to it first.

SG Client 3, female, 18, took twelve aspirin tablets after an argument with her boyfriend. She took the tablets in full view of a roommate who stopped her before she could take more tablets.

SG Client 4, female, 18, took twelve pain-killers and stated that she knew it would not be lethal but had some problems, one of which was pregnancy. The clinician described her as a very manipulative person.

SG Client 5, female, 17, superficially lacerated her left wrist at dorm-closing hour when her roommates were returning.

SG Client 6, female, 18, took twenty-eight aspirin tablets and stated that she definitely did not want to die. She came to the S.H.H. by herself and was not particularly sick at the time.

Predictions

Previously, it was stated that serious suicidal behaviour takes place in the context of (a) social conceptual disorganization, (b) constriction in the application of concepts and (c) constriction in the content of concepts. In the context of this hypothesis, the following specific predictions were made: SA 5 will have a higher rank average score on the three measures (a), (b) and (c) than other groups. These differences will be significant ($p = 0.05$ or better) as determined by the Mann-Whitney U test (Siegel, 1956). Further, it was predicted that SA 5 will have a higher score on a measure in which the three variables are combined.

We also predicted that LT 24 will have a higher rank average score on measures (a), (b) and (c) than BA 10. Further, it was predicted that MM 12 of the LT 24 group will have a higher rank average than LM 12 and BA 10.

Results

Disorganization: FIC (cp)

SA 5 has a higher rank average than other groups. It is significantly higher than SG 6, LM 12 and BA 10, but is not significantly higher than SI 5 ($p < 0.07$), MM 12 and PR 11. (Note Table 6.1, Where statistics are reported only for the primary hypothesis.)

TABLE 6.1   Disorganization scoring: FIC (cp) distribution differences between suicidal (SA 5) and control groups

Groups	SG 6	SI 5	LT 24	MM 12	LM 12	PT 11	BA 10
	U 5	U 6	U 41 Z 1.1	U 23	U 13	U 16	U 11
SA 5							
	p0.04	p0.07 ns	p0.13 ns	ns	p0.05	ns	p0.05

SA 5 rank average > other groups
U refers to Mann-Whitney U statistic

TABLE 6.2 Constriction scoring: combined 'N' and '?' distribution differences between suicidal (SA 5) and control groups

Groups	SG 6	SI 5	LT 24	MM 12	LM 12	PT 11	BA 10
SA 5	U 4	U 3	U 23 Z 2.1	U 13	U 14	U 10	U 12
	$p0.02$	$p0.02$	$p0.01$	$p0.05$	ns (13 = 0.05)	$p0.05$	ns (11 = 0.05)

SA 5 rank average > other groups

LT 24 has a significantly higher rank average than BA 10. MM 12 has a higher rank average than LM 12 and BA 10, and is significantly higher than BA 10.

Constriction: non-application (N and ?)

SA 5 has a higher rank average on 'N' and '?' totals than the other groups. It is significantly higher than SG 6, SI 5, LT 24, MM 12 and PT 11, but is not significantly higher than LM 12 and BA 10. However, the difference between SA 5 and LM 12, BA 10 is close to significance. (Note Table 6.2.)

LT 24 has a higher rank average than BA 10, but the difference is not significant. MM 12 does not have a higher rank average than LM 12, but does have a higher rank average than BA 10. The latter difference is *not* significant.

Constriction: concreteness

SA 5 has a higher rank average than other groups. It is significantly higher than LT 24, LM 12 and BA 10, but is *not* significantly higher than SG 6, SI 5 ($p < 0.07$), MM 12 and PT 11. (Note Table 6.3.)

LT 24 does not have a higher rank average than BA 10. MM 12 has a higher rank average than LM 12, but does not have a higher rank average than BA 10. Differences between MM 12 and LM 12, BA 10 are not significant.

Combined scoring

The next step was to empirically establish a best cutting point for differentiating SA 5 from SG 6 on each of the three variables. The following scoring points were

TABLE 6.3 Constriction scoring: concrete description differences between suicidal (SA 5) and control groups

Groups	SG 6	SI 5	LT 24	MM 12	LM 12	PT 11	BA 10
SA 5	U 11	U 5	U 24 Z 2.1	U 15	U 8	U 19	U 8
	ns	$p0.07$ ns	$p0.01$	ns	$p0.01$	ns	$p0.02$

SA 5 rank average > other groups

TABLE 6.4   Combined disorganization and constriction scores: differences between suicidal (SA 5) and control groups

Groups	SG 6	SI 5	LT 24	MM 12	LM 12	PT 11	BA 10
SA 5	U 2	U 2	U 10 Z 2.8	U 5	U 4	U 8	U 3
	$p0.01$	$p0.01$	$p0.002$	$p0.01$	$p0.01$	$p0.02$	$p0.01$

SA 5 rank average > other groups

used: FIC (cp) scored 21 points or more; 'N' plus '?' scored 61 points or more and 'concreteness' scored 2 points or more. Combining this scoring, a subject was given 1 point for each criterion score reached. The range of scoring is 0 to 3.

Using this multiple scoring, SA 5 has a higher rank average than the other groups and the differences are significant in every comparison. (Note Table 6.4.) Four SA 5 clients reached the criterion score on the three predictive variables. Two PT 11 clients also reached the criterion level on the three variables. (See Table 6.5.)

MM12 of the LT 24 group had a higher rank average than LM 12 and BA 10. However, MM 12 was not significantly higher than the other groups. All maladjusted groups had higher rank averages than BA 10. However, SA 5 was the only group that could be significantly differentiated from BA 10.

FIC and case severity

Since the FIC (cp) score differentiates LT 24 from BA 10, one may question how much case severity contributes to the suicidal level FIC scoring. To partially answer this question, we asked Miss Trixie Austin, State Hospital psychologist, to administer Rep Tests to six non-suicidal hospitalized patients. These patients had a mean age of 31, high school or college educations, and were given such diagnostic labels as: schizoid, depressive, drug-addicted, schizophrenic and sociopathic. Five of these patients were considered chronically anxious. None were backward patients. Their FIC (cp) scores of 5, 7, 14, 14, 16 and 17 did not reach the suicidal FIC (cp)

TABLE 6.5   Number of subjects in each comparison group scoring* 0, 1, 2, 3 on combined measures

Comparison groups	Scores on combined measures			
	0	1	2	3
SA 5	0	1	0	4
SG 6	3	3	0	0
SI 5	2	3	0	0
LT 24	8	12	4	0
MM 12	4	5	3	0
LM 12	4	7	1	0
PT 11	6	3	0	2
BA 10	5	4	1	0

*FIC (cp) 21 = 1 point, N + ? = 1 point, concrete poles
2 = 1 point

score level of 21. An additional protocol, that of a 52-year-old 'binge type' alcoholic male, did show suicidal level scoring.

Bannister (1962), working within personal construct theory but using grid methodology somewhat different from that used in the present study, i.e. providing constructs and asking subjects to respond to photographs of unknown people, found evidence to support the fragmented social construing of thought disorder schizophrenics. Control groups of normals, non-thought disordered schizophrenics, depressives and neurotics could be differentiated from the thought disordered but not from one another. Neurotics tended to be more highly organized than other groups.

Discussion

Although theorists maintain that suicidal behaviour is associated with social failure, hopelessness, depression, hostility, psychosis and 'a cry for help', these conceptions apparently are not defined in ways which allow clinicians to more clearly differentiate between those who will actively try suicide and those who will threaten with gestures or with words. Clinicians talk knowledgeably about suicide, yet comprehension of this problem area is shaky. Why else would N.I.M.H. devote an entire journal to it?

It can be anticipated that the many studies of suicidal behaviour which will fill our journals in the coming years will give false hope. We will rediscover something that we already know — that post-diction is easier than prediction,— and the hypotheses and methods of the present study may prove to be only part of that chaff of investigative effort. Nevertheless, it is necessary that we confront baffling problems with new theories and methods or with formulations that give a new twist to old ideas. The hypotheses and methods of the present investigation provide that new twist to old ideas. For example, the social alienation and meaning deprivation hypotheses of suicidal behaviour are encompassed by the disorganization—constriction hypothesis, although it is contended that the suicidal act takes place within the framework of a personal anticipation of failure of one's system of social meanings and a desire to avoid such failure. Personal construct system disorganization and constriction are the indices of this failure which gives rise to the dread of a total breakdown of one's structure for comprehending life. Suicidal behaviour, then, may be viewed within two interrelating hypotheses, one of *context*, which we have investigated, and the other one of *purpose*. If the purpose of acutely suicidal behaviour is to validate one's social meaning system or to prevent its further invalidation, then one important context which may lead to desperate validational assertions is the imminent deterioration and failure of that system.

Presumably, this contextual hypothesis is the least controversial of the two hypotheses. Even so, one may be critical of it because it does not include statements about hostility and depression, characteristics commonly associated with the suicidal act. Have we not seen the hostility and depression of suicidal patients? Yes, the suicidal patient often is hostile and depressed. However, *most* hostile and depressed patients are not acutely suicidal, and it may be hypothesized that their systems of social construction either are well integrated or are not constricted. Furthermore, clinical observation suggests that the manic-depressive is more prone to suicide at the point of transition from a more disturbed state to one of greater normality. Perhaps it is in this point of transition from one emotional state to its opposite that the patient experiences his greatest sense of uncertainty and his personal construct system is most vulnerable to invalidation.

Summary

A major hypothesis concerning the nature of suicidal behaviour was derived from statements of personal construct theory. It was hypothesized that serious suicidal attempts occur in the context of social conceptual disorganization and constriction as measured by the role construct repertory test (Rep Test). This hypothesis was tested in relationship to a serious suicidal student group, a gesture group, an ideation group, a long-term therapy group, a group of premature terminators from long-term assignment, a better adjusted control group and a group of hospitalized patients. Data were collected within the contexts of a rather unique theory and an uncommon method. Moreover, an attempt was made to more carefully differentiate actively suicidal persons from those who are not really intent on such behaviour and in the context of ostensibly more normal personalities.

References

Ansbacher, H. L. (1969). *Suicide as Communication: Adler's Concept and Current Applications.* Paper read at the Fifth International Convention for Suicide Prevention, London, September 24—27, 1969.

Bakan, D. (1966). *The Duality of Human Existence,* Rand McNally, Chicago.

Bannister, D. (1962). 'The nature and measurement of schizophrenic thought disorder'. *J. Mental Science,* 108, 825—842.

Berkowitz, L. (1962). *Aggression: A Social Psychological Analysis,* McGraw-Hill, New York.

Dublin, L. (1963). *Suicide: A Sociological and Statistical Study,* Ronald, New York.

Kelly, G. A. (1955). *The Psychology of Personal Constructs,* Vols. 1 and 2. W. W. Norton, New York.

Kelly, G. A. (1961). 'Suicide: the personal construct point of view'. In N. L. Farberow and E. S. Schneidman (Eds.), *The Cry for Help,* McGraw-Hill, New York.

Landfield, A. W. (1965). 'Franklin Shaw: the emergence of man and theory'. *J. Humanistic Psychol.,* 5, 91—102.

Landfield, A. W. (1971). *Personal Construct Systems in Psychotherapy,* Rand McNally, Chicago.

Schneidman, E. S., and Farberow, N. L. (Eds.) (1957). *Clues to Suicide,* McGraw-Hill, New York.

Siegel, S. (1956). *Nonparametric Statistics for the Behavioral Sciences,* McGraw-Hill, New York.

Weiss, J. (1959). 'The suicidal patient'. In S. Arieti (Ed.), *American Handbook of Psychiatry,* Vol. 3, Chapter 8, Basic Books, New York.

7

MONITORING CHANGES IN THE MENTAL STATE OF A PATIENT UNDERGOING PSYCHIATRIC TREATMENT

Patrick Slater

Summary

Changes in a patient's mental state while undergoing psychiatric treatment were monitored by means of a personal questionnaire with seventeen scales recording his self-evaluations in terms of the symptoms he mentioned in describing his disorder. Records were obtained on twenty-four occasions, before and after sessions of psychotherapy and occupational therapy. The data were analysed as a grid. Measurements were obtained of the extent and direction of the changes which occurred, and were mapped to show how they related to the general aggravation or relief of the symptoms and their reference to external or internal conditions. The path they follow is clearly defined, though it is devious and movements along it are sometimes forward, sometimes backward. It proved possible to compare the immediate effects of the two treatments and show that psychotherapy was the more powerful and flexible form of treatment in this case. Questions concerning generalizations of the results are discussed. (P.S.)

The source of the data

A patient admitted to the Bethlem Royal Hospital with a diagnosis of neurotic depression in an immature personality characterized by morbid jealousy was made the subject of a single-case research designed and supervised by Monte Shapiro (Shapiro, 1969, case A). Felix Post was the consultant in charge of treatment; psychotherapy was conducted by B. Woody and occupational therapy by C. Carsley. One of Shapiro's students constructed a personal questionnaire consisting of seventeen symptom scales, using the terms in which the patient himself described his disorder. Each scale has a range from 4, for the acutest form of the symptom, to 1, for its complete remission (see Shapiro, 1961).

Sessions of occupational therapy and psychotherapy were alternated during the course of treatment, and the therapist responsible administered the questionnaire before and after each session to record how the patient evaluated his mental state at that precise time. When the record was terminated by the patient's discharge, data had been collected on twenty-four occasions. They were very kindly placed at the disposal of the author, who is solely responsible for the analyses and the discussion which follow.

TABLE 7.1 Results from a series of personal questionnaires

Symptoms	Tues. 4 April PT		Fri. 7 April OT		Tues. 11 April OT		Fri. 14 April PT		Tues. 18 April PT		Fri. 21 April OT		Tues. 25 April OT		Fri. 28 April PT		Tues. 2 May PT		Fri. 5 May OT		Tues. 9 May OT		Fri. 16 May PT	
	B	A	B	A	B	A	B	A	B	A	B	A	B	A	B	A	B	A	B	A	B	A	B	A
a My stomach keeps plunging	4	4	3	2	2	2	3	1	3	1	2	2	4	4	2	2	1	1	2	1	1	2	2	2
b I feel on edge all the time	4	3	1	1	2	1	1	1	4	1	1	1	3	2	1	1	1	1	1	1	1	1	1	1
c I feel very bad in the evening	4	4	4	2	2	2	4	2	4	4	4	4	4	4	4	1	1	1	2	1	1	2	1	1
d I feel depressed	3	2	1	1	1	1	2	1	4	1	1	1	4	3	1	1	1	1	1	1	2	1	1	1
e I am worried about the future	4	4	4	4	4	4	4	4	4	4	4	4	4	4	4	4	4	2	4	4	3	3	3	3
f I feel jealous of my wife	3	3	2	1	1	1	1	1	1	1	1	1	1	1	1	1	1	1	1	1	1	1	1	1
g I feel like hitting people who annoy me	3	3	1	1	1	1	1	1	1	1	1	1	1	1	1	1	1	1	1	1	1	1	1	1
h I feel unhappy	4	2	1	4	1	1	1	1	3	2	1	1	4	4	1	1	1	1	2	1	1	1	1	1
i I don't feel like ever doing my job again	4	4	4	4	4	4	4	4	4	4	4	4	4	4	4	4	3	1	3	3	4	3	4	3
j I don't want to read the papers	4	4	4	4	4	3	1	1	4	4	2	1	4	4	3	1	1	1	1	1	1	1	1	1
k My thoughts always go to seeing my wife with the other man	4	3	2	1	3	1	2	1	3	3	3	2	4	3	2	1	2	2	2	2	2	2	2	2
l I can't concentrate	4	2	1	2	1	3	2	1	1	2	1	1	4	3	2	1	1	1	1	1	1	1	1	1
m I feel jealous of my wife's success	3	3	1	1	1	1	1	1	1	1	1	1	3	3	4	1	1	1	1	1	1	1	2	1
n I can be hurt extremely easily	4	4	4	4	2	2	4	4	4	4	3	3	3	4	4	1	1	1	2	1	2	1	2	1
o I get confused	2	2	1	2	2	2	1	1	2	3	1	1	4	4	3	1	1	1	2	1	2	1	1	1
p I feel tense	3	3	2	1	2	2	1	1	4	1	1	1	1	4	3	2	1	1	1	1	1	1	1	1
q I feel my heart beating fast	4	3	3	1	1	1	2	1	4	2	2	1	4	3	2	1	1	1	1	1	1	1	1	1

PT = psychotherapy, OT = occupational therapy, B = before a treatment session, A = after a treatment session

The table containing the data (Table 7.1) is a particular form of grid, where the constructs are the symptom scales and the elements are the informant's mental states at the times when he recorded them. It has one exceptional feature: the elements are not put in order arbitrarily but belong in a temporal sequence related to concomitant events.

The data are put through a principal component analysis and the results are used to describe the fluctuations in the patient's mental state measured on the scales of the two major components; they are then subjected to statistical analyses.

Results from the principal component analysis, concerning the dimensions of the symptom space

The results show that 60.5 per cent. of the variation occurs along the axis of the first component and another 11.2 per cent. along the axis of the second. The remaining variation spreads out over the axes of another fourteen components, diminishing gradually. Finally, there is one axis where no variation occurs, since the readings obtained from the symptoms 'I feel jealous of my wife's success' and 'I feel like hitting people who annoy me' do not vary independently; they are exactly the same.

The scale of the first component is a weighted sum of the measurements on all the symptom scales, the weights being the entries in its vector, Table 7.2. As the readings on the symptom scales are highest when the symptoms are most acute, the weights assigned to them must be negative if general improvement in the patient's mental state is to be expressed as a positive value. In sum, the component scale measures aggravation of the symptoms negatively and improvement positively.

The second component contrasts some symptoms with others. A general impression of the nature of the contrast can be gained by comparing those which

TABLE 7.2   The construct vectors of the first two components

Symptom scale (construct)		Component 1 Vector	Component 2 Vector
a	My stomach keeps plunging	−0.27	−0.11
b	I feel on edge all the time	−0.25	−0.29
c	I feel very bad in the evening	−0.34	+0.44
d	I feel depressed	−0.24	−0.30
e	I am worried about the future	−0.11	+0.26
f	I feel jealous of my wife	−0.10	−0.03
g	I feel like hitting people who annoy me	−0.09	−0.08
h	I feel unhappy	−0.29	−0.22
i	I don't feel like ever doing my job again	−0.11	+0.23
j	I don't want to read the papers	−0.38	+0.12
k	My thoughts always go to seeing my wife with the other man	−0.19	−0.19
l	I can't concentrate	−0.23	−0.13
m	I feel jealous of my wife's success	−0.09	−0.08
n	I can be hurt extremely easily	−0.31	+0.55
o	I get very confused	−0.21	−0.07
p	I feel tense	−0.28	−0.22
q	I feel my heart beating fast	−0.32	−0.09

have the highest positive weights with those that have the largest negative ones:

	Construct	Weight
n	I can be hurt extremely easily	0.55
c	I feel very bad in the evening	0.44
e	I am worried about the future	0.26
i	I don't feel like ever doing my job again	0.23
		. . .
p	I feel tense	−0.22
h	I feel unhappy	−0.22
b	I feel on edge all the time	−0.29
d	I feel depressed	−0.30

The contrast appears to be between constructs which refer to external circumstances and ones that are directly self-referent.

Further evidence on the relationships between the symptom scales comes to light when their dispersion in the space of the three major components is examined. By including the third, another 7.2 per cent. of the observed variation is taken into account. Figure 7.1 is a map of the dispersion projected onto one surface of a sphere. The axis of the first component runs from front to back, with the negative pole foremost; and as the prevailing direction of all the symptom scales is the same (from aggravation to relief) they all appear on the visible surface. The axis of the second runs from left to right and of the third from top to bottom.

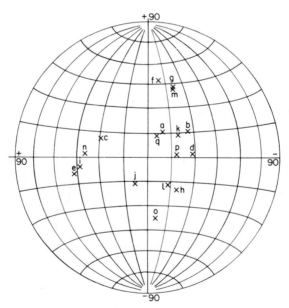

FIGURE 7.1   The dispersion of the symptom-scales in the space of the three major components represented as the negative aspect of a sphere

The four symptoms referring to external circumstances, which have already been noted as the ones with the highest positive weights for the second component, namely c, e, i and n, appear as a separate cluster near the positive pole of the horizontal axis. The three which form a separate cluster near the positive pole of the vertical axis, namely f, g and m, have stability as their common characteristic. While other symptom scales record fluctuations, they remain constant and thus constitute a null class in effect. They can be left out of account.

The construct vectors and element loadings of the components constitute their operational definitions; the interpretations — of the first as a scale for measuring aggravation or relief of symptoms in general and of the second as a scale for measuring the relative strength of externally and internally referred symptoms — are supplied speculatively by the author, not elicited from the patient. They are introduced merely for descriptive purposes.

Much can be gained from replacing the original symptom scales by the derived scales of the major components:

1. The crude four-point scales referring to particular symptoms are converted by weighted summation into finely graduated and more extensive scales which define and measure the main directions in which variation occurs.
2. Most of the information about the simultaneous variation on all the original scales can be gathered by examining the variation on a few component scales.
3. Since the component scales are strictly orthogonal, conclusions drawn from one are additional to any drawn from another, whereas conclusions drawn from different symptom scales are metrically confounded because such scales are intercorrelated.

Results (continued): fluctuations in the patient's mental state revealed by the components

The element loadings in Table 7.3 record the patient's mental state on different occasions, as measured by the two major components. The sequence of the

Table 7.3   The element loadings of the first two components

| | | Component 1 | | Component 2 | |
| | | Before | After | Before | After |
Date	Treatment	treatment	treatment	treatment	treatment
4 April	PT	−6.23	−4.20	−1.64	−0.08
7 April	OT	−1.54	−0.67	2.09	1.07
11 April	OT	0.13	0.70	−0.12	0.17
14 April	PT	−0.16	2.05	1.64	1.67
18 April	PT	−4.77	−1.42	−0.89	1.98
21 April	OT	0.32	1.22	1.56	1.71
25 April	OT	−6.05	−4.85	−2.17	−0.41
28 April	PT	−1.11	3.06	1.94	−0.53
2 May	PT	3.25	3.68	−0.84	−1.84
5 May	OT	1.83	3.25	−0.25	−0.84
9 May	OT	2.80	2.74	−1.24	−0.77
16 May	PT	2.66	3.30	−0.43	−1.75

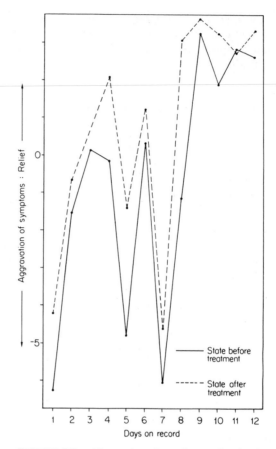

FIGURE 7.2   Fluctuations from day to day in the patient's mental state, measured on the scale of the major component

measurements on the scale of the first is traced in Figure 7.2 by two lines: the continuous line connects the measurements before treatment and the broken line the ones after.

The patient's mental state fluctuated widely during April, the period that includes the first eight sessions, but there is no convincing evidence of any lasting relief from the symptoms. His state at the beginning of the seventh session is almost the same as it was at first. However, his state after the eighth was the best recorded for the period, and it remained at this satisfactory level during May, which includes the last four sessions before discharge.

Improvements were recorded after treatment at every session, with the trivial exception of the eleventh. During the first period the improvement was sometimes quite conspicuous, but during the second, when a satisfactory mental state was being maintained, the beneficial effects of treatment were naturally much slighter.

Figures 7.3 and 7.4 are maps of the plane in the symptom space defined by the

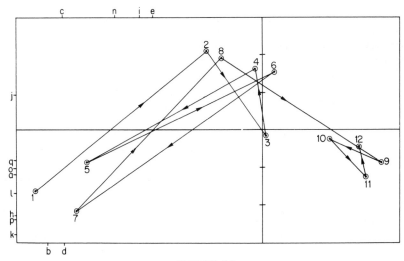

FIGURE 7.3

axes of the two major components. The letters a, b, . . . , q on the margins mark the relative orientations of the symptom scales (the three null scales, f, g and m, are omitted). Aggravation of a symptom corresponds with movement towards its point on the margin away from the point of intersection of the axes, and relief corresponds with movement in the opposite direction.

Readings at each session before treatment are plotted in Figure 7.3, and connected by a line from one to the next with an arrowhead on it to show the direction of the change which occurred meanwhile. Readings after treatment are omitted. The immediate effects of treatment are indicated by similar directed lines

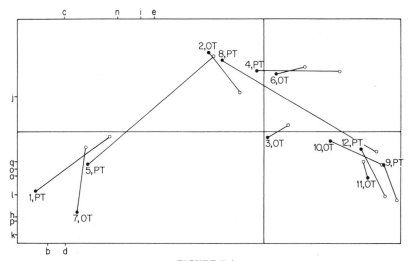

FIGURE 7.4

in Figure 7.4. The state at the beginning of the session is indicated by a solid circle, marked with the number of the session and a PT or an OT to show the nature of the treatment — psychotherapy or occupational therapy. The state at the end of the session is indicated by a hollow circle, so the line connecting the two points indicates the extent and direction of the immediate change.

A very conspicuous and quite unexpected feature of both the diagrams is the appearance of a well-marked, indirect course of change. Tempestuous as the fluctuations are, straying backwards and forwards along it, they keep quite closely to it. It could perhaps be described as a circuitous course or one that turns a corner — whatever else it may be it is certainly not straight. It may be tempting to indulge in speculations and to look for analogies and explanations in the literature of psychiatry in the attempt to interpret it, but perhaps it would be wiser to keep to the evidence as closely as possible.

The course has a fairly well-marked starting point, mid point and end point. During April the patient's mental state fluctuates between the start and the mid point, being back near the start at the beginning of sessions 5 and 7, and near the mid point at the beginning of the other five sessions; after the eighth it moves over to the end point, where it remains. At the starting point a high level of disturbance is shown on almost all the symptom scales; at the mid point the scales referred internally record more relief than the ones referred externally; and at the end point almost all the scales record relief. So a sufficient explanation for the shape of the course is that the internally referred symptoms were the ones most easily relieved in this case. It is also the explanation why the externally referred symptoms form a separate cluster (see Figure 7.1) and define the axis of the second component by contrast with the others.

Evidence for comparing the two forms of treatment can be found in Figure 7.4. The largest and most beneficial effects were due to psychotherapy, both in the transition from the starting point to the mid point and from the mid point to the end point. It proved more powerful and more flexible than occupational therapy in this case.

Results from statistical tests

This report is a review of a previous one on the same data (Slater, 1970; see also Rump, 1974, and Slater, 1974). Analysis of variance was applied there to the loadings of the elements on the two major components, and some small amendments ought to be made in their details. However, the conclusions are not affected and they are all that need to be noted here.

The investigation was originally planned with the intention of applying an analysis of this kind to the data. For example, the treatments are alternated orthogonally to the course of time in days (Tuesdays and Fridays) and months (April and May). The total observed variation on any of the scales can be partitioned into the variation between sessions and between occasions at the same session; and the variation between sessions can be partitioned further into the variation between treatments and between months. Moreover, the interaction between these two main effects can be found. The variation between occasions at the same session can be partitioned similarly into the variation between times (before and after treatment); and the first-order interactions of times with treatments and with months can be found, together with the second-order interactions of these three main effects.

When this analysis is applied to the measurements of the elements on the scale of the first component, the observations reported descriptively in the previous section can be verified statistically. The tests prove that the null hypothesis cannot account at an acceptable level of probability for:

1. The correlation between the two series of records shown in Figure 7.1. This evidence of the short-term test—retest reliability of the questionnaire amply satisfies the standards maintained for psychometric tests in general.
2. The difference in level between the two series, which shows that immediate improvement has occurred regularly after treatment.
3. The difference in the extent of immediate improvement, which shows that psychotherapy was more beneficial than occupational therapy.
4,5,6. The differences between the periods, which show that relief was greater, a more stable state was maintained and the effects of treatment were smaller in the second.

A different kind of analysis is required for the measurements of the elements on the axis of the second component. The variation along it cannot be said to measure changes for better or worse according to their direction, since it is orthogonal to the axis of the first, which measures aggravation—relief of symptoms. The questions to be considered statistically concern the relative amounts of variation from different sources. The largest of these is the ratio comparing the variances between the measurements in the two periods ($F = 5.87$, $n_1 = 15$, $n_2 = 7$), which shows that the patient's mental states during the second period were significantly more stable than in the first. Both treatments produce changes in both directions. The changes after psychotherapy are larger and more evenly balanced in direction; those following occupational therapy are mostly shown as directed upwards in Figure 7.4, thus recording relatively greater relief of the internally referred symptoms. However, the variance ratio ($F = 4.17$, $n_1 = n_2 = 5$) is not large enough to prove that the two treatments differ significantly in this respect. Thus, the results from the second component are not negligible; they supplement the results from the first though, as one might expect, they contribute less.

Statistical proof that the course from starting point to end point mapped in Figures 7.3 and 7.4 is circuitous, not straight, can be obtained by fitting a second-order polynomial to the measurements on the two components and calculating how much of the variation of the second can thus be attributed to regression on the first. The amount is almost half. Rectilinear regression, of course, does not account for any.

Methodological points needing consideration

The analysis has rested on the assumption that the scales have remained stable throughout the course of treatment and that all the variation recorded is due to changes in the patient's mental state. If it could not be accepted, there would be no certainty about what the variation shows, so it is necessary as a working assumption. Admittedly, the contrary cannot be completely disproved, but there is no evidence to substantiate it, while arguments in support of the assumption can be found in the procedure and the results.

The interview guards against inconstancies in the use of the scales by asking patients to make paired comparisons between statements describing different degrees in the severity of the symptoms (Phillips, 1976); thus there is evidence that the patient has used the scales consistently. Moreover, unreliabilities in the use of the scales could not have produced the systematic pattern we have observed in the results, but would have obscured it.

The application of statistical tests raises a further question. How far can conclusions be generalized which have been reached by applying them to results of experiments like this? How far, for example, can the conclusion that psychotherapy gives more relief than occupational therapy be generalized from the evidence that a significant difference was found here between the averages for the two treatments?

Statistical tests apply to experiments which involve sampling a universe, and an effect observed in one is considered significant if probability theory indicates that it is not likely to disappear when the experiment is replicated with another sample drawn by the same procedure from the same universe. So a reasonable paraphrase for the question 'How far can a conclusion from an experiment be extended?' is 'What are the boundaries of the universe sampled in it?'.

Uncertainties about the boundaries of universes sampled in experiments with repertory grid technique form a major source of difficulty in deciding how probability theory should apply to them. In the present experiment, however, the universe is evidently definable as the complete series of mental states through which the patient passed during the course of his disorder. The conclusions that he benefited more and in a greater variety of ways from psychotherapy than from occupational therapy are therefore ones that do not go beyond the boundaries of the universe sampled and can hardly be considered open to doubt. Any further extension of them can only be tentative and dependent on analogies drawn from wider experience. Thus, the evidence might be quoted to support an argument that the prognosis for psychotherapy is favourable in some other case, on the strength of whatever valid analogies could be found between it and this.

General discussion

The results from this research seem promising enough to prompt the question 'How far they are likely to be repeatable?', and several related problems are thereby brought into consideration.

To answer the preliminary question 'How far can personal questionnaire techniques be generalized?', we need to consider the essential properties of such a questionnaire. It is constructed from statements made by a patient describing the psychological symptoms of his illness during the course of an open-ended interview, and consists of a set of scales which can be used by him to register the severity of his symptoms at any particular time. It is not considered suitable for patients who show clinical signs of thought disorder and is probably not adaptable for ones who are retarded mentally (Litman, 1971), but it is not subject to other restrictions and could presumably be extended to study any illness with important psychological concomitants and to monitor the effects of any treatment. For example, it might be used to monitor the after-effects of a surgical operation such as hysterectomy.

Phillips (1976) has discussed the generalization of the technique with particular reference to alternative ways of graduating symptom scales, but has not gone on to consider the next question of whether principal component analysis is appropriate for data obtained by the technique.

Being an idiographic multivariate scaling system, a questionnaire automatically generates an array of data in the form of a grid when it is used repeatedly. So any data obtained in this way can be analysed by the method exemplified here.

A characteristic of such arrays, that their elements are ordered in time, is essential but not exclusive to them. If an informant completes a grid with m elements and n constructs on o occasions, the data will form a three-way array which can be partitioned into m sections each showing the changes in the evaluation of a particular element in terms of the n constructs on the o occasions. Or an array can be formed from the differences between two such sections. In this way, for instance, changes in the relationship between a patient and his therapist could be measured over a course of time.

Evidently, personal questionnaires constitute one of a great many different sources of data which take the form of grids. There is nothing unique about them that precludes them from the same form of analysis. It may seem a puzzle why the INGRID program, which had already proved widely acceptable for grids of other kinds in its 1967 version and had been shown to be applicable to data from personal questionnaires when the results reviewed here were first published (Slater, 1970), has not since been applied more extensively to such data. Actually, the program was being used by G. K. Litman and D. A. Shapiro for analysing their data shortly afterwards. It may seem even more of a puzzle why their results were not reported and discussed in their theses (1971). Anyone who seeks a strictly scientific explanation in the literature is likely to remain dissatisfied; only a historian with an interest in personalities and an eye for what goes on behind the scenes could discover the complete explanation.

Principal component analysis is recommended here as the optimum, i.e. mathematically canonical procedure for simplifying a systematica and potentially exhaustive examination of the data (see Slater, 1976). Other procedures may conceivably be better for particular purposes, but most run greater risks of leaving important aspects of the data unexamined. In comparing proposed methods, what is overlooked needs to be noted as well as what is found.

As results from INGRID analyses of personal questionnaires have not been published and results from other analyses do not take their place, the ones reviewed here have remained for five years a solitary example of the measurements obtainable; and in the meantime interest in the potentialities of personal questionnaire technique has tended to decline — possibly because grid technique has greater resources. No other diagrams for comparison with Figures 7.1 to 7.4 are yet available from parallel researches using data from personal questionnaires; but Ryle and Lipshitz have recently (1975) used a dyadic grid similarly to monitor changes in the way in which husband evaluated the relationship between his wife and himself during a course of treatment.

Answers to the final question of whether parallel researches may be expected to show parallel results must accordingly be couched in extremely speculative terms.

It is perhaps reasonable to expect that symptom scales will usually form configurations roughly resembling the one in Figure 7.1 — all tending to cluster on one hemisphere, leaving the opposite one empty. This is because the rule for constructing a scale is that it is to be graduated from maximum severity to complete remission. Scales referring to the same illness are therefore all likely to be orientated in approximately the same direction, and the major dimension of variation in the patient's mental states will tend to be between aggravation and relief of most symptoms concomitantly. However, more complicated patterns are conceivable; they could occur if remission of some symptoms is accompanied by aggravation of others. This might indicate the presence of a psychological trap like ones noted by Rowe and Ryle, where, for instance, a patient sees strong people as cruel, and kind as weak and sickly, and is accordingly confronted with a dilemma in choosing what role to adopt. Or it could indicate that the treatment being followed is not completely successful and has some unfortunate side-effects. Or, again, it could correspond with a deliberately phased course of treatment such as may be followed for a drug addict, when one drug is replaced by another less addictive one in order to provide some temporary relief from acute withdrawal symptoms.

There is really not much reason to suppose that the path mapped in Figures 7.2, 7.3 and 7.4 is a typical one for fluctuations in other patients' mental states to follow, even if their diagnoses and treatments could be matched to this one's. Only the main outlines of the procedure adopted here are repeatable; each application of it must be adapted to a different person and the results will then become incorporated in another case history. If one record is not like another, more than one explanation of the differences is likely to be admissible. It would be prudent, for the present, to expect maps constructed from them by the same methods as these to take many different forms.

The path can be mapped, whatever form it takes. The method of analysis does not postulate any hypotheses about it — or, in other words, attempt to impose any particular form on it. Thus, it is not committed to any model of remedial change, but could be applied when mood-swings occur spontaneously and have no definite start or end point, e.g. during the menstrual cycle. If the user decides after inspecting the results in a particular case that some particular kind of regression equation would fit them well, he will find the measurements on the scales of the components more convenient for the purpose than those on the symptom scales, because the components are strictly orthogonal and fewer will need to be considered.

Conclusions

Contemporaneous measurements of the extent and direction of changes which actually occur in the state of mind of an individual are desirable when he is subjected to any treatment which is intended to, or liable to, produce such changes. Ideally, perhaps, no such treatment should be attempted unless its direct effects and side-effects are measurable at the time.

The need is clearest, of course, when the symptoms displayed are predominantly psychological, being expressed as anxiety states, guilt feelings or depression. In other cases. where mental disturbances accompany behavioural anomalies, as in agoraphobia or anorexia nervosa, the behavioural changes are commonly taken as the criteria of the efficacy of the treatment and the mental changes may be regarded as incidental. Evidence of the former is readily observable and can be described as objective, while evidence of the latter, based on clinical impressions, is not easily recorded and may be considered suspect and anyhow superfluous. Yet the opinion may be tenable, in some cases at least, that the mental changes are critical and the behavioural changes are merely incidental. In the treatment of alcoholism, for instance, it seems necessary that the patient should first accept the idea that he is desperately in need of treatment. Then medical and physical treatments directly aimed at altering behaviour may produce dramatic results rapidly, but may soon be followed by a relapse if the patient does not accept the idea that he is still an alcoholic and must continue to leave all alcoholic refreshments alone. Thus psychotherapy is an important part of the treatment and the psychological changes which occur during it appear to be the critically important ones. They should be treated as independent variables and measured directly, not regarded merely as dependent functions of observed variations in behaviour. When comparisons are being made, it is as reasonable to ask what are the psychotherapeutic effects of behaviour therapy as what are the effects of psychotherapy on behaviour.

In deciding on a course of psychiatric treatment for a patient, the consultant is bound to rely primarily on statistical generalizations (unless he is convinced that one particular treatment, psychoanalysis for instance, is the panacea for all mental ills). From the evidence available, he will draw the conclusion that a certain diagnosis is correct. He will recall evidence of a statistical kind that some other patients with that diagnosis have benefited from a certain treatment, and choose it as the best for his case. Once the course of treatment has begun, statistics are hardly likely to be of any further help to him. He is no longer concerned with speculating on the probable effects of the treatment on other patients but with observing its actual effects on his own. He is entitled to expect the psychological changes accompanying the treatment to be measured as directly, promptly and precisely as possible. Otherwise, he might persist ill-advisedly with a treatment that is not proving beneficial.

When suitable methods of measurement have been developed sufficiently, other applications may be found for them, e.g. in studying the effects of different kinds of corrective training for criminals and delinquents. It may be just as ill-advised to persist with an expensive treatment for them if it is not proving beneficial.

Personal questionnaire technique and other forms of grid technique can help in monitoring psychological effects of treatment, as this paper shows.

References

Litman, Gloria K. (1971). *An Investigation of Some Psychological Variables Affecting Symptom Fluctuation in Neurotic Depressives.* Ph.D. Thesis, University of London.

Phillips, J. P. N. (1976). 'Generalised personal questionnaire techniques'. In *The measurement of intrapersonal space by grid technique: dimensions of intrapersonal space* ed. P. Slater. John Wiley, London.

Rump, E. E. (1974). 'Cluster analysis of personal questionnaires, compared with principal component analysis'. *Br. J. soc. clin. Psychol.,* 13, 283–292.

Ryle, A., and Lipshitz, Susan (1975). 'The marital reconstruction grid.' *Br. J. med. Psychol.,* 48, 39–48.

Shapiro, D. A. (1971). *The Measurement and Investigation of Psychotherapeutic Change*. Ph.D. Thesis, University of London.

Shapiro, M. B. (1961). 'A method of measuring psychological changes specific to the individual psychiatric patient'. *Br. J. med. Psychol.*, 34, 151–155.

Shapiro, M. B. (1969). 'Short term improvements in the symptoms of affective disorder'. *Brit. J. soc. clin. Psychol.*, 8, 187–188.

Slater, P. (1970). 'Personal questionnaire data treated as forming a repertory grid'. *Brit. J. soc. clin. Psychol.*, 9, 357–370.

Slater, P. (1974). 'Cluster analysis versus principal component analysis: a reply to E. E. Rump'. *Brit. J. soc. clin. Psychol.*, 13, 427–430.

Slater, P. (1976). *The measurement of intrapersonal space by grid technique: dimensions of intrapersonal space*, John Wiley, London.

8

STUDIES OF THE PSYCHIATRIST'S INSIGHT INTO THE PATIENT'S INNER WORLD

Dorothy Rowe, Patrick Slater

Summary

Grid technique can be used to measure a psychiatrist's understanding of his patient. Two studies of this kind are reported. In the first, a psychiatrist was given a list of the elements and constructs in a grid completed by a patient he had selected, and was asked to fill it in as he supposed his patient had. Though he showed a fair degree of insight on the whole, there was one area where he had misconstrued his patient's views. In the second study, grids were completed by a psychiatrist and his patient before and after a two months' course of treatment, following the same procedure. Several comparisons could be made. In this case, both the psychiatrist's estimates came closer to the patient's grids, and the second improved on the first. But again the discrepancies, which are examined in detail, prove to contain features of psychological interest; they are not merely random deviations. (P.S.)

Introduction

In therapy the psychiatrist is concerned to understand how the patient views himself and the significant people in his environment. It is of some importance to develop measures of the accuracy of the psychiatrist's understanding. Grid technique is suitable for this purpose.

The patient can describe his private world in terms of the elements and constructs of a grid. His personal construct system has its own inner logic, a set of relationships and values which he has built from his experience. The system is not necessarily consistent throughout, since human beings have been capable of holding contrary opinions long before Orwell named it 'doublethink'; but even with its internal inconsistencies each person's system hangs together as a whole. To understand another person we need to see the inner logic which makes the construct system complete and interrelated. We cannot understand another person by imposing the inner logic of our own construct system onto his behaviour. His values may well be different from ours.

The word *values* is stressed here since it is not the case that personal construct theory is a purely cognitive theory of behaviour, as people often view it. Generally, an individual's constructs assign a value, a quality of goodness or badness of the elements they apply to, in relation to his own image of himself. Similarly, when emotional states are used as constructs, subjects experience no difficulty in applying them to the relevant elements.

The extent of a psychiatrist's understanding of his patient's world can be investigated by comparing a grid completed by the patient with one referring to the same elements and constructs, completed by the psychiatrist in the way he supposes the patient has done it. Of course, the elements and constructs chosen from the patient's system must be ones that come to the attention of the psychiatrist during therapy.

Two studies of this kind have been made. The first was originally reported in 1971; the second is presented for the first time here.

The first study

Method

The psychiatrist selected a patient who was known to him over a period of eight months. This patient was administered a repertory grid using the split-half method (Bannister and Mair, 1968).

The patient was required to select twenty people who were significant figures in his past and present environment, including himself and his ideal self. These are the elements listed in Table 8.1. Eight constructs and their contrasts were elicited from the patient and seven constructs were supplied by the tester. The elicited constructs were evaluative while the supplied constructs are as shown in Table 8.2. The patient was then required to sort the twenty elements into two groups of ten for each of the constructs and its contrast. Each sort was marked on a grid.

A list of the patient's elements and constructs was given to the psychiatrist, who then predicted into what groups of ten and ten the patient had sorted the elements on each construct. His predictive sorts were marked on a grid.

TABLE 8.1   Differences between patient's and psychiatrist's evaluations of elements

1.	Self	6
2.	Ideal self	7
3.	Wife	4
4.	Daughter	4
5.	Father	4
6.	Mother	5
7.	Sister-in-law	7
8.	Brother	8
9.	Brother	5
10.	Sister	5
11.	Brother-in-law	7
12.	Grandmother	7
13.	Colleague	5
14.	Colleague	2
15.	Colleague	1
16.	Friend	4
17.	Psychiatrist	4
18.	Woman patient	10
19.	Friend	5
20.	Father-in-law	2

TABLE 8.2   Correlations between patient's and psychiatrist's evaluation of constructs

Elicited constructs

1.	Runs things efficiently/actors	0.60
2.	Sense of humour/have missed opportunities in life	0.40
3.	Inferiority complex chip on shoulder/mix easily	0.20
4.	Serious minded/relaxed	0.40
5.	Put themselves first/nice person	0.20
6.	Helped me/didn't help me	0.40
7.	Has knowledge and experience not in a book/hasn't	.00
8.	I respect/I don't respect	0.40

Supplied constructs

9.	I fear these people/I don't	0.20
10.	I have affection for these people/I don't	0.80
11.	These people make me angry/they don't	0.20
12.	I want these people's approval/I don't	0.20
13.	These people make me feel guilty/they don't	0.20
14.	I would like to be like these people/I wouldn't	0.20
15.	These people are like me/they aren't	0.40

The patient's grid and the psychiatrist's grid were analysed separately on the INGRID 67 program and compared on the DELTA program.

The case history

The patient was a 44-year-old man who had been admitted to the clinic with a diagnosis of anxiety state, following a severe panic attack. He was described by the psychiatrist as a compulsive, driving individual. He had spent his childhood in a poor part of Glasgow but had achieved a grammar school education and had become managing director of a company. However, business difficulties arose and the company went into liquidation. His marriage was unhappy. His wife opposed his ambition to move up the social scale and at one time he had an extra-marital affair. At the time of this study he had been observed to spend a great deal of the time in the hospital with a woman patient.

Results

The agreement between the patient's grid and the psychiatrist's is limited and rather patchy, but not negligible. The general degree of correlation between the two listed in the output from DELTA was 0.32. As shown in Table 8.2, the correlations between the patient's and the psychiatrist's evaluations of the constructs were all positive except for construct 7 ('has knowledge and experience not in a book'). Table 8.1 shows the differences in the patient's and psychiatrist's evaluation of the elements. These differences tended to be small, except for the difference (see Table 8.3) on element 18 (woman patient).

The principal component analysis of the grid of differential changes showed that in component 1, which accounts for 27 per cent of the total variation due to differences between the psychiatrist's grid and the patient's grid, the major element

TABLE 8.3   Comparison of patient's and psychiatrist's description of element 18 (woman patient)

Patient	Psychiatrist
Has missed opportunities in life	Sense of humour
Inferiority complex	Mixes easily
Someone who puts themselves first	Nice person
Didn't help me	Helped me
Lacks knowledge and experience	Has knowledge and experience not in a book
I don't respect	I respect
I have no affection for	I have affection for
These people make me angry	These people don't make me angry
I don't want these people's approval	I want these people's approval
I don't want to be like these people	I want to be like these people

loading is on element 18 (0.47) and the major construct loading is on construct 7 (−0.51). Thus the major shift from the patient's grid to the psychiatrist's grid is related to the application of element 18 and construct 7 in the psychiatrist's grid. The individual analysis of each grid showed that construct 7 had a high loading in components 1 and 2 of the patient's grid, but it is not represented at all in components 1 and 2 of the psychiatrist's grid. Construct 7 can be regarded as being of central importance in the patient's construct system. Comparison of the constructs which describe the first two components in each grid show that the patient's constructs form a consistent, meaningful relationship while the psychiatrist's are less consistent and meaningful (see Table 8.4).

TABLE 8.4   Comparison of first two components on the patient's grid with the first two components on the psychiatrist's grid

Patient	Psychiatrist
Component 1	*Component 1*
Actors	Runs things efficiently
Someone who puts themselves first	Has missed opportunities in life
Lacks knowledge and experience not found in books	Serious minded
I don't respect	I fear these people
I have no affection for these people	These people make me angry
I don't want these people's approval	These people are not like me
I don't want to be like these people	
Component 2	*Component 2*
Runs things efficiently	Inferiority complex
Serious minded	Have not helped me
Helped me	I don't respect
Has knowledge and experience not found in a book	I have no affection for these people
I fear these people	I don't want these people's approval
These people are like me	

Conclusion

Thus it appears that, while the psychiatrist has a fair degree of insight into the patient's construct system, the differences between the two grids are not wholly due to chance but indicate systematic errors in the psychiatrist's perception of the patient. The psychiatrist consistently underestimated the importance of the patient's construct 'Has knowledge and experience not in a book'. Such a construct is ego-supportive to a man who feels that his educational attainments do not match his level of aspiration.

The patient had been observed to spend considerable time with a woman patient, so it is not surprising that the psychiatrist would predict that she would be placed on the favourable end of most constructs. However, the observed behaviour of a patient in a psychiatric hospital may not always reflect the real nature of his attitudes, since the range of behaviour possible in a hospital is very limited. In this case, the patient may have been lying, but if the necessity to deceive himself affects the patient's perception of the world the psychiatrist should ideally be aware of it and take it into account in completing the grid in the way he supposed the patient would. Perhaps, too, the psychiatrist might have considered whether a patient, who, in a typically depressive manner, undervalues himself, will associate only with people whom he can denigrate as he denigrates himself.

The second study

The remarkable amount of interesting material obtained from the simple study just described prompted a second one with a more elaborate design. Two grids were obtained from the patient, one before and one after treatment, and on each occasion the psychiatrist was asked to complete the grid in the way he thought the patient would.

The case history

The patient, Tom, was a 24-year-old miner. He was referred by the G.P. after he complained of impotence, heavy drinking and depression. He reported that he had masturbated since he was twelve, but had always regretted it afterwards and felt that masturbation had contributed to his impotence. When Tom was nineteen he had a girlfriend, Lily, with whom he had had intercourse, with varying degrees of success, over a period of six months. He attempted sexual intercourse only when drunk and had difficulty in maintaining an erection. He was very angry and distressed when Lily became pregnant and a subsequent paternity suit revealed that it was unlikely that he was the father of the child.

A year before presenting for treatment, he met a girl, Anne, whom he now wished to marry. Despite her assistance, attempts at sexual intercourse with her had failed and he felt that he should not expect her to marry him.

Tom lived at home with his parents and for the previous six months had been working day-shift only at the mine. He spent a lot of time drinking, but, while often drunk, did not get into fights or into trouble with the police. He said that his mother expressed a great deal of anxiety about his drinking. His closest friend was a workmate, Peter.

The grid

A dyad grid (Ryle and Lunghi, 1970) was used for the experiment. If one considers that the problems of people who became psychiatric patients arise, at least in part, from hurtful relationships with others then it seems more relevant to take as the elements of the grid relationships between people rather than the people themselves. One finds in clinical practice that while psychiatric patients know of a number of people they see themselves as a member of very few relationships. A dyadic relationship grid for a psychiatric patient is therefore likely to be small. The constructs in such a grid are the feelings that can form part of the experience of a relationship.

The dyadic grid used here was one which had been used with a number of psychiatric patients (Rowe, 1972). Unlike the type of dyadic grid used by Ryle, the patient is a member of every relationship included in the grid. His reciprocal relationships with his parents, psychiatrist, spouse and two other people important to him form the elements. The twelve constructs were selected by the psychologist as important feelings commonly associated with relationships. The relationships which were included in the grid and the constructs applied to them are listed in Table 8.5.

TABLE 8.5

Elements		Constructs	
A	Tom's relationship to his mother	1	Good friend
B	Mother's relationship to Tom	2	Makes happy
C	Tom's relationship to his father	3	Gets angry with
D	Father's relationship to Tom	4	Wants to be like the other
E	Tom's relationship to Dr. D	5	Can trust
F	Dr. D's relationship to Tom	6	Gets frightened of
G	Tom's relationship to Anne	7	Admires
H	Anne's relationship to Tom	8	Feels guilty about
I	Tom's relationship to Lily	9	Is kind to
J	Lily's relationship to Tom	10	Can talk to
K	Tom's relationship to Peter	11	Has affection for
L	Peter's relationship to Tom	12	Is patient with

Procedure

Tom was seen by the psychiatrist, Dr. D, for an initial interview. On the same day he was seen by the psychologist and given the grid. Tom was relectant to include Lily in the list of elements and had to be persuaded that certain people can be important to us and can affect our lives, although we do not like them. He used a seven-point scale for rating the elements.

After Tom had completed his grid, the psychologist gave the list of elements to the psychiatrist, who rated them on the constructs in the way in which he thought the patient had done. The psychiatrist was acquainted through Tom's descriptions with all the people in the grid except Peter. The psychologist described Peter to the psychiatrist as 'a workmate, a close friend'.

Two months later, the patient again rated the elements on the constructs. then the psychiatrist rated the elements on the constructs in the way he thought the patient had done on the second occasion.

Psychiatric treatment and outcome

The patient was admitted to the clinic for a fortnight, during which time he had a number of discussions with his psychiatrist. These revealed that Tom had several misconceptions about sexuality and contraception. Advice was given to Anne about obtaining and starting a course of oral contraceptives. At the end of the fortnight, Tom said that he felt well and happy. He returned to work and arranged to take Anne to a holiday resort for the Easter vacation.

On his return, Tom saw the psychiatrist at the Clinic. He said that while on holiday he had tried to have sexual intercourse with Anne but had failed. He thought now that it would be unfair to marry her, and to leave his mother to cope with his father who was ill.

It had been arranged that Tom would see the psychologist for testing after seeing Dr. D, but it was obvious that when Tom presented himself in the psychologist's office that he was too miserable and anxious to be subjected to testing. However, he clearly wished to talk to someone and this the psychologist let him do. Instead of discussing his sexual problems, he talked about his difficulties at work, what an effort it was for him to go down the mine and how he was completely unable to stay down the mine at night. He described periods of overwhelming fear, feelings of being alone, vulnerable, diminished and abandoned. He spoke of fear again in the context of fearing to bring Anne, as his wife, into his mother's house and of his mother's fear of him, of what he might do when he got drunk.

The psychologist discussed this conversation with the psychiatrist. The question was considered of whether the cornerstone of Tom's difficulties was the nature and intensity of his relationship with his mother. If this were so, then his impotence served the purpose of solving the problems arising from this relationship. Thus, by being impotent, he could act fairly to Anne by not marrying her and avoid bringing another woman into his mother's home. He could avoid the necessity of becoming a separate, mature individual and remain in the safety of his boyhood home, at the same time being protected by his impotence from giving expression to the incestuous desires of himself and his mother. (The psychiatrist had noted on one occasion that when describing the situation where Anne was undressing, Tom used the word 'Mother' instead of 'Anne'.)

Tom was seen by the psychiatrist for further discussions. By the time of the second administration of the grid, Tom was engaged and planning to get married in three months. He could discuss with Dr. D the difficulties he experienced in his relationship with his mother and her jealousy of Anne. Sexual intercourse with Anne was proving satisfactory.

Three months later Tom had obtained a flat and he and Anne were married as planned. He was no longer depressed, he drank less and was able to work all shifts down the mine.

TABLE 8.6

Tom's grids First (T1)

First grid

Constructs	A	B	C	D	E	F	G	H	I	J	K	L
1	7	7	6	6	5	5	7	7	1	1	7	7
2	7	7	6	4	7	7	7	7	1	3	7	7
3	1	1	2	2	1	1	1	1	5	7	2	1
4	3	4	7	1	6	6	5	1	1	5	6	1
5	7	7	7	7	7	7	7	2	1	1	7	7
6	1	1	1	2	1	1	1	1	1	1	1	7
7	7	7	7	2	7	7	7	3	1	1	7	7
8	5	3	2	2	1	1	2	7	4	4	1	4
9	3	7	3	6	5	7	7	4	1	1	7	1
10	5	5	5	5	7	7	7	4	7	7	7	7
11	7	7	5	6	7	7	7	1	1	1	7	7
12	6	7	5	7	7	7	7	3	1	1	7	7

Second (T2)

Constructs	A	B	C	D	E	F	G	H	I	J	K	L
1	1	7	3	7	7	7	7	4	1	1	7	7
2	1	3	3	3	7	7	7	3	1	1	7	7
3	7	5	5	5	1	1	1	1	3	5	1	1
4	5	3	3	5	7	2	7	7	6	3	6	4
5	5	6	7	7	1	7	7	1	1	7	7	7
6	5	7	1	1	1	1	1	2	3	4	1	1
7	6	7	5	7	1	1	2	1	1	1	1	1
8	3	2	2	1	1	1	1	3	3	3	3	7
9	1	6	3	6	7	7	7	1	1	1	1	7
10	1	5	2	3	7	7	7	3	1	1	7	7
11	5	7	5	6	7	7	7	2	1	1	7	7
12	5	6	6	6	7	7	7	3	1	1	7	7

The psychiatrist's grids First (D1)

First grid

Constructs	A	B	C	D	E	F	G	H	I	J	K	L
1	6	6	4	4	4	5	6	7	1	1	6	7
2	2	4	4	3	4	5	4	7	1	1	4	7
3	1	6	1	6	4	3	5	4	5	1	1	1
4	4	1	5	1	1	5	2	4	1	7	7	3
5	6	2	5	4	4	4	1	4	4	4	7	7
6	1	1	1	1	1	4	2	6	4	1	1	7
7	5	3	5	3	1	7	5	1	6	1	1	4
8	7	5	3	5	4	6	4	6	5	1	7	1
9	2	6	4	3	4	6	7	1	1	5	5	7
10	4	5	2	1	4	4	7	1	1	5	5	7
11	7	6	5	3	4	7	7	1	1	1	7	6
12	4	5	4	4	4	5	7	1	1	7	7	7

Second (D2)

Constructs	A	B	C	D	E	F	G	H	I	J	K	L
1	2	3	6	5	4	5	7	7	3	1	6	6
2	2	2	3	4	4	5	6	7	1	1	5	6
3	6	7	2	5	3	1	1	3	4	5	1	1
4	2	1	3	4	6	1	6	4	4	5	1	1
5	3	1	5	4	6	1	5	1	5	2	6	6
6	6	5	2	2	4	1	1	1	2	2	2	1
7	3	1	4	3	5	1	7	5	1	1	7	2
8	7	4	5	3	1	6	6	6	1	1	1	1
9	2	5	4	5	4	6	5	7	1	1	5	6
10	1	2	2	1	6	7	6	7	1	1	6	6
11	5	6	6	6	4	5	7	1	1	1	6	6
12	2	2	4	4	5	5	6	7	1	1	6	6

The grids

Tom's two grids and the psychiatrists' are listed in Table 8.6.

The general plan of the analysis

The four grids were analysed individually by INGRID 72. The differences between T1 and D1, T2 and D2, T1 and T2, D1 and D2 were analysed by DELTA. A grid of second-order differences was also formed to compare the differences between T1 and T2 with the differences between D1 and D2, with the intention of studying how closely the changes between the psychiatrist's two grids agreed with the changes in the patients. A set of one hundred 12 x 12 grids of random numbers was generated by GRANNY, which summarizes the results of analysing them for comparison with ones obtained from the experiment.

The results reported here are the ones which appear most interesting from the psychological point of view.

Results

A comparison of the experimental grids with grids of random numbers

Naturally the dispersion in the random grids is not distributed evenly in all directions, but tends to be ellipsoidal in form. The amount of variation from grid to grid is limited. Table 8.7 gives the average amount per component as a percentage of the total per grid, with the standard deviation of the variation about the average and its upper and lower limits. The percentages for the experimental grids are given in Table 8.8.

When the two tables are compared, it can be seen that the only experimental grid which resembles the random grids in the general form of its dispersion is the grid of second-order differences. In all the others, the first component carries much more variation and the remaining components correspondingly less.

TABLE 8.7   A set of 100 random 12 x 12 grids

Root	Mean	S.d. of variation about mean	Limits Upper	Lower
1	27.96	3.41	36.88	22.08
2	20.36	2.20	28.99	15.88
3	15.93	1.60	20.55	11.38
4	12.02	1.37	15.92	9.62
5	8.65	1.27	11.63	5.64
6	6.14	1.08	8.57	4.12
7	4.12	0.93	6.70	2.05
8	2.61	0.75	4.71	0.99
9	1.41	0.55	3.47	0.41
10	0.64	0.37	1.67	0.09
11	0.15	0.14	0.65	0.00

TABLE 8.8 Latent roots of experimental grids as percentages of the total variation

Root	INGRID results				DELTA results				
	T1	T2	D1	D2	T2−T1	T1−D1	T2−D2	D2−D1	(T2−T1) −(D2−D1)
1	72.43	72.94	60.19	63.59	63.78	48.49	40.57	58.29	31.37
2	9.04	10.80	17.44	12.86	11.95	18.73	21.63	20.06	24.43
3	6.79	7.83	8.80	10.70	11.40	12.57	12.95	7.32	17.00
4	5.38	5.23	7.20	6.17	4.70	7.40	10.32	5.41	9.24
5	3.65	2.03	2.59	2.80	4.00	7.08	6.79	4.62	7.13
6	1.48	0.94	1.93	2.01	1.97	2.90	4.43	2.47	4.70
7	0.64	0.19	1.02	1.19	0.89	1.27	1.55	0.70	3.39
8	0.37	0.03	0.44	0.40	0.81	0.89	0.83	0.59	1.74
9	0.19	0.00	0.25	0.15	0.43	0.48	0.54	0.40	0.60
10	0.03	0.00	0.11	0.12	0.06	0.11	0.39	0.08	0.29
11	0.00	0.00	0.02	0.00	0.00	0.09	0.01	0.07	0.11

Patient's grids = T1 and T2; psychiatrist's = D1 and D2

Accordingly, the theory that they are just arrays of random numbers cannot be applied to the four original grids or most of the ones derived from them; and the alternative opinion that they contain psychologically meaningful material is supported. But it remains doubtful whether mathematical operations of any kind can separate the variation they record into psychologically meaningful and meaningless parts. Ideally, every part of it should be searched for information. It is not safe to assume, for instance, that the meaningful material is confined to dimensions where the variation is relatively large. Contrarywise, there are three dimensions in the component space of T2 where no variation occurs at all, a fact which can hardly be less inconsistent with the theory that the grid is an array of random numbers than the fact that its major component contains 73 per cent. of its total variation. Both facts should stimulate curiosity. A psychological explanation for the absence of any variation in one of the dimensions of the component space will be encountered later.

Tom's first grid

The graphic representation of the data in Tom's first grid (Figure 8.1) shows very close convergence between all the constructs except 6 (with 3 and 8 forming approximate bipolar contrasts to the others) and very little variation between the elements, except for three salient ones: his mother's relationship to him (B) and the relationships between him and Lily (I and J).

These two dominate the variation along the axis of the first component. Briefly, Tom and Lily do not get on well together; the others do, except that there is a special connection between construct 6 and element B. It refers to the exceptionally large entry of 7 in row 6, column 2, which conveys the information that Tom believes his mother gets extremely frightened of him. This is the source of most of the variation in the second component.

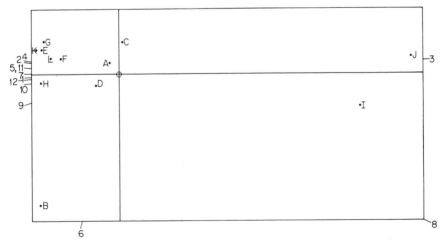

FIGURE 8.1   Tom's first grid. The dispersion of the elements in the sub-space of the first two components, with the orientation of the axes of the constructs indicated in the margin

TABLE 8.9   Distances between certain elements, expressed proportionately to the unit of
expected distance (listed above the diagonal for T1 and below for T2)

Elements		E	F	G	H	K	L
E	Tom to psychiatrist		0.513	0.280	0.296	0.210	0.545
F	Psychiatrist to Tom	0.505		0.504	0.419	0.555	0.183
G	Tom to Anne	0.000	0.505		0.265	0.236	0.470
H	Anne to Tom	0.101	0.515	0.101		0.256	0.377
K	Tom to Peter	0.101	0.404	0.101	0.143		0.524
L	Peter to Tom	0.303	0.202	0.303	0.320	0.202	

Note. For comparison, the proportionate distances in the set of random grids vary about a
mean of 1.000 with s.d. 0.073; and 98 per cent. of the 6 600 recorded values lie within the
range 0.60 to 1.40.

The comparatively small distinctions between other elements are exemplified in
Table 8.9.

The correlations among the constructs and elements are summarized by noting
the ones that are exceptionally close, i.e. outside the range ±0.70, which includes
just over 99 per cent. of the values found in the random grids. Tom's reciprocal
relationship with Mary and Peter are closely correlated with positive feelings. He
associated with his relationship to the psychiatrist feelings of wanting to be liked,
not feeling guilty, being able to talk to and being patient with, but he did not see
the psychiatrist's relationship to him as closely associated with any of the
constructs. Similarly, his reciprocal relationship with his father and his relationship
to his mother were not associated with any of the constructs. He put the negative
feelings of no friendship, unhappiness, anger, distrust, no admiration, guilt, inability
to talk to, no affection and impatience onto his relationship with Lily, and, except
for guilt, saw similar feelings emanating from her relationship to him. His mother's
relationship to him had only one close correlation and that was the feeling of fear.

Tom's second grid

As Figure 8.2 shows, all the elements lie at roughly the same distance from the
centre of the dispersion except three: Tom's relationship to his mother (A), his
relationship to Lily (I) and her relationship to him (J). His mother's relationship to
him (B) is no longer a particularly conspicuous element. The three salient elements
are all seen as unsatisfactory in terms of the first component: J, the most, and A
and I to about the same extent. The construct vector for this component is
approximately the same as in the first grid (correlation 0.95). In other words, the
major dimension of the construct space has remained quite stable.

Elements A and I mark the opposite poles of the second component. Tom's
relationship to his mother and Lily are both unsatisfactory, but for different
reasons. He gets angry with his mother and frightened of her (constructs 3 and 6).
He does not react to Lily so much in these ways, but he does not want to be at all
like her, cannot trust her and does not admire her as he does his mother (constructs
4, 5 and 7). He still reports that his mother gets extremely frightened of him, so
element B remains near the negative pole of component 2 and its construct vector

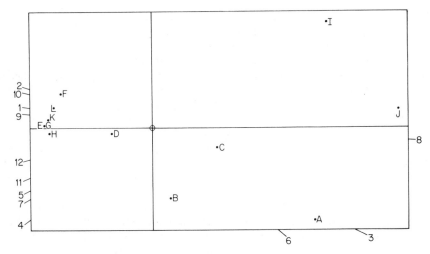

FIGURE 8.2   Tom's second grid. The dispersion of the elements and the orientation of the constructs in the sub-space of the first two components

converges with the vector of the second component in the first grid to some extent, though not closely (correlation 0.30).

The distinctions between the elements listed in Table 8.9 for T2 are even smaller than those for T1. Tom does not distinguish at all in his second grid between his feelings for his psychiatrist and the girl he is going to marry. They are both perfect in every respect. This equivalence accounts for the disappearance of variation along one of the axes in the component space.

Now Tom saw that his feelings of guilt, anger and fear are linked together and involved in his reciprocal relationship with his mother and Lily. He now saw that in his relationship with his mother he made her unhappy, was unfriendly, got very angry with her, was frightened of her, felt guilty about her, was unkind and could not talk to her.

Comparison between Tom's two grids

The differences between these two grids record the changes Tom reports in his relationships with the other characters, between the first occasion and the second. Quantitative differences are noted first and then psychological implications discussed afterwards.

The output from DELTA begins by listing the differences between the means and variances of the constructs. The most marked changes in the means, taking the first grid from the second are:

Construct	Change	S.e. of difference
4	1.25	0.4626
8	−0.83	0.3445
10	−1.00	0.4082

The variance of all the constructs are approximately equal on the first occasion and remain about the same on the second, except for construct 8, where there is a drop from 3.73 to the exceptionally low value of 0.79.

The changes on construct 4 show that Tom admitted wanting to be like other people rather more on the second occasion (mean increase 0.5), but was readier to suppose that they wanted to be like him (mean increase 2.0). The changes in the mean and variance of construct 8 show that his guilt feelings are greatly diminished all around and no longer play an important part in determining his attitudes to other people or his estimates of their attitudes to him. The changes in construct 10 are corroborated by parallel though smaller changes on construct 2. Its mean change is -1.16 with s.e. 0.6376 and its correlation with construct 10 is 0.79. In both, the changes refer specifically to the relationships between Tom and his parents and indicate greater estrangement.

Next to come out are changes referring to the elements. Much the bigger are shown in Tom's relationship to his mother. They account for 39 per cent. of the total variation in the grid of differential changes. Tom is no longer a good friend to his mother, he does not make her so happy, he gets angrier with her, is more 'frightened of' her and finds it more difficult to talk to her. This increase in hostile feelings is accompanied by a decreased sense of guilt. The next largest are in his attitude to Lily. They are more favourable: he is more of a good friend to her, readier to make her happy and less liable to get angry with her. They, too, are accompanied by a decreased sense of guilt.

It turns out to be important to distinguish between outward-directed relationships, expressing Tom's attitudes to other people, and inward-directed ones, expressing their attitudes to him. Each of the outward relationships is more salient than the corresponding inward one; altogether they account for 74 per cent. of the total variation. The most salient of them are Tom's relationships to his mother and Lily, and correspondingly their relationships to him are the most salient of the inward ones. The reversal of this general tendency in construct 4 (mentioned earlier in this section) is exceptional.

These changes set the pattern for the dispersion of the elements in the construct space (see Figures 8.3 and 8.4). The location of an element here indicates how far its evaluation has changed and in what direction.

The salient elements at the positive and negative poles of the first component are A and I respectively. So it contrasts two outward-directed elements: Tom's feelings towards his mother and Lily. The constructs with the highest loadings are 1 and 2 negatively and 3 positively. Referred to the elements, they show that Tom has ceased to be a good friend to his mother or make her happy, and his attitude to Lily has changed conversely. Other changes along this axis are comparatively small.

Constructs 4 and 6 are the ones with relatively high loadings on the second component and both are positive; the salient elements at its positive and negative poles are J and B respectively. Thus this component differs from the first in relating to the contrast between the two corresponding inward-directed relationships: his mother's attitude to Tom, and Lily's. He reckons that Lily wants more to be like him, while his mother wants less; she also gets more 'frightened of' him, while his mother still remains as frightened as before.

The third component refers particularly to guilt feelings in which pronounced changes have already been demonstrated. Construct 8 has the highest positive

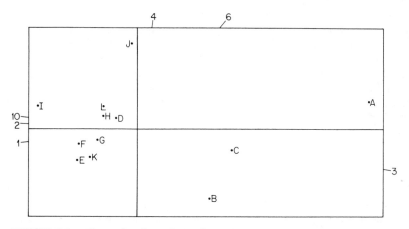

FIGURE 8.3   The major dimensions of the changes between Tom's first grid and his second. The dispersion of the elements and the orientation of constructs in the sub-space of the first two components of the grid of differential changes. Note: Constructs 5, 7, 8, 9, 11 and 12 are omitted because they contribute very little (only 7.5 per cent.) to the variation in the space of the first two components. Constructs 5, 7, 9, 11 and 12 record very little change at all, while changes on construct 8 appear mainly in the dimension of the third component

loading; constructs 4 and 6 also have relatively large loadings, positive and negative respectively. The only salient element is I, at the negative pole; the rest form a contrasting cluster. The evidence indicates that Tom's guilt feelings towards Lily have decreased greatly. He also wants less to be like her and gets more frightened of her.

In his first grid, Tom reported that he enjoyed good relationships with his parents, fiancee and closest friend. It was only from Lily that he saw unpleasant feelings emanating towards him. This was a simple picture, and such simplicity can imply strength and stability. But two things suggested that his view of his world was not as strong and stable as he would wish. His mother was intensely frightened of him and he felt guilty about her. To maintain a balance it seems that it was

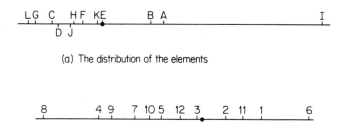

(a) The distribution of the elements

(b) The distribution of the constructs

FIGURE 8.4   The third component of Tom's grid of differential changes

necessary to project onto Lily much of the unpleasant feelings he experienced in the relationship with his mother. By the time Tom completed the second grid, he was able to admit the direction of his negative feelings, namely that he was angry with and frightened of his mother and that his affectionate feelings for her were limited. Then he no longer needed to project so much of his own fears and angers onto Lily, where they would appear to emanate from her, and, instead, he could see her feeling more benignly towards him. He could admit his fear of Lily and hers of him. Such changes in perception would appear to be related to the successful outcome of therapy.

Psychiatrist's first grid

The correlations among the elements and constructs showed that the psychiatrist saw the positive feelings of making happy, being kind, talking to, having affection and being patient associated with Anne's and Peter's relationship to Tom, and these feelings negatively correlated with Tom's reciprocal relationship with Lily. He saw Tom as feeling trust and admiration in his relationship with Mary and Peter. He did not associate the reciprocal relationship of Tom and his mother with any other relationship or construct. He associated the father's relationship to Tom with not wishing to be like, not admiring and not being able to talk to. Tom's relationship to his father he sees as close to Tom's relationship to himself, and both these relationships he associates with the feeling of fear.

Psychiatrist's second grid

The correlation among the elements and constructs showed that now the psychiatrist saw Tom's relationship to his mother as important, being closely related to making her unhappy, getting angry, feeling frightened of, feeling guilty about, being unkind to and being unable to talk to. He saw the mother in her relationship to Tom as being angry, untrusting and frightened. In contrast, Tom's relationship to his father is no longer seen by the psychiatrist as important, since it does not relate closely to any element or construct. Tom's relationship to him the psychiatrist now sees as being close to Tom's relationship to Peter. That is, the psychiatrist perceives Tom as seeing him more like a friend and less like a threatening father-figure.

Comparisons between the psychiatrist's and Tom's first grids

The DELTA program applies to the differences between two grids, not their similarities. So in this context, it analyses how far and in what ways the psychiatrist misunderstood the patient's view of the relationship between himself and the other people concerned on the first occasion. It would be misleading to discuss the differences in detail without first mentioning that his estimates mostly came quite close to the mark. The general degree of correlation between Tom's ratings and his was 0.60.

It is immediately apparent from looking at all four grids that the psychiatrist has not perceived how Tom sees his world in extremes of good and bad. The psychiatrist uses the 7 and 1 grades more sparingly and the intervening grades more

TABLE 8.10 Correlations between Tom's and the psychiatrist's ratings of the elements on the same construct

	Occasion	
Construct	First	Second
1	0.94	0.67
2	0.70	0.87
3	0.18	0.66
4	0.63	0.76
5	0.50	0.61
6	−0.33	0.71
7	0.54	0.47
8	0.65	0.77
9	0.72	0.86
10	0.78	0.93
11	0.80	0.87
12	0.81	0.84

frequently. But the output from DELTA shows that the total variation about the construct means is approximately the same in the first pair of grids and remains so in the second pair.

On the first occasion, the psychiatrist tended to underestimate the strength of Tom's feelings (or his expressions of them). His average ratings are appreciably lower than Tom's on constructs 1, 2, 5, 7, 9, 10, 11 and 12 and about the same on constructs 4 and 6. It is only on constructs 3 and 8, expressing feelings of anger and guilt, that he tended to overestimate.

His ratings correlate closely with Tom's on all the constructs except 3 and 6 (see Table 8.10). The errors in his estimates for construct 3 are numerous, but none are exceptionally large. His estimates in construct 6 are more erratic and include two gross mistakes: he did not expect Tom to report that his mother got extremely frightened of him and expected him to report that he got frightened of Lily, and so put 1 for B where Tom put 7 and 6 for J where Tom put 1. The distinction between outward and inward relationships appears to affect differences in Tom's and his use of this construct. Tom does not admit to being frightened of anyone but reckons that some people, most of all his mother, are frightened of him. The psychiatrist expected him to report being more frightened of them than they of him. The averages are:

	Outward	Inward
Tom	1.0	2.3
Psychiatrist	3.5	1.6

The psychiatrist saw Tom as being frightened of his father, the psychiatrist, Anne and Lily. Here the psychiatrist has not distinguished between what, for him, was implied in his interview with Tom and what had been openly stated.

His error in estimating how Tom would apply it to element B affects later results from the analysis. B comes out as the most salient element: that is to say, the relationship the psychiatrist misunderstood most is Tom's mother's relationship to him as he described it. It appears again as the element with the largest loading on the first component.

The other outstanding elements are D and J. D appears with B near the positive pole of the first component, which refers to constructs 5, 6 and 7; and J appears at the negative pole, which refers primarily to construct 3. Thus the component links together the evidence that the psychiatrist:

(a) Underestimated how far, according to Tom, his parents trusted and admired him as well as got frightened of him,

(b) Overestimated how much they got angry with him; and, conversely,

(c) Overestimated how far Lily trusted, admired and got frightened of him, and

(d) Underestimated how much she got angry with him.

Comparisons between the grids on the second occasion

The psychiatrist's estimates mostly came closer to the mark on the second occasion. The general degree of correlation is 0.73.

He still tended to underestimate the strength of Tom's expressions of his feelings. His average ratings were appreciably lower on constructs 2, 4, 5, 7, 9, 10, 11 and 12, about the same on constructs 1, 3 and 6 and only higher on 8, the feelings of guilt.

His ratings correlate more closely with the patient's on constructs 2, 3, 4, 5, 6, 9, 10, 11 and 12, but less on constructs 1, 7 and 8 (see Table 8.10). The improvement is not consistent throughout. The biggest changes are up from −0.33 to 0.71 for construct 6 and down from 0.94 to 0.67 for construct 1. The total variation of the differences provides the most convenient basis for comparison: the drop from 94.9 to 22.9 for 6 and the rise from 6.25 to 37.67 for 1 are both substantial.

The sums of squares are lower for all the elements except A, C and E; none of the changes either up or down is exceptionally large.

The results imply that the psychiatrist tended to misconstrue the same elements to about the same extent, proportionately, on both occasions, but to do so in terms of different constructs. For example, element B, which has the largest sum of squares on both occasions (82.5 first, 52.8 second), was misjudged most in terms of constructs 6, 5 and 3 the first time and constructs 7, 5 and 1 the second time. Similarly, the errors for element C were largest on constructs 4 and 6 the first time on constructs 1 and 3 the second.

B and J appear, as before, at the opposite poles of the major axis of the dispersion. B is at the positive pole, where the constructs with the highest loadings are 7, 1 and 5. C appears with J at the negative pole, where 3 is again the only construct with a high loading. So this component associates the evidence that the psychiatrist:

(a) Underestimated how far, according to Tom, his mother admired him, was a good friend to him and trusted him, and

(b) Overestimated how much she got angry with him; and that he

(c) Misconstrued Lily's relationship to Tom and Tom's relationship to his father conversely.

With the marked improvement in his estimates of Tom's use of construct 6, the evidence of a distinction between outward and inward relationships there has disappeared. But it emerges on construct 7. Tom recorded a high level of mutual admiration in all the relationships except the ones between him and Lily, and considered that everyone admired him at least as much as he them, some even more. The psychiatrist put the relationships at a distinctly lower level on the whole and expected Tom to admit that other people generally admired him less than he them. The averages are:

	Outward	Inward
Tom	5.5	6.0
Psychiatrist	4.5	2.16

Changes in Tom's compared with changes in the psychiatrist's two grids

The plan to compare changes of this kind by using the DELTA program to calculate and analyse a grid of second-order differences came to grief. The grid calculated as $(T2 - T1) - (D2 - D1)$ can also be defined as $(T2 - D2) - (T1 - D1)$, i.e. the grid of differences between the errors made by the psychiatrist on the two occasions. Finding that it resembles grids of random numbers in the form of its dispersion is thus not very surprising. It is also to be expected if the errors on the two occasions are independent. There may be some circumstances in which a grid of second-order differences is worth examining, but these are not.

Therefore, another method was adopted for comparing the changes. The construct vector of the major component of Tom's grid of differential changes was used as a reference scale and the points were found on it where Tom and the psychiatrist had located the elements in their grids. The results are listed in Table 8.11. The changes in the locations given by the psychiatrist correlate 0.74 with those given by Tom. If he had not misjudged how Tom would construe his relationship to his father, the correlation would have been even higher. The vector contrasts construct 3 with constructs 1 and 2, i.e. getting angry with being a good

TABLE 8.11   Location of the elements on the major axis of Tom's grid of differential changes

		Tom's grids			Psychiatrist's grids		
Elements		First	Second	Change	First	Second	Change
A	Tom to his mother	−0.44	1.75	2.19	−0.38	1.30	1.68
B	Mother to Tom	−0.17	0.47	0.64	−0.03	1.18	1.21
C	Tom to his father	−0.08	0.75	0.83	0.36	−0.18	−0.54
D	Father to Tom	−0.11	−0.27	−0.16	0.67	0.29	−0.38
E	Tom to psychiatrist	−0.38	−0.88	−0.50	0.24	−0.02	−0.26
F	Psychiatrist to Tom	−0.45	−0.92	−0.47	−0.12	−0.79	−0.67
G	Tom to Anne	−0.53	−0.88	−0.35	−0.52	−1.19	−0.67
H	Anne to Tom	−0.51	−0.82	−0.31	−0.79	−1.08	−0.29
I	Tom to Lily	1.60	0.69	−0.91	1.42	1.05	−0.37
J	Lily to Tom	2.06	1.91	−0.15	1.37	1.29	−0.08
K	Tom to Peter	−0.37	−0.89	−0.52	−0.87	−0.82	0.05
L	Peter to Tom	−0.62	−0.91	−0.29	−1.35	−1.03	0.32

Note. Change is defined as second reading minus first.

friend to the other and making him happy. The psychiatrist expected a change for the better; Tom recorded a change for the worse. In spite of this, the changes given by Tom can be discerned, if only as through a glass, darkly, in the differences between the psychiatrist's grids.

Conclusions

The guesses and predictions a person makes about another person's behaviour depend on the perceptions, the constructs, the first person has about the second. Here the psychiatrist's predictions depend on his perception of the patient. The predictions he made tell us not only something about his ability to predict his patient's behaviour but also something about the psychiatrist's own construct system. In the first study, it was found that the psychiatrist had not seen how important the construct 'has knowledge and experience not in a book' was to the patient. This psychiatrist was much respected in the hospital for his research and erudition. It is often painful for the therapist to recognize that the person whom he is trying to help can both accept the help and resent the therapist for offering help. The patient, to protect himself from being overwhelmed by guilt at accepting help from such a totally good person, will perceive the therapist in some less-than-perfect way. Here, the patient, by valuing non-academic experience, both increased his own stature and made a mild criticism of the psychiatrist. The psychiatrist, whose life to that stage would suggest to the observer that he placed a high value on academic achievement, did not see how important non-academic achievement was to his patient. This may have been no more than a simple difference in construct systems or it may have been an example of selective perception, a turning away from a possible hurtful implication.

Similarly, in the second study, it seems that the psychiatrist's initial perception of the patient's predicament reflected two aspects of his own personal construct system: one, an aspect of his system to do with paternal figures and the other, to do with sexual potency. Psychiatry in Britain is a paternalistic profession, both in the way in which its members are trained and in the way in which the role of the psychiatrist is usually defined. The perception of another person's relationship to oneself always involves a degree of projection. Here the psychiatrist, seeing himself as a paternal figure, to some measure unconsciously expected the patient to see him as like a father, although consciously he would never have claimed the sexual precocity such a relationship would have implied. Paternalism, for the psychiatrist, was not entirely benign. His construct system included the premise that 'sons are afraid of fathers'. He was right in recognizing how important fear is in the functioning of human relationships, but it was his experience to associate fear more with fathers than with mothers.

One mark of the competent therapist is his readiness to recognize his ideosyncratic perceptions. Here the psychiatrist recognized and so changed his perceptions both of the patient's relationship to him and of the patient's symptom of impotence. The presenting problem, while it might, for the patient, encapsulate and symbolize his entire predicament, may appear to the psychiatrist as a single entity — a problem, a complaint. Impotence might be no more than a minor problem, linked to a specific situation, as terms like 'wedding night nerves' and 'brewer's droop' imply. As such, it should respond to the carrying out of sensible advice. But when the symptom does not respond to sensible advice it needs to be looked at in a wider setting, to see what meaning the symptom has for the patient and how it fits into his private system of inner logic. This the psychiatrist set about doing in his sessions with Tom by relating the impotence to his feelings of guilt and fear in his relationship with his mother. Such an exploration of the meaning of the symptom seems to have been effective in resolving it. However, the changes that occurred did not involve any major change in Tom's construct system. As was noted in Tom's second grid, 'the construct vector for this component is approximately the same as in the first grid. In other words, the major dimension of the construct space has remained quite stable'.

It would seem that the successful outcome of therapy here did not require a major alteration of Tom's construct system, since his construct system, as it was sampled here, did not reveal any major inconsistencies, either internally or in its relationship to reality. An example of a major internal inconsistency was given by Rowe (1971) when she described a depressed woman patient whose grid revealed that she divided the people in her world into good and bad. All the good people were 'poorly'; the bad people were well. To date, all attempts to transform her into a well person (and therefore a bad person) have failed. An inconsistency with external reality was found with an anorexic, 11-year-old girl (Rowe, 1973) whose situation grid showed that she associated all happy situations with being with her father and all unhappy situations, including eating, with being with her mother. Her mother had custody of her.

Therapy, in construct theory terms, involves enabling the patient to modify his construct system. The patient's construct system not only has its own peculiar logic but, as this study and the work of Ryle and Breen have shown, it also is less differentiated in structure than a non-patient's system. What are here called 'constructs' Piaget (1954) called 'schemata'. He pointed out that 'the more schemata are differentiated, the smaller the gap between the new and the familiar becomes, so that novelty, instead of constituting an annoyance avoided by the subjects, becomes a problem and invites searching'. We are all familiar with the way in which the neurotic patient avoids novelty, even when the experiences may offer release from neurotic misery. In our second study here, the psychiatrist, having more differentiated schemata and being thus less afraid of new experiences, was able to assimilate a new experience, to modify his schemata in the direction of understanding his patient better and, through these new insights, to help his patient accept a novel experience and the modifications it brought.

One important aspect of this type of inquiry has not been examined here, namely how the psychiatrist and the patient perceived the psychologist. How much did they modify what they said according to their expectations of her criticism of them? Psychologists can no longer pretend that how the subject perceives the experimenter is not relevant to the outcome of the experiment. One of the advantages of the repertory grid is that it provides a technique for examining this variable.

Acknowledgement

The authors thank the Editor for permission to reprint extracts from the article by Dorothy Rowe, 'An examination of a psychiatrist's predictions of a patient's constructs', which was published in the *British Journal of Psychiatry*, **118**, 231–234 (1971).

144

References

Bannister, D., and Mair, J. (1968). *The Evaluation of Personal Constructs*, Academic Press, London.

Piaget, J. (1954). *The Construction of Reality in the Child*, Basic Books, New York.

Rowe, D. (1971a). 'An examination of a psychiatrist's predictions of a patient's constructs'. *Brit. J. Psychiat.*, **118**, 231–234.

Rowe, D. (1971b). 'Poor prognosis in a case of depression as predicted by the repertory grid'. *Brit. J. Psychiat.*, **118**, 297–300.

Rowe, D. (1972). *The Individual Microcosm. A study of the Psychiatric Patient's Private World*. Ph.D. Thesis, University of Sheffield.

Rowe, D. (1973). *A Study of an Anorexic Child*. Unpublished case study, St. John's Hospital, Lincoln.

9

SEX DIFFERENCES IN STEREOTYPING
THE ROLES OF WIFE AND MOTHER

S. Jane Chetwynd

Summary

About 200 men and women were shown simplified line drawings of six distinctive female physiques and asked to evaluate them on ten descriptive scales including 'like a wife' and 'like a mother'. Despite the extreme simplicity of the drawings, the informants did not hesitate to place such interpretations on them.

Men and women both proved to have stereotyped views of these roles, but their views were different. The men consistently placed a higher value on 'wife'. They saw her as more attractive, less prudish and less socially deviant in terms of alcoholism, and saw the fatter and less attractive physiques as less likely to be wives. In contrast, the women consistently rated 'mother' higher. They saw the less extreme and more attractive physiques as more likely to be mothers, and saw the mother role as more attractive, more like themselves and their ideal selves, and less socially deviant in terms of alcoholism and lesbianism than did the men. In comparing the two roles the women saw little difference between 'wife' and 'mother', but the men saw a wide contrast.

The relevance of these findings in areas such as the study of marital discord, adjustment to parenthood, etc., is discussed and the process of acquiring sex-role stereotypes is reviewed. (P.S.)

In that area of psychology known as person perception, the act of consistently attributing certain characteristics to a particular concept such that all members of that class of concept are also assumed to portray those characteristics is known as stereotyping. In real life, the act frequently takes on an evaluative connotation and it is then known as either discrimination or prejudice. It is very strange that much has been written about prejudice and much about discrimination, but relatively little about stereotyping. It is equally strange that what is written about prejudice and discrimination tends to get dismissed by 'authorities' and labelled as emotive and biased, yet what is written about stereotyping tends to be acknowledged as scientific fact. For these reasons, this study is concerned with stereotyping and an attempt will be made to avoid such words as prejudice or discrimination. Nevertheless, it is a study, although based on scientific facts, concerned with the real life situation.

The particular area of stereotyping under study is that of the female social role, so the study is concerned with the attribution of certain characteristics to a woman, simply because she is fulfilling a particular social role. The two roles chosen for study are those basic to our present-day society — those of 'wife' and 'mother'.

As far back as we care to think, we have been encouraged to conceive of a woman as a being distinct and infinitely different from a man. In Genesis, woman is described as an afterthought, created from one of Adam's spare parts, solely to act as a companion to man. In the ancient Jewish religion, men's attitude to women is revealed by the fact that they gave thanks that they were Jew no Gentile, free not bond, and man not woman.

The concept of 'wife', however, has had an even lower evaluation than that of 'woman'. The Ten Commandments indicated that a wife was a form of property like a house, an ox or a servant, and an ancient Chinese maxim taught that 'A woman married is like a pony bought, to be ridden or whipped at the master's pleasure'. To this day, on the Channel Island of Sark, 200 miles off the English coast, a married woman is considered her husband's chattel and as she has no separate identity cannot legally hold a Bank Account, buy property or goods, make a will or sign any deed in her own name.

This study assumes that attitudes to woman, in England at least, have progressed somewhat beyond this level and attempts to look at the 'wife' and 'mother' roles in terms of the aesthetic, personality and characterological traits which are attributed them. It particularly looks at any differences between men and women in this attribution.

For investigating the stereotyping procedure, a method of grid technique was employed. The elements used were a range of six female physiques, differing in body size, but standardized for height, hairstyle, etc. (see Figure 9.1). These line drawings were strictly reproduced so that there were two representatives of each of the somatotypes: Endomorphs, Mesomorphs and Ectomorphs. Within each pair there was one extreme representative and one not so extreme. (Sheldon's (1963) figure numbers are given in parenthesis under each physique in Figure 9.1.) The elements were evaluated in terms of the constructs by comparative grading on a seven-point scale.

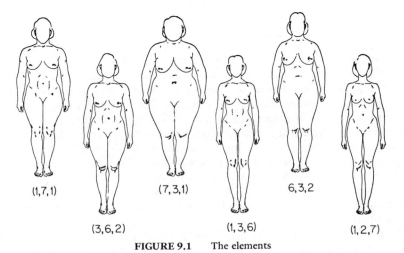

(1,7,1)   (7,3,1)   6,3,2

(3,6,2)   (1,3,6)   (1,2,7)

FIGURE 9.1   The elements

TABLE 9.1   Constructs used in the stereotyping
process

Construct		Classification
1	Like a wife	Social role
2	Like a mother	Social role
3	Attractive	Evaluative
4	Cruel	Evaluative
5	Alcoholic	Social deviancy
6	Lesbian	Social deviancy
7	Like Me	Identification
8	Like I would like to be	Identification
9	Influential	Potency
10	Prudish	Morality

The ten constructs included were selected from those used in previous studies of the stereotyping process (e.g. Powell, Stewart and Tutton, 1973; Stewart, Tutton and Steele, 1973) because it was thought they would be both interesting and relevant for this particular study. The constructs are shown in Table 9.1. Two constructs examined the sex roles ('like a wife' and 'like a mother'), two were of an evaluative nature ('attractive' and 'cruel'), two measured social deviancy ('alcoholic' and 'lesbian'), two measured identification ('like me' and 'like I would like to be'), and the remaining two were concerned with potency ('influential') and morality ('prudish'). By looking at the relationships between the social-role constructs and the other constructs, as well as the attribution of the physiques to the social roles, an examination of the stereotyping process was possible.

The 203 subjects who took part in the study (112 females and 91 males) were drawn from a variety of social and occupational backgrounds and covered a fairly wide age range, though the majority were between nineteen and twenty-five and were unmarried. The mean age for the men was 23.0 and that for the women 22.3.

The first stage in the analysis of the data was to look for evidence that these two social roles were actually being stereotyped in terms of the physiques attributed them. That is to say, the grids were examined for consistent evaluations of the physiques in terms of the social-role constructs. A one-way analysis of variance was performed on the male and female groups separately, using the SERIES program, and F-ratios calculated. Table 9.2 shows these results.

TABLE 9.2   Results of one-way analysis of
variance to assess the difference between mean
gradings attributed the physiques for the two roles

Role	F-ratios	
	Males	Females
Wife	21.43*	13.19*
Mother	17.84*	17.20*

*indicates $p < 0.005$

At a probability level of 0.5 per cent. stereotyping of the social roles in terms of which body sizes were commonly associated with each was displayed by both the men and the women. The men presented a more consistent stereotype of the 'wife' role than did the women, but there was a similar degree of homogeneity in the two groups for the stereotype of the 'mother' role.

The next stage of the analysis was to examine the stereotypers held in more detail by establishing which physiques were commonly attributed each role. Table 9.3 shows the mean evaluation given the six physiques by the men and women for the two social-role constructs. The lower the numerical value of the mean, the greater the appropriateness of assigning that physique to that role.

Significant differences between the sexes were present for both roles. The men saw the endomorphic or fat physiques as less likely to be wives than did the women, whereas they saw the least extreme of the mesomorphic and ectomorphic physiques as less likely to be mothers. It seems from this that men have a more attractive conception of the body image of a 'wife' than do women, but a less attractive conception of that of 'mother'. (The attractiveness of the physiques was ascertained by examination of the evaluations on the 'attractive' construct.)

The analysis then went on to examine the relationships between the social-role constructs and the descriptive and characterological constructs. The COIN program was employed to obtain intercorrelations between the constructs for each individual grid and, from these, the average correlations for the male and female groups obtained with the use of the angular distance transformation procedure. Z-tests were used to assess the significance of sex differences in these correlations. The correlations and Z-test results are shown in Table 9.4. Concerning the wife role, differences between men and women were found on its relationship with the 'attractive', 'alcoholic' and 'prudish' constructs. The men saw the 'wife' as more attractive, less prudish and less like an alcoholic than did the women, which seems to indicate a generally higher valuation of the wife role by men than by women. On the other hand, the women seemed to give a higher valuation to the mother role than did the men. They saw it as more attractive, more like themselves and their ideal selves and less like an alcoholic or a lesbian than did the men.

The intercorrelation between the 'wife' and 'mother' constructs was also of interest; the women displayed a much higher relationship in their conceptions of the wife and mother roles than did the men.

So, at this point, to sum up the findings of importance: throughout all aspects of the analysis there were repeated evidences of the discrepancy between mens' and womens' evaluations of the wife and mother roles and the interrelationship of these two. The men consistently gave a more positive valuation to the concept of 'wife'. They saw the fatter and less attractive physiques as less likely to be wives and they saw the wife role as more attractive, less prudish and less socially deviant in terms of alcoholism than did the women. In contrast, the women consistently gave a more positive valuation to the concept of 'mother'. They saw the less extreme and more attractive physiques as more likely to be mothers and they saw the mother role as more attractive, more like themselves and their ideal selves, and less socially deviant in terms of alcoholism and lesbianism than did the men. In terms of the relationship between the two, the women saw relatively little conflict between 'wife' and 'mother', but the men saw the two roles very differently.

It is interesting to speculate on the importance and origins of such discrepant

TABLE 9.3   Mean evaluations given the physiques

Physique		Wife Men	Wife Women	Wife Significance of difference	Mother Men	Mother Women	Mother Significance of difference
Endomorph	1	4.07	3.12		2.73	2.67	
	2	5.36	4.34	*	3.96	3.79	
Mesomorph	3	3.36	3.12		3.37	2.93	
	4	4.04	4.11	*	3.44	3.91	*
Ectomorph	5	4.00	3.93		4.74	4.36	
	6	3.16	3.00		4.00	3.50	*

*indicates $p < 0.05$

TABLE 9.4   Intercorrelations between the social role constructs and the other constructs and the Z-test comparisons between men and women

Construct	Correlation with 'wife' Men	Women	Z	Correlation with 'mother' Men	Women	Z
Attractive	0.53	0.34	2.33**	−0.05	0.09	1.72*
Cruel	−0.16	−0.18	0.22	−0.27	−0.37	1.45
Alcoholic	−0.34	−0.21	1.60*	0.00	−0.26	3.19***
Lesbian	−0.37	−0.37	0.00	−0.25	−0.42	2.07*
Like me	0.28	0.33	0.91	−0.03	0.17	2.45**
Like I would like to be	0.25	0.29	0.77	−0.05	0.09	1.72*
Influential	0.25	0.18	0.72	0.10	0.10	0.00
Prudish	−0.20	−0.02	2.22*	−0.12	−0.08	0.55

Correlation between 'wife' and 'mother' roles		
Men	Women	Z
0.43	0.62	2.32**

*indicates $p < 0.05$, **indicates $p < 0.01$, ***indicates $p < 0.001$

evaluations. The higher evaluation of the wife role by men can be interpreted as indicating that the men are construing 'wife' in a more idealistic and ethereal manner than women, who have a more realistic attitude. Whereas the women take a more 'middle of the road' conception of both 'wife' and 'mother', the men seem to polarize the roles much more, with the 'wife' at the positively valued end and 'mother' at the negative end.

One wonders what role the media may play in the proliferation of such stereotypes. Advertisments constantly push the young, slim, attractive female as the only successful and socially acceptable wife image and perhaps, as a result of this, men do hold an idealized conception of a wife. On the other hand, women who either fulfil the role or may have aspirations of doing so, tend to bring down the image to a more attainable level and so conceive of it in a more realistic light.

What might be the consequences of such differences in mens' and womens' perceptions of these primary social roles? It can be immediately hypothesized that such discrepant attitudes may be an important factor in problems of marital harmony. There are two aspects of these findings which might be a cause of conflict in a marital relationship. The first concerns the discrepancy between men and women in their perceptions. Successful marital relationships exhibit a varying degree of common attitudes, tastes, affiliations, etc., between the two partners, but it has been shown in previous studies that a certain degree of shared stereotypes are important for marital harmony. For example, the Drewery and Rae (1969) study showed that a shared conception of masculinity was an important factor in marital success. So it can surely be proposed that a shared conception of the two basic female roles in a marital relationship is of great importance for the success of that relationship. Our research suggests that such perceptual differences between men and women may be quite widespread, but their exact contribution to marital discord remains to be investigated.

The second aspect of these findings which may be a cause of conflict between man and wife is the discrepancy between the conception of the wife and mother roles as displayed by the man. This discrepancy may be an important factor in the role adjustment necessary in a harmonious marital relationship. Again, further research is necessary to investigate the exact influence of such differences, but one possible model is as follows. It can be proposed that too much discrepancy in the evaluation of the wife and mother roles causes problems of role adjustment. It is when a woman's role changes from solely that of wife to both wife and mother that the dangers to the marital relationship are fully felt. The man faced with such changed circumstances finds his wife is now fulfilling two roles for which he has conflicting stereotypes. To overcome this conflict, he either adapts his stereotype of one or both of the roles until they are seen as compatible, or, more likely, he changes his perception of his wife until she fits in more with his stereotype of a mother, and this is equivalent to devaluing his wife. When a man takes this latter alternative and the woman is unaware of her husband's change of perception, then marital discord may result and seriously affect the continuity of the relationship. Further research is needed to discover how effective counselling would be in modifying these perceptions and avoiding or relieving marital distress.

It is interesting to speculate on the development of such differences in mens' and womens' perceptions. In a previous study (Powell, Stewart and Tutton, 1973), it was shown that young boys of nine or ten valued the mother role more positively than did girls of the same age. For adolescents, the value of the mother role was about the same for boys and girls. And now in this study the findings show that in adulthood the mother role is devalued more for males than females. So it appears that there is a general downward trend in attitudes toward the mother role from childhood to adulthood for both males and females. However, whereas the trend tends to flatten out for females about adolescence, it continues to descend for males, dropping below that of the females and resulting in the discrepancy in evaluations in adulthood.

Concerning the relationship between the two social roles, for both boys and girls 'wife' and 'mother' were seen as less similar in early childhood than they were in adolescence. But again, after adolescence there was a sharp drop in the relationship for men, whereas for women the degree of relationship stayed fairly constant. So again it appears that the crucial time for the development of this difference between men and women is in the years between adolescence and early adulthood.

The influence of the perception of age on the stereotyping process cannot be disregarded here. In a previous study (Stewart, Tutton and Steele, 1973) where the constructs 'young' and 'old' were included, it was found that the men saw the wife role as positively correlated with 'young' and the mother role positively correlated with 'old', whereas for the women the relationship between 'young' and 'wife', although positive, was significantly lower than that of the men, and they in fact saw 'mother' as being positively correlated with 'young' as well.

This correlation between 'mother' and 'old' for the men may explain, at least in part, their devaluation of the mother role. In this society, age is not a highly valued commodity, and it may be its association with the maternal construct which accounts for such negative traits attributed to the mother role by men. In contrast, youth is a highly valued and positively associated attribute, and similarly the high correlation between 'young' and 'wife' displayed by the men may account for the high valuation given to the wife role by the men.

It is hoped in this study to have shed some light on this rather complex field of female social-role stereotyping. Particularly, it is hoped to have made an objective contribution in a field which tends to abound with what has been described as subjective speculation. Generally speaking, many of the contributions in this area are valid assessments of the true situation, but their credibility is heightened when they can be shown to be based on scientific facts. And in this respect grid technique is a useful tool. It provides a method of exploring attitudes and opinions in a subtle and relatively indirect way, and the analyses available enable detailed and complex inspection of the data.

Acknowledgements

This work was carried out in association with Bob Stewart and Graham Powell of the Institute of Psychiatry, London, S.E.5.

References

Drewery, J., and Rae, J. B. (1969). 'A group comparison of alcoholic and non-alcoholic marriages using the interpersonal perception technique'. *Brit. J. Psychiat.*, **115**, 287–300.

Powell, G. E., Stewart, R. A., and Tutton, S. Jane (1973). *The Stereotyping of Physiques: Investigations into the Processes Involved and the Implications for Social Behaviour*. Paper read at British Association for the Advancement of Science, Canterbury.

Powell, G. E., Stewart, R. A., and Tutton, S. Jane (1973). *The Development of Person Perception: A Grid Study*. Paper read at the London Conference of the British Psychological Society, London. Also in *Bulletin of the British Psychological Society*, 1974, **27**, 149 (Abstract).

Sheldon, W. H. (1963). *The Varieties of Human Physique*, Hofner, New York.

Stewart, R. A., Tutton, S. Jane, and Steele, R. E. (1973). 'Stereotyping and personality: 1. Sex differences in perception of female physiques'. *Perceptional and Motor Skills*, **36**, 811—814.

10

OF ATTITUDES AND LATITUDES: A REPERTORY GRID STUDY OF PERCEPTIONS OF SEASIDE RESORTS

Stuart Riley, John Palmer

Summary

This paper reports a study using repertory grid technique to map respondents attitudes to seaside resorts. The technique is used in full, not merely as a device for construct elicitation, and various complementary types of analysis are applied to the data. The results indicate considerable pay-off to extending this 'qualitative' technique into the quantitative area. Future analytic developments are considered briefly, as is the decisional outcome of the research. (P.S.)

Introduction

One of the most persistent themes in market research is the division of projects into 'qualitative' and 'quantitative' phases. As the names suggest, the former is concerned with generating an understanding of the situation — or, to put it more crudely, deciding what questions are to be asked — and the latter with describing the extent or frequency of occurrence of the key aspects of the situation — or, in other words, obtaining answers to the questions. In practical terms the division is apt to be quite rigid. The qualitative phase is often commissioned and paid for separately from the quantitative, and the research agency often submits a detailed research report on the qualitative work done before the quantitative phase is commissioned. The qualitative stage is small-scale, both in terms of sample and of budget; the quantitative stage may involve a national survey of several thousand persons.

In the qualitative stage, the methods employed often include loosely structured interviews and group interviews or discussion groups, and the interviewers are highly qualified, must understand the research objectives in detail and write interpretative discursive reports on their interviews. In the quantitative stage, the interviewers are less highly qualified, may be kept deliberately ignorant of major facts about the research objectives and are trained to ask standard-form questions and record the answers in pre-specified categories.

Most British market researchers would recognize the repertory grid as a technique which belongs to the qualitative rather than the quantitative phase. Its use in the former phase tends to take the following form. From prior knowledge of the market, or perhaps on the strength of information from unstructured interviewing, a list of competing products is drawn up, the client's product naturally being included. Each 'repertory grid' respondent is shown this set of products, either as names printed on cards or, in suitable cases, as actual packages or articles, and by the application of Kelly's (1955) method of triads is asked to furnish as many constructs as possible. These are recorded as pairs of contrasted properties. Application of this procedure with a number of respondents – say, twenty to eighty – yields a list of opposed pairs of epithets. From these are selected the appropriate words to use in a battery of bipolar or unipolar rating scales in the questionnaire for the quantitative stage. (It is likely that this battery may be further refined by trying it out on a small sample and subjecting it to various quantitative item analysis procedures before the main survey is begun.)

Analysis of grids

In the foregoing description we have deliberately passed lightly over the process by which the grids are analysed. In this area there have been considerable variations in practice. It seems, however, from various publications that there has been a tendency away from formal analysis of grids in recent years. (Indeed, there appears to be a belief among some market researchers that repertory grid technique is synonymous with construct elicitation.) For instance, Frost and Braine's (1967) paper devotes a considerable section to the ways in which the grids can be analysed. Such analysis implied, of course, that the respondents must complete the construct vectors, i.e. rate every product on every construct produced. More recent papers, however, have tended to concentrate on construct elicitation more than analysis of grids. In Nolan's (1971) review of construct elicitation procedures, the purpose of completing the vector was more recreational than scientific, and in Sampson's (1972) description the completion of the grid is not referred to at all.

In our work, we have had the grids completed in full and subjected to full analysis. By doing this, one can describe in some detail the structure of the perceptions and attitudes which people have about the differing brands in the product class. The result of the grid analysis is a substantial enrichment of the information which is obtained from the 'qualitative' stage. In fact, such an analysis introduces a 'quantitative' element into the qualitative stage. It enables firmer decisions to be taken about the form of the later quantification and, furthermore, it can be valuable when funds are limited and a full-scale quantitative attitude survey is out of the question, while 'impressionistic' reports on attitudes derived entirely from unstructured or 'depth' interviewing are felt to be inadequate.

A practical example

In the rest of this paper, we shall describe the analysis of repertory grids for market research purposes as we have practised it, illustrating the process with an actual study in which we were both concerned. This study was part of a programme of research carried out by the Tourism Research Unit directed towards assisting in planning the future of a seaside resort, but in this paper we describe it as if it stood entirely alone. We are thus in the situation referred to previously of seeking a quantified description of the perceptions of resorts from a small sample of respondents.

The phrase 'repertory grid' refers to a technique rather than to a particular procedure and, consequently, it is necessary to spell out the particular variations of the technique which we used. First of all, our application was to a group of respondents; the technique was developed for psychiatric use and, in this setting, application was to a single individual. Secondly, the objects, or 'elements', in our grid were the names of seaside resorts. They were, thus, verbal representations of the objects under investigation, rather than the actual objects or photographs which are sometimes used. Thirdly, the constructs were elicited from respondents by the method of triads and each respondent produced his own set of constructs. We, therefore, had as elements of the grid a variety of British seaside resorts chosen to exemplify all parts of the country; they were twenty-one resorts which had been most frequently recorded in a national survey of holiday destinations. To introduce a further axis of comparison, four European resorts were added, making a total of twenty-five objects.

The respondents were sixty people who had taken a holiday of at least four nights away from home in the last twelve months, living in six major cities (Birmingham, Cardiff, Glasgow, Leeds, London and Manchester). Within each city we interviewed a quota of ten people: five men and five women, five aged 25—44 and four aged 45—64, five from non-manual occupational classes and five from the skilled manual classes.

The interviewing technique included a number of features which we do not consider invariable or necessarily optimal. We believe that considerable scope for modification and improvement may exist in this area; however, the procedures used here do seem to be quite adequate. The triadic method of eliciting constructs was used, although other methods are possible (Nolan, 1971, gives a number of alternatives). The construct vectors were completed using a three-point scale, using 3 for the preferred property or epithet, 2 for 'neutral' and 1 for the rejected or disapproved property. Thus, if a construct was defined as 'noisy/peaceful' and 'peaceful' was positively evaluated, resorts classed as 'peaceful' were rated as 3, 'noisy' ones as 1 and the remainder (the in-betweens or those out of the range of convenience, i.e. those to which that construct was not applicable) as 2.

A further feature that was adopted exceptionally, for this study only, because of the large number of objects, was to allow each informant to discard the seven to nine resorts least familiar to him at the outset of the interview and to complete his grid on the remaining sixteen to eighteen resorts. The omitted objects were all rated 2 on each of his constructs. However, the interview procedure satisfied the essential requirements, which are that there must be produced a set of constructs for each respondent, each having a rating for every object.

The analysis of the grids was carried out according to the principal components procedure developed by Dr. Patrick Slater using a computer program written by him (a modification of PREFAN, which accepts larger arrays of data and lists some additional results). The program normalizes the construct vectors, setting each to zero mean and standard variance, finds the principal components of the normalized grid and relates every object and every construct to the principal components, the latter having a function similar to a map grid. The program also provides detailed specifications for making a three-dimensional map of the data on a geographical globe, treating the first three components as orthogonal axes of the globe.

As mentioned above, an important feature of the market research application is that we have several respondents, in this study sixty, and thus several grids. The data have a three-way character; they consist of ratings *of* objects *on* constructs *by* persons, and since the constructs vary in both meaning and number between persons, the data do not form a straightforward three-way matrix or 'block'. There is scope for a good deal of ingenuity in dealing with such data and we do not think that we have arrived at a definitive procedure. However, since the first objective is generally to describe the differing images of the object, rather than to investigate the differences between people in the way the total set of objects is differentiated, it is usually satisfactory, in the first instance at least, to analyse all the constructs produced by all the respondents together, as if they constituted a single grid. In the present study, with twenty-five objects and sixty informants yielding an average of about eleven constructs each, this meant analysing a 'great grid' of order 25 x 672.

In this great grid, it is possible that some constructs will be verbal repetitions of each other. We do not permit an informant to repeat himself, i.e. he may not use the same construct twice. However, it is entirely possible that a different informant may hit upon the same distinction. Thus, the same construct may, and usually does, appear more than once. Since all constructs are set to equal variance, repeated concepts are weighted according to the frequency of their repetition – which appears not illogical. It is appropriate that a distinction which is noted by 80 per cent of people should be given more weight than an idiosyncratic construct noted by only one person.

The 25 x 672 grid has twenty-four principal components (see Table 10.1). From the commercial standpoint, the ability of the program to produce a 'best approximation' to the total 24-dimensional configuration in only three dimensions is a great advantage. It can be valuable when presenting results to have a succinct graphical or solid representation of the relationships in the data. However, it can leave nagging doubts in the researcher's mind to rely too heavily on the three-dimensional approximations, particularly when, as in the present case, the first three components account for only 37 per cent of the total variance, and a number of objects project further into the subsequent dimensions than into any of the first three. In situations of extreme multivariability, we often find a simple taxonomic analysis of the objects is valuable, because it can show very simply a set of relationships which involves many dimensions.

The hierarchical 'cluster analysis' of Figure 10.1 is based on the linear

TABLE 10.1   Cumulative percentages of total variation explained by different numbers of components

Number of components	Percentage of total variance
1	16
2	27
3	37
4	43
5	48
6	52
10	67
15	81
24	100

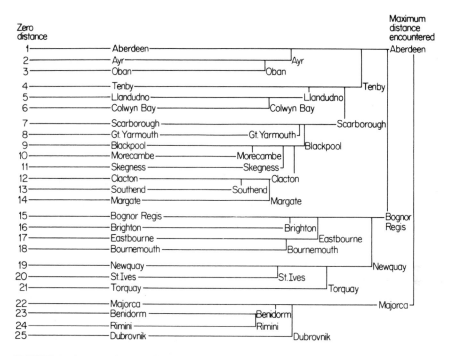

FIGURE 10.1   Dendrogram by McQuitty's replacement method: analysis by 'distance' between resorts

(Euclidean) distances between the resorts in the total 24-dimensional space. As a consequence of the way in which the constructs are scored, the linear distance between any two objects is a measure of their general perceived dissimilarity. A large distance implies that the two objects have been given different ratings on many constructs, a small one that they have been given similar ratings on many constructs. Our clustering method is one which tends to produce compact rather than straggling groupings; it is a simple method well adapted to hand calculation as well as electronic computing, described by McQuitty (1960) as 'hierarchical syndrome analysis'. (The computer realization of this procedure is a subroutine attached to Dr. Slater's program which takes as its starting data the linear distances between the objects in the 24-dimensional space. The routine could also be adopted to perform an analysis in the angular distances between the objects.)

In the present case, the interpretation of the dendrogram is quite simple. There are six groups of resorts and the basis of each is geographical. From top to bottom they are Scottish, Welsh, Middle England, South Coast, West Country and Europe. This sixfold classification gives a hint that an adequate description of the data may be possible in about five dimensions, since if we consider only the centres of the six groups there must be a five-dimensional space in which they can be located. When we look at the loadings of the resorts on the first five dimensions, furthermore, the supposition of a neat five-dimensional description seems quite plausible. For instance, the distinction between the Mediterranean resorts and the British — the

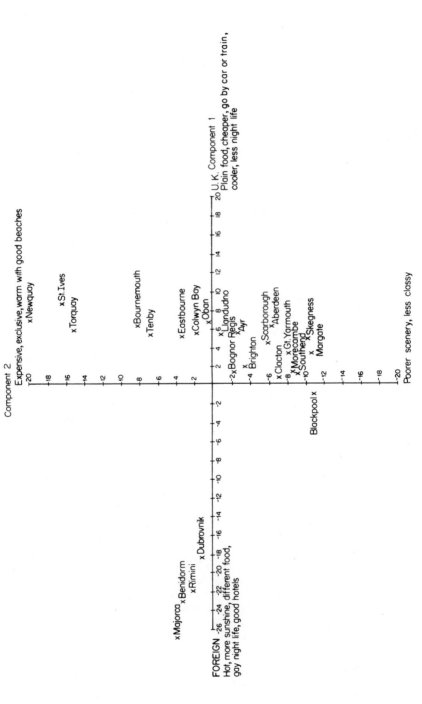

FIGURE 10.2   Principal components analysis: component 1 against component 2

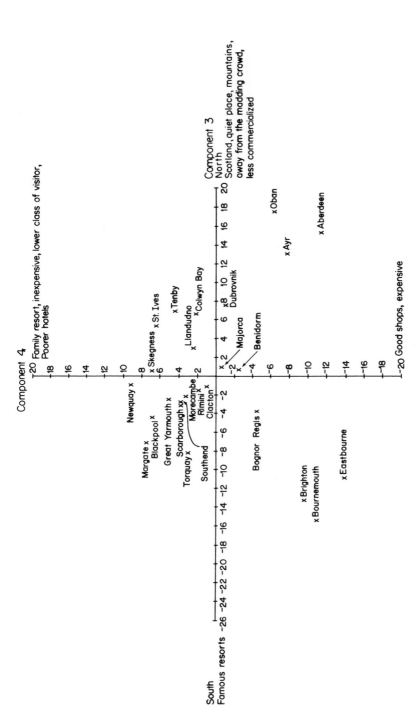

FIGURE 10.3   Principal components analysis: component 3 against component 4

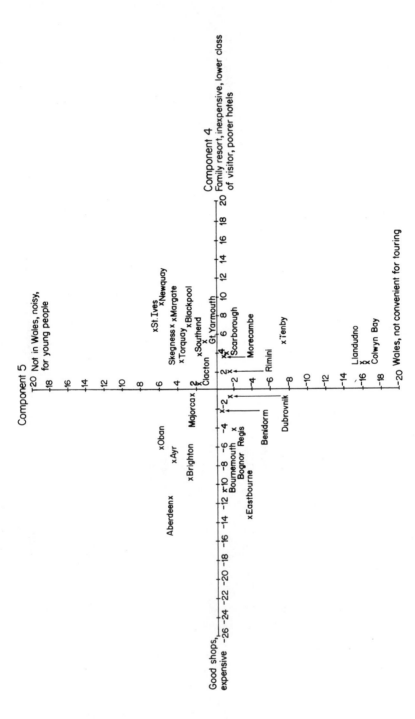

FIGURE 10.4　Principal components analysis: component 4 against component 5

lowest fork of the tree, as it were — is clearly identifiable with the first component (Figure 10.2). The second component is particularly associated with the West Country group of resorts.

We can also see (Figure 10.3) that the South Coast group is distinguished from the Scottish group by the third component, and that these two groups are separated from all others by the fourth component. In Figure 10.4, we can see that the fifth component is specifically associated with the Welsh group of resorts. The Middle England group is relatively close to the centre on most components, but tends to be opposed to the West Country on the second component.

There is then a strong indication that an adequate interpretation has been achieved using five dimensions. We do not attempt any statistical justification for this dimensionality; in principle, all components are potentially meaningful if one is prepared to search deeply enough for meaning. It does appear, though, in this case that the effort may not be well rewarded after the fifth component.

It is instructive at this point to see how well the five dimensions are presented in a three-dimensional figure. Figure 10.5 shows a geographical projection of the three-dimensional global map on which the locations of the resorts have been indicated. It will be seen immediately that the six clusters are located each in its own well-defined area of the globe's surface. This is true in spite of the 'compression' into three dimensions. However, it should be remembered that the clusters were arrived at by employing the total dimensionality and that an attempt to *define* clusters using only the three-dimensional representation could be dangerous or misleading. Once, however, a grouping has been arrived at, it is entirely justifiable to demonstrate the way in which it presents itself in the simpler three-dimensional map.

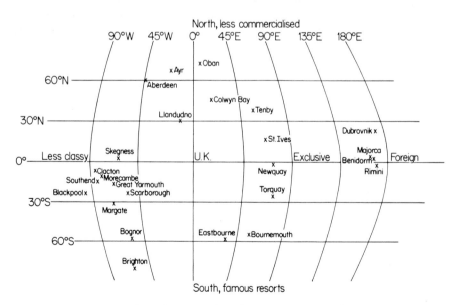

FIGURE 10.5   A projection of the location of the resorts on the first three components (modified Gall projection)

So far the resorts have been grouped according to their relationship with one another. The next step is to attempt to interpret the components in terms of the constructs which they represent. For instance, the first component is associated with constructs of the following general character: 'heat', 'sunshine', 'different food', 'gay night life' and 'good hotels', all these properties being associated with the Mediterranean rather than Britain. The second component relates to such terms as: 'expensiveness', 'exclusiveness', 'good beaches' and 'warmth', these being attributed to the West Country in distinction from the rest of Britain.

There is, however, rather more difficulty describing the adjectival content of the third and following components. Principal components are, after all, not factors in 'simple structure', and there is no guarantee that any will be particularly easy to interpret.

One possible solution to this problem of interpretation of components is available by returning once more to the globe. Both poles of each construct can be represented as points upon the globe's three-dimensional surface. Each pole has the character of an adjective applicable to resorts, and each adjective is located, in theory, closest to the resort to which it is particularly relevant and furthest from those to which it has the least application. At least this would be true if we could construct a 24-dimensional globe; in three dimensions distortions are inevitable.

However, given a computer there is no particular difficulty in exploring the surface of a 24-dimensional globe. We simply program the computer to report to us which properties (or epithets) lie within a given radius of any specified point on the surface of the globe. The points we choose to specify are, naturally, the locations of the different resorts. The radius is specified in degrees of arc or as the cosine of an angle subtended at the centre of the globe; the latter can be interpreted as a correlation. Choice of a suitable radius is a matter of convenience, but in the present case a cosine of 0.5 (corresponding to an angle of approximately 60°) turns out to produce lists of constructs of convenient length which are sufficiently distinctive for each resort. A list of constructs for a single Middle England resort is shown in Table 10.2.

Thus we can produce a 'characteristic description' for every object, using the original words that the informants employed to define their constructs. Of course, a similar procedure can be performed in three dimensions; in fact, it can be carried out by eye on the globe, once all the objects and constructs have been plotted. However, it is safer to use the computerized 'hyperdimensional' globe to arrive at one's conclusions, which can then be illustrated on the three-dimensional globe, with an awareness of the distortions which the neglect of minor dimensions has produced.

Our Middle England resort, whose attributes were listed above, proves to be somewhat negatively regarded in comparison with other resorts. The resort shows a strong tendency to be associated with the negative, or 'rejected', ends of most constructs. This does not mean to say that nothing good can be said about it, but it does indicate that it is far from being thought of as a first choice within its field.

Before we leave the basic model there is a further feature which can be given a distinctive interpretation. Since all the construct vectors were set to a standard length, they all extend to the same distance from the origin in the 24-dimensional space. The same is not true of the resorts. Their vectors have very different lengths. The figures, given in Table 10.3, are the squares of the vector lengths, i.e. the sum of

TABLE 10.2 Characteristics associated with the resort

Characteristic associated with the resort	Opposite characteristic
Stony beach	Sandy beach
More life	Dull
Colder	Warmer
Rowdy	Sedate
Commercialized	Tranquil
No sails by boat	Sails by boat
Not abroad	Is abroad
I don't like them	I quite like them
Are flat places but are also attractive	Is hilly and attractive
Is a flat place	Aren't flat places
Is seaside I know	Is seaside I don't know
Full of juke boxes and amusement arcades	No juke boxes and amusement arcades
No nice scenery	Lovely scenery near to
For youngsters	For the older people, middle aged
They are in England	It's abroad
I've been there on holiday	I haven't been there
Is on a different coast from the other	Not on the same coast
Teenager	Mature people
Noisy	Restful
Does not have cliffs	Has cliffs
Has a lot of evening shows	Does not have shows to a great extent
Over commercialized	Not commercialized
Has a funfair	Hasn't a funfair
Not such warm weather	Generally warmer weather
Not such a good beach	Lovely sandy beach
I've been there	I've not been there
I didn't like it	I don't know
Not such good scenery	Has lovely scenery
I haven't been told it's lovely	I've been told it's lovely
I know something about it	I don't know about it
Not an interesting place	Is an interesting place
Are common places	Are better class

TABLE 10.3 Resorts ranked by 'definiteness of image'

Resort		Sum of squares	Resort		Sum of squares
1	Majorca	1073	14	Margate	592
2	Benidorm	828	15	Colwyn Bay	589
3	Newquay	806	16	Llandudno	572
4	Torquay	770	17	Gt. Yarmouth	562
5	Bournemouth	768	18	Ayr	557
6	St. Ives	768	19	Scarborough	557
7	Rimini	764	20	Skegness	553
8	Aberdeen	756	21	Blackpool	520
9	Dubrovnik	755	22	Southend	455
10	Oban	710	23	Bognor Regis	441
11	Brighton	689	24	Morecambe	438
12	Eastbourne	617	25	Clacton	378
13	Tenby	615			

squares for each item or the diagonal elements of the product total matrix by items. The closer a resort is located to the origin — the smaller its sum of squares — the less distinct is its perceived image or the less is the interest taken in it. An object about which informants have no distinctive opinions at all would be located *at* the origin. An object with a very clear image — whether good or bad — will be located far from the origin. It will be noted that the Middle England group tend to be closer to the origin than many others, which suggests that they are 'grey', indistinctively regarded compared to others.

Discussion

What has been done in the foregoing analysis is, of course, to describe the perceptions of a hypothetical average person. The grids of sixty individuals have been pooled and analysed as a single great grid. Such a procedure is likely to represent the actual perceptions of each person accurately only if individuals' perceptions are quite similar to each other. If, however, we have pooled together grids which are substantially different, it may be that we have described a pattern of thought which is average but represents nobody accurately. The problem of differences between individual persons' grids has been left till last, mainly because in the small-sample application we are considering, the scope for identifying distinctive types of people is very limited. However, the technique may not always be applied to small samples, and even among sixty people there may be a chance of finding distinctive types of personal grid.

There seem to be three possible approaches to the investigation of personal differences in this context. They are put forward tentatively here as they represent an area in which we are currently working.

The first is the atomizing approach, to analyse each person's grid on its own instead of pooling the grids. This is likely to make more problems than it solves, because the common frame of reference provided by the common set of principal components is destroyed. The principal components of each grid may differ sharply from one to another, and if the number of constructs in an individual grid is less than the number of objects minus one, even the number of principal components will be altered.

The second approach is to form a typology of persons and to pool into great grids only the grids of those persons who seem fairly similar to each other. The basis for a typology of the persons must lie in the objects, for the constructs are not the same for each person. The criterion of similarity between grid structures must be that the matrix of inter-object linear distances for each person shall be similar to that for each other person to be pooled. Attempts to use this approach have tended to indicate that the usual finding is a central group of broadly similar persons, with a few deviant cases, the latter being individual outliers rather than a second homogenous type. This finding, if correct, suggests that it is reasonable to pool all persons into a single grid.

The third possibility, which seems to us to have more usefulness, is to retain the common principal component frame of reference derived from the great grid and to indicate upon it the distortions or strains which occur if we choose to consider not all the respondents but only particular groups or individuals among them. If there are differences of any importance between, say, older and younger informants, it should be possible to indicate the nature of these differences by indicating alternative positions for objects on the same fixed principal component structure. There could also be a possibility of defining the individual preference vector of a person as the resultant of all his constructs, given that the positive end of each construct is always the preferred one. Whether or not such preference axes bear any relation to actual choice (e.g. places to take a holiday in) is one which we intend to investigate further.

Outcome of the research

As has been reported earlier, the project was carried out with a view to informing the policy- and decision-making management of the resort. The project is similar in many ways to that reported on by Samuels (1973); it is different in that operating from a university and having a continuing relationship with the client provided greater opportunities for seeing what decisions followed from the research.

The only thing that can be said with certainty is that nothing happened as a direct result of the project. There has been no change in the copy of the resort's advertising, although the results have an immediate bearing on this. Some indirect effect may have been achieved but we have no evidence of this. The lack of action resulting from the research confirms us in the view, deriving from Channon (1968) and developed by Samuels in his paper, that research performs many functions other than the provision of information for better decision-making. In this case, the function of the research can only be guessed at, but it is likely that the client hoped the research, begun some years ago, would strengthen the case being made for independence under Local Government Reorganization. That case having failed, the role of the research (and of the researcher) is having to be rethought.

What can be learned from this situation? It is clear that market research is not quite as straightforward in its relation to the decision-making systems which it serves as many market researchers think. In many ways market research findings need to be marketed. This does not just mean effective presentations; it means providing the right people with the right information at the right time, and the achievement of such a goal requires more concentration by market researchers on clients and less, this paper notwithstanding, on techniques.

References

Channon, C. (1968). *The Role of Advertising Research in Management Decision Making*. Proceedings of the Eleventh Annual Conference of the Market Research Society, Market Research Society, London.

Frost, W. A. K., and Braine, R. L. (1967). 'The application of the repertory grid to problems in market research'. *Commentary*, 9, 161–175.

Kelly, G. A. (1955). *The Psychology of Personal Constructs*, W. W. Norton, New York.

McQuitty, L. L. (1960). 'Hierarchical syndrome analysis'. *Educational and Psychological Measurement*, 20 (2), 293–303.

Nolan, J. A. (1971). *Identifying the Dimensions of Brand Image, Vol. 2*. Proceedings of the ESOMAR/WAPOR Conference, Helsinki, pp. 255–277.

Sampson, P. (1972). 'Using the repertory grid test'. *J. Marketing Res.*, 9, 78–81.

Samuels, J. A. (1973). *Research to Help Plan the Future of a Seaside Resort*. Proceedings of the Sixteenth Annual Conference of the Market Research Society, Market Research Society, London.

11

CONSTRUCT THEORY AS AN APPROACH TO ARCHITECTURAL AND ENVIRONMENTAL DESIGN

B. Honikman

Summary

This paper is intended to establish the value and importance of applying personal construct theory and grid technique in studies of environmental meaning. An architect makes his plans, whether large or small, for a city or a kitchen, to fit the needs of the people they affect, and should attempt to understand how they see their environment. The problem is a complicated one. The environment combines many features into a coherent whole. Each individual has a personal way of construing it in the light of his particular needs. Thus, different elements of the environment should not be considered in isolation and it is unsafe to assume that everyone uses the same terms in evaluating them. The argument is illustrated by a study of the ways in which living-rooms are construed. In the conclusion, general strategies are outlined for research in environmental psychology. (P.S.)

Introduction

I recall how during my undergraduate architectural education there existed, almost like an unwritten law, the assertion that an architect was able to understand and respond to peoples' needs, even and particularly those of which they themselves were not aware. Furthermore, it seemed that this ability was developed by the specialized character of architectural education. It was not that professors and practitioners made this claim in a blatant or confident manner. Instead, it was one of those things that was quietly understood and doubtlessly accepted by those involved. Probably, it was a perfectly natural consequence of the growing conviction that architecture was firstly for people. Ironically, there was nothing at all within the typical architectural school curriculum in the 'forties and 'fifties which prepared the student to understand or define peoples' needs. Nonetheless, the architect felt a very clear responsibility. He sensed that the only justifiable role he could play in society was to use his skills as a designer in a way that no other professional could. His direction was clear and, even though he lacked social science experience, he began to develop fairly sensitive insights into the workings of those individuals and groups to which his own life style related. The professional responsibility of architecture, of course, extends well beyond the architect's own society, so that although he was keenly aware he was less than adequately prepared either to analyse or appreciate professionally the environmental needs of many of the other groups within society as a whole.

In the introduction to *Sceptical Essays*, Bertrand Russell (1935) proposes the following doctrine, 'that it is undesirable to believe a proposition when there is no ground whatever for supposing it to be true'. He admits that if this proposition became universally accepted, it would transform our social and political systems. The incomes, he explains, of clairvoyants, bookmakers, bishops and others would be drastically reduced. Architects could well have been included in this group. One has only to think of some of the subjective statements of internationally renowned architects such as Neutra or Wright to realize that Russell's scepticism is indeed appropriate.

The architect's influence on the social and urban quality of life is considerable. He has a good training in the mechanics of construction and the visual subtleties of form and shape. He has had little or no education to prepare him to identify the kinds of grounds necessary for proposing and supposing a human environmental proposition to be true.

It is difficult to say exactly when social science/environmental design research began. Over the last fifteen years, however, quite considerable changes may be observed in the form and shape of architectural education. Today, students at all stages are concerned with 'Why should we build?', 'What should we design?' and 'How will it fit into individual, group and social patterns?'. The question of how to deploy the techniques and materials with which design and environmental policy are implemented within a human urban context is fundamental.

In other words, environmental design has assumed a strong social science orientation. The nature of this orientation differs at the various scales of environmental problems. For instance, at the macro-scale of urban policy planning, the concern tends to be with generalized community and group characteristics. On the other hand, with micro-scale, architectural decisions, the concern may be with individual environments – neighbourhoods, homes and rooms.

Barker (1968) points out in *Ecological Psychology* that it is impossible to separate a behaviour from its milieu. The behaviour and the setting interact. How to understand this interaction is the problem. The physical aspects – mechanical needs and human performances – may be ascertained through observational research techniques. More important, perhaps, are the non-physical aspects. These include how each individual assesses his needs and his level of awareness. These are personality issues and involve a study of individual anticipation, understanding and interpretation.

I have tried to outline an argument for research into environmental meaning. Social scientists are, and have been, interested in Man's interaction with the environment and research has been conducted from a psychological or sociological viewpoint. Usually, the resolution of designers' and policy makers' problems has not been the main objective. At the same time, the band of environmental researchers has grown and a wide variety of social science theories has been the basis of their research.

Unfortunately not all research is relevant to design problems. Consequently, I have developed a set of three criteria. These criteria are, in a sense, conditions. I argue that a social science-based, environmental research study which fulfils the requirements of the criteria will provide an architect with useable information. The criteria are explained and discussed in the next section. This is followed by a description of a study of the construing of living-rooms. This study indicates the value of applying personal construct theory (Kelly, 1955) and repertory grid technique in meeting the requirements of the criteria. It also illustrates one way in which construct theory and repertory grid technique may be applied. In essence, the study was a methodological investigation and the results were not intended to establish infallible information about the meanings the living-rooms had for the social groups to which the informants belonged. For this reason, the study is most appropriate to a discussion focussing on the application of construct theory, repertory grids and principal components analysis in the architectural and environmental design spheres.

Criteria for architecturally relevant environmental meaning

The phrase 'architecturally relevant' is used to refer to the kind of problems which face an architect when involved in designing. He or she is trying to create a comprehensive solution which responds to all the requirements of its future inhabitants. Many of the health and safety issues may be resolved empirically. Those relating to the quality of the design *vis-à-vis* the values and emotions of the people who are going to use it are collectively an area of doubt and mystery. The purpose of architecturally relevant research is to give the designer some firmness upon which to base his decisions. Traditionally, architectural taste has been the guide and this cannot be considered to have been entirely satisfactory. The criteria were developed as a result of frustration which, as an architect and designer, I experienced with research and theorizing in the broad area of people—environment integration. The criteria relate not so much to whether the study is reputable or interesting as a contribution to knowledge in the social sciences as to the extent to which it is architecturally relevant.

They help to define the scope of personality information which relates to designers in addition to illustrating the variety of ideas which have to be included in an architecturally relevant research package. The criteria are as follows.

The evaluation—physical characteristic criteria

A study should attempt to deal with the relationship between definable physical characteristics of an environment and the personal structure of evaluation by which it is assessed. In other words, it was important for the architect to be able to gain some appreciation of the responses which his use of, say, yellow brickwork in triangular patterns would invoke in the minds of those who were to use the environment.

It seemed entirely reasonable to suggest that, if we were to begin to make progress in understanding environmental evaluation, we should be able to relate the tangible physical components and characteristics which cohesively interact to form an environment to the way people see it and interpret it.

The whole environment criteria

Studies should deal with the environment as a cohesive whole and component parts should be considered within the total context.

On first reading, this criterion may appear to contradict the first criterion or, at least, seem paradoxical. The argument is that the role of particular physical characteristics of environment should be studied within their overall environmental context. This point is strongly reinforced by Barker (1968). He argues that if we wish to understand the interactions between Man and any environment, we must consider both as whole total entities; each piece of behaviour has a physical setting and the characteristics of each are dependent upon those of the other. The usual research approach in which a problem or phenomenon is dissected by analysis into manageable sub-problems or components is virtually impotent in the environment/behaviour context.

Barker (1968) supports this position by explaining that if one wanted to study the behaviour of a baseball player, it would be folly to focus only on him and conduct an analysis of his activities. The number of balls he caught or runs he made would explain very little of the nature of his behaviour. The researcher would be better served by observing the whole game, what each player did, which equipment was used and the role of the stadium in which it took place. The whole game in its context and including equipment, people, weather and location is, in Barker's terms, a 'behaviour setting'. The activities of the people are, of course the behaviour, and all the physical items, bats, balls and clothes, including the grass field and stadium itself, are called the 'milieu'. The study of behaviour settings requires a simultaneous consideration of both behaviour and milieu for as long as the behaviour setting exists as a discrete entity. In the case of the baseball game, the behaviour is connected with the day's game and it ends when the last person leaves the stadium. Careful and thorough observation of all people involved for the duration of the behaviour setting enables a series of deductions to be made about how the environment is used. Both the needs of all participants and the nature of their participation may be described as a result of such observations. What will not be revealed is the meaning that everything associated with the behaviour setting has for everyone involved in it. (This, of course, is the reason for the third criterion.)

Many studies have been concerned only with, for example, light or space or even arrangement of chairs in a seminar room and related it to the position of the lecturer in a study of the choice of seating positions by students (Canter, 1970). Although this work was concerned with the investigation of environmental evaluation, the researcher did not include the other characteristics and influences of the seminar room in his considerations. Canter was interested in the way people made their decisions about enviroment. He was comparing the experiences of people treated as subjects with the behaviour of people treated as objects in an evaluation of two approaches to environmental investigation. Perhaps the presence of a bright light over a particular seat, the proximity of a window or the effect of the light, the window and the carpet could have influenced not only the choice of seat but the user's whole attitude to the room as a place for seminars or even just as a place to be in.

The Gestaltists argued that people were capable of a free introspective view of events as wholes. They contended that people themselves are more than the sum of their physical and mental characteristics. When all the characteristics are grouped together, the total configuration has its own uniqueness (Sarason, 1966).

As the evaluation of an environment is dependent on how it is perceived by people, it should also be treated as a whole, the attributes of which amount to more than the sum of the attributes of its parts. In perceiving an environment, the person sees the whole and its parts at the same time. He sees and evaluates the whole environment. Each of the parts which register significantly in his perceiving are evaluated according to the way he considers they contribute to the formation of the whole. Information deriving from a specific study of an isolated part of an environment, e.g. colour, would therefore seem to have only a limited contribution to make toward the understanding of environmental evaluation.

The personal criterion

The study should allow the informants to operate in experiments or surveys in their own personal and unique manner. This criterion derives from one of my original motivations for embarking on this kind of inquiry. Traditionally, it seemed that the small part of architectural activity devoted to the spatial and environmental design of a building was channelled through the architect's own perception. It seemed that he was almost like a behavioural psychologist who built a maze in which his rat would run predetermined patterns. Admittedly, the architect tried to anticipate the patterns that he thought the rat wanted to run. Sometimes he even asked him about his needs, but, as I have already mentioned, he frequently seemed to believe that his special training and capabilities equipped him to understand user needs better than the user himself. In the same way that most psychological trends, from subjective Gestaltism onwards, questioned and doubted behaviourism, it seemed that architecture's attempts at forecasting the environmental user's interpretations and experiences were equally open to question. Until relatively recently, there was little in the architect's education to equip him to do more than make his own subjective interpretations about the needs of his clients. People usually spend a number of years in their houses and during that time form them into homes for themselves. This implies that each individual must make a personal interpretation of the accommodation and his or her needs in order to make it make sense. This need not be obvious or logical to the outside observer. Lynch's (1960) methodology for studying towns acknowledges that citizens probably see their environment very differently from visiting observers. Local inhabitants are interviewed and asked to draw maps describing the route from one part of the town to another. Frequently they nominate cues, such as a red letterbox or a patch of cobbles, the importance of which, or even the existence of which, may have escaped the external observer.

Terence Lee (1963) has observed that local social involvement was related to the physical patterns of the personal environment. After the war, planners proposed the urban neighbourhood unit. They assumed that the drab uniformity of the housing of the 'thirties had destroyed the identity of neighbourhoods. Lee found that a high proportion of the housewives he interviewed had a clear view of their neighbourhoods and were able to draw them on a map. When he superimposed the maps they were found to vary greatly, and the conclusion drawn was that neighbourhoods, in addition to having clear identities, were also personally unique.

Reference to this study reinforces the two points which underline the third criterion. The first is that the observations made about an environment by people who are visiting it may differ greatly from the way its inhabitants conceive of and evaluate it. The second is that each individual's view of an environment is affected by the uniqueness of his own personal experience.

Application — The living-room study

The living-room study is really a study of methodology and was designed to satisfy the three criteria. It was aimed at developing a tool which would tell a designer about relationships between the physical items he could control and manipulate and the patterns of personal evaluation of the people who used his designs.

Keven Lynch (1960) in *The Image of the City* triggered the idea to explore a construct theory approach. In trying to understand what a city meant to its inhabitants, he asked them to use a sketch map to describe the routes they took on various trips. In doing this, they mentioned all kinds of physical features of the city, many of which were not always obvious to a visitor. The descriptions of these physical features and accompanying interviews yielded rich information about the way the citizens ascribed personality and meaning to their city (in this case, Boston).

Recently the work of George Kelly (1955) has become increasingly well known. *The Psychology of Personal Constructs* deals with Kelly's approach for treating his patients by helping them to see how they construed their worlds. 'Man differs from all other animals in that he is always trying to make sense of his world' and 'people anticipate events on the basis of their previous experiences' are statements basic to Kelly's philosophy.

The living-room study was intended to investigate a method for exploring the nature of the sense people made out of environmental events. Kelly explains how anticipation may be considered as a series of mental templates. As the person experiences a new event, he evaluates it by seeing how well his templates fit it. Other words, such as schemata (Lee, 1963) are sometimes used instead of templates, but I prefer to think of them as an hierarchical system of understandings and meanings — a construct system. Each construct is a dimension for evaluation because the sense made of an event depends upon the relationship between the anticipation and the actual experience. When small differences occur of relatively subordinate importance, adjustments may easily be made to the system to accommodate the change. This is how a construct system changes and grows with each experience. When the experience begins to relate to more superordinate constructs, then change and adjustment become more difficult.

An example of a superordinate environmental construct is the standard of hygiene and cleanliness evident in a doctor's surgery. Someone approaching the surgery anticipates a behaviour setting (Barker, 1968) which includes the surgery, the doctor and the treatment he will receive. If on arrival he finds the hygenic standards far, far below the level he anticipated, his confidence in the doctor and the treatment could be seriously reduced. He may well go to another doctor, and if he finds that all doctors in town have unhygienic surgeries he could become very anxious. If the treatment he needs is crucial, he may have to change his required level of hygiene and accept reality (or admit changes to his system of constructs).

In the context of this example, the living-room study attempted to identify the following:

(a) The superordinate constructs in the system or network with which the respondent anticipated and reconstrued events such as living-room, home, house, etc.

FIGURE 11.1 Photographs of two living-rooms, used as elements 1 (above) and 2 (below) in the living-room study (originally in colour)

(b) The sub-structure of subordinate constructs in such a way that the roles and importance of physical characteristics, items and features could be understood.

The process began by selecting a series of colour photographs of living-rooms and using these to elicit constructs by means of Kelly's (1955) triad method. There were seventeen colour photographs in the eliciting process. One of these was selected to be the focus of the study in terms of the goals stated above. For purposes of identification it is referred to as element 2 in this paper.

In almost every case this technique resulted in the establishment of superordinate constructs. These were bipolar ('formal/informal', for example) and represented the 'important ideas' (superordinate constructs) with which the informant evaluated living-rooms. Each construct was then subjected to Hinkle's (1965) 'laddering' technique to establish its subordinate network of constructs. Laddering is an important technique in this study because it enabled the 'physical characteristic constructs' to be elicited. It is appropriately named because it allows the informant to nominate a series of constructs in an upward or downward sequence within his overall hierarchy of construing the event in question.

In the living-room study, laddering was used to elicit subordinate constructs. The informant was asked to consider the initial constructs, elicited by the triad method, and to indicate which of the two poles he preferred. For example, he might prefer the 'formal' pole of the 'formal/informal' construct and 'organized' pole of the 'organized/disorganized' construct. The informant was then asked why he or she considered element 2 to be 'formal' or 'organized' or characteristic of any of the other constructs which he or she could associate with it. The answer to this question was usually another construct. An informant might say that the living-room (element 2) was 'organized' because there was 'a place for everything'. The question was then repeated and the answer might be that there was 'a place for everything' because there were 'cupboards and shelves'. In this way, I was able to ladder-down from a superordinate construct like 'organized' to a subordinate one which also identified a tangible physical feature or characteristic of the element.

Next, the informants used their constructs as seven-point rating scales to complete repertory grid evaluations of each living-room photograph. The same elements were used for each informant's repertory grid. These consisted of ten colour photographs selected from the original set of seventeen used for eliciting.

Ten of the superordinate constructs elicited from each informant became the personal bipolar rating scales for his personal repertory grid. The repertory grid therefore consisted of each informant's personal set of evaluative constructs used to rate a common set of elements. Two other grids were completed, the first a resistance to change grid to confirm the hierarchical status of each construct within the network and the second to identify implied relationships between constructs in different parts of the network. (See Figure 11.2 and Bannister and Mair, 1968.)

The repertory grid scores were analysed by the INGRID program. Earlier in this section I have explained that the main objective of this study was to relate the physical environment to the construed environment. The INGRID analysis enables the major characteristics of each person's construct network to be charted. Firstly, the relationship of each of ten elicited constructs to principal components indicated the number of superordinate dimensions that each informant used to evaluate the living-room photographs (Slater, 1969a, 1969b, 1972).

Plotting both elements (photographs) and constructs in the construct space provided a graphic display of how meaning and importance was shared among the ten elicited constructs and how each element was treated in relation to this meaning. This technique is simple and yet provides the researcher with most interesting graphic displays. The physical world, being limited to three dimensions, imposes limitations on the number of dimensions that may be represented graphically. Slater uses all three and has evolved a method for plotting elements and constructs on a sphere. In the living-room study, the three-dimensional sphere was not used. The spread of variance for each individual respondent was such that, without exception, at least 60 per cent was accounted for by the first two principal

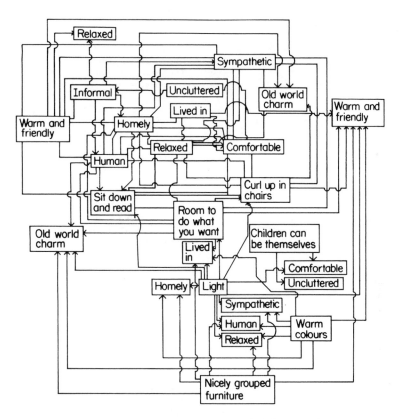

FIGURE 11.2   Implication network (informant 6)

components. In most cases, the three principal components accounted for between 80 and 90 per cent of the variance. It seemed that the subtleties of meaning reflected in the remaining variance were not usefully relateable to the physical characteristics of the living-rooms and, consequently, the construct space diagrams were two-dimensional. The two principal components were used as the major axes of the graph and the constructs and elements were plotted by virtue of their loadings to each component. The third principal component was also included on the diagram, but not in a three-dimensional configuration (Figure 11.3).

To summarize, then, initial bipolar constructs were elicited from each informant and the preferred pole of each construct was identified. These were then subjected to a laddering process which established chains of subordinate constructs, emanating from each initial construct. In almost every chain, as the constructs descended in ordinacy they became clearly identified with the physical character-istics (e.g. rough bricks) of the living-room being considered (element 2). Next, ten of the photographs were used as elements with the ten initial constructs in a bipolar repertory grid. The ten initial constructs were then combined with ten laddered constructs in the resistance-to-change and implication grids (Hinkle, 1965; see also Bannister and Mair, 1968).

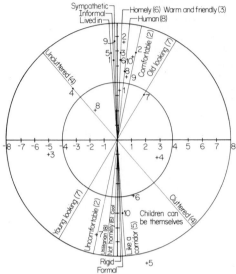

Second
principal component

Key for reading diagrams
The heavy axis lines represent the principal components and are divided into scales of 8 units. The light lines are the construct lines representing dimensions running between the opposite poles of each construct.
+9 = location in construct space of element 9

Second
principal component

Note. The vertical heavy line in both diagrams is the first principal component, the horizontal heavy line is the second principal component. For reasons of clarity, the third, less important, principal component is excluded.

Amounts of variance included in each principal component
Informant 6
72.76% in first principal component
12.69% in second principal component
8.00% in third principal component*

Second
principal component

Informant 29
42.51% first principal component
21.85% in second principal component
16.03% in third principal component*

*Note. It has not been possible to include the third principal components in these diagrams. The original construct space diagrams were much larger.

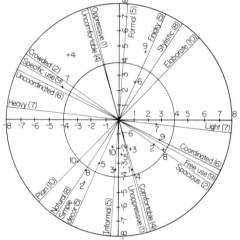

FIGURE 11.3   Elements in the construct space (informants 6 and 29)

The raw scores of the repertory grids were then analysed by the INGRID principal components program and here the relationship between element and principal component was established. The program provides loadings for both elements and constructs on principal components. It was thus easy to establish a connection between the living-room being considered (element 2) and the main areas of meaning (principal component) of each informant. This was called link type 1 — a link by component loading. The second link type (link type 2) was a link by eliciting. Here the connection is made because the eliciting of a construct could be traced directly to one of the elements. Laddering also constituted a link between constructs and this was link type 3. Through the identification of these 3 link types it was possible to construct linear link diagrams showing relationships among element 2, the three principal components (major areas of evaluation) and their constituent constructs at decreasing levels of ordinary.

In this way part of the study objectives were fulfilled. It was possible to trace the development of a meaning pattern from the physical characteristic, e.g. 'fireplace' through increasing levels of ordinary, e.g. 'centrality of focus', 'friendly' to the superordinate area of evaluation (principal component), e.g. 'sense of home, security and family'.

There were two further link types and both related to types of implication. Obviously people do not think only in terms of linear chains. Constructs have implications of other constructs which in some cases belong in other principal components. Implications can be either parallel (A implies B but B does not imply A) or reciprocal (A and B imply each other). These implication links are called types 4 and 5. With their introduction the linear diagram is converted into a more interesting cross-lattice (Figure 11.2).

The resistance-to-change grid was used to confirm levels of ordinary. In most cases, the initial constructs turned out to be superordinate but occasionally a particular laddered construct was, in fact, much more important to the informant than many of the initial constructs. An example of this was the importance to a librarian of the presence of books in the living-room (element 2). 'Books' was a construct identified rather late in the laddering process, yet it ranked second in importance in the informant's set of twenty elicited and laddered constructs. The level of ordinary of a construct is established by virtue of the number of other constructs over which it is preferred in the paired comparison process of the resistance-to-change grid.

Figure 11.3 is a diagram of the elements and constructs in the construct space. The interest value of this diagram lies in its capacity to synthesize and depict the construing process. It shows the relative importance and the comprehensive meaning of each principal component. It provides comparisons among and between constructs and elements merely by looking at their physical location in the diagram. It indicates to the designer how many areas of meaning are important to the informant, together with their identity and composition. Once he has studied these diagrams, reference to the linear link and inplication diagrams will tell him something about how the main areas of meaning are represented by the physical characteristics of the room.

This, then, is how the construct theory and principal component techniques were used in the living-room study. The research may be criticized from many standpoints. For example, the sample tested was entirely composed of middle-class professional people. All were interested in the study and were prepared to spend time on the somewhat exacting interview process. It has been stated that members of other socioeconomic groups may neither be prepared nor able to carry out the interview, and these are the people about whom designers know the least. Another criticism concerns problems of relating data to a general population. The very basis of construct theory makes this extremely difficult. Despite these criticisms, the study does fulfil the three criteria — something that had not been achieved without the use of personal construct theory and its related techniques. The criticisms amount to areas for further methodological experiment and research. I have chosen to leave these issues and devote the final part of this paper to other kinds of areas for further research — namely the potential for attacking the issues of planning and designing the built environment.

Potential and further research

Ironically, it was a colleague who was neither a designer nor a social scientist who stated most clearly and simply the major issues in which the application of social science theory and techniques would assist the environmentalist. He is a systems engineer and he summarized the information about people that designers needed by identifying four major issues:

1. People's basic physical or ergonomic needs,
2. What people thought their needs were,
3. The performance of people in an environment and the dimensions of the physical spaces needed to accommodate it, and
4. Levels of awareness and sensitivity.

The four issues cover a range of interlocking questions and each tends to head a hierarchy of subordinate issues. The results of a study which focuses on these issues should enable a reduction to be made in the subjective guesswork in the design decision-making processes. At the same time, the results will not dictate to the designer. They tend to be descriptive of the person or group studied and, therefore, unlike technological or engineered calculations, do not impose empirical, inflexible requirements upon the design of form and space. In other words, I am claiming that the results of enquiry centred upon these four issues will be informative rather than definitive in character. It will still be up to the environmentalist or designer to use his creative and professional abilities to interpret trends and characteristics in the development of designs and/or policy.

Examination of the four issues suggests two basic research strategies. Issues 1 and 3 would be most appropriate for observational or ecological (Barker's use of the word, 1968) study. Issues 2 and 4 are clearly related to the interpretation of personal meaning. It is in these areas that I believe the potential of cognitive environmental research lies. In particular, it is directly appropriate to research related to issues 2 and 4, and in general the research findings about the first and third issues would be enriched when viewed in concert with findings in the second and fourth areas of issue.

Consider two levels of application. The first could be at a research design or methodology level. Here the combination of personality theory and grid analysis techniques with other approaches could greatly enhance a researcher's ability to respond to the four issues. A number of conglomerate research techniques could be developed and applied to such environmental problems as housing, education, urban renewal and even land-use zoning. It would be totally impractical to suggest that research of this magnitude should be carried out as a prelude to each design project. The contention is that large-scale investigation of typical communities and socioeconomic groups could result in banks of continually updated information. Designers and other environmental policy makers could draw upon this and even small-scale projects with limited resources would benefit. The implication of this first level of appreciation is establishment of national environmental design and policy investigation agencies. They could be either state-supported or private enterprises. These ideas are intended to suggest a possible large-scale operational outlet for construct theory research within a comprehensive environmental strategy. I will resist the lure of further speculation in this direction, except to note that the scale of the building, urban and environmental 'industries' should make such an operation financially viable, even if society continues to pay only lip-service to the value of an enhanced environment.

The second level of application would be at a small personal scale and could relate to specific projects. Social science is beginning to feature in the curricula of many architectural schools. Today's graduates, particularly those with advanced degrees, have been encouraged to undertake various forms of analysis in order to formulate goals and objectives for their designs. An architect could easily include some form of personal construct study within his user requirement analysis for even a relatively small project. It should be easy for simple forms of construct inquiry to be carried out by individual designers or planners if they have access to on-line computing facilities offering principal component analysis and other appropriate programs.

At present, particularly in the U.S.A., research organizations operate as contractors to federal and local government and many other agencies. The Environmental Research and Development Foundation is one such organization. Based in Kansas City, it undertakes research for large urban and housing authorities. Most of the techniques are based on Barker's behaviour settings approach. This is essentially an observational technique and, because of Barker's (1968) very clear understanding of Man—environment interactions, it relates very well to the first and third issues stated above.

The purpose of this discussion has been to argue the proposition that it is contributing to the investigation of the second and fourth issues simultaneously that repertory grid and principal components analysis, based upon cognition theory (such as personal construct theory), can have its most telling application in the field of environmental policy and design.

Potential

Potential is not really an accurate heading for this, the final part of the paper. In it, I describe two current researches in the hope that they stimulate the reader to imagine a wider potential than I could describe.

The four major issues seem to apply to environmental research at macro (urban and community)- and micro (individual and building)-scales. Clearly, each scale of consideration has its own particular kind of milieu. The meaning and definition of a community within an urban district (macro) probably includes a less specific evaluation of detailed milieu components than would be the case in a micro-environment such as a house or church. Although the difference in scale and consequent differences in degrees of detailed construing may involve adjustments in technique, the four issues still pertain, as does the pertinence of the combination of observational and cognitive research.

Behaviour setting research is not, of course, the only approach with which cognitive studies can combine. This paper concludes with brief descriptions of two other conglomerates. These, by virtue of the differences between the problems they explore, indicate something of the breadth and range of scale of environmental research that was undertaken.

The first research responded to the high rate of mobility among Americans and investigated housing preferences. Paradoxically, it seemed that although 40 million people moved their place of residence at least every five years, the sales and location of mobile homes bore no relationship to this trend. Using the faculty of the university as a population, highly mobile, moderately mobile and low mobility groups were identified. Personal construct theory was used to compile construct networks of the concept 'home' and this technique was combined with demographic and mapping techniques to trace the residential trends of the various mobility groups in Lawrence, Kansas (Rawson, 1973).

The second study looks at the entirely different issue of the way people design. Here construct theory was used to compare the construing of architectural students using formal systematic design methods. The students were working on the design and construction of a portable temporary building. This was to be erected and lived in on an island in a nearby lake. Here construct theory, combined with certain aspects of cognitive complexity, enabled some indication to be formed about the different ways that different kinds of student used formal design methods. This is still very much a pilot study, but initial results indicate that some students are unable to think in evaluative terms at all. These students merely assess in terms of undeniable facts and make no judgement. It seems that these students have difficulty with design and architecture and see it merely as a form of physical engineering assessable only in empirical terms (measured characteristics), such as 'How large?', 'How heavy?' or 'How weather resistant?'. The group that were able to evaluate in terms of judged qualities varied in terms of cognitive complexity. The more complex students were continually conscious of a number of dimensions which were important in the formation and assessment of their designs. They were able to make imaginative leaps in designing without comprising important considerations. The less cognitively complex students tended to evaluate in terms of one heterogeneous dimension. All important considerations or design goals were lumped together in this one area and consequently none maintained a clear individual identity in the student's mind. Without the use of a formal design method framework, important issues tended to be overlooked. If one of these students was investigating, for example, the aesthetic form of his building, he was quite likely to reach a decision which neglected a major aspect such as structural stability. These students were able to reinforce the overall competence of their work by deploying design method and organizational devices. The more cognitively complex group did not need these devices in the same way and sometimes expressed frustration or claimed creative inhibition when the instructor required that they be used.

Throughout this section of the paper my intention has been to evoke interest in the potential of construct theory and its related research techniques. The purpose of the paper was to argue the need for this kind of research in the environmental design and urban planning spheres, and to demonstrate how it can be applied. The whole problem of improving the quality of life in cities could be said to relate directly to the meanings that peole see in the various urban phenomena which surround them. It matters little that the architect, planner and engineer feel that they have made an important breakthrough unless the design is recognized, understood, approved of and used by the people for whom it was intended.

References

Bannister, D., and Mair, J. (1968). *The Evaluation of Personal Constructs*, Academic Press, London.

Barker, R. (1968). *Ecological Psychology*, Stanford University Press.

Canter, D. (Ed.) (1970). *Architectural Psychology*. Proceedings of the Conference held at the University of Strathclyde, 1970, RIBA Publications, London.

Hinkle, D. (1965). *The Change of Personal Constructs from a Viewpoint of Theory Implications*. Unpublished Doctoral Thesis, Ohio State University.

Kelly, G. (1955). *The Psychology of Personal Constructs*, W. W. Norton, New York.

Lee, T. (1963—4). *Psychology and Living Space*, Vol. 2. Transactions of the Bartlett Society, University College, London.

Lynch, K. (1960). *The Image of the City*, MIT Press, Boston.

Rawson, K. (1973). *Residential Mobility and Housing Preferences*. Unpublished Thesis, School of Architecture, University of Kansas.

Russell, B. (1935). *Sceptical Essays*. Allen & Unwin, London.

Sarason, I. G. (1966). *Personality: An Objective Approach*, John Wiley, New York.

Slater, P. (1969a). *The Principal Components of a Repertory Grid*. Privately published under a grant from the Medical Research Council of the United Kingdom.

Slater, P. (1969b). 'Theory and technique of the repertory grid'. *Brit. J. Psychiat.*, 115, 528.

Slater, P. (1972). *Notes on INGRID 72*, St. George's Hospital Medical School, London.

12

REPERTORY GRIDS IN THE STUDY
OF ENVIRONMENTAL PERCEPTION

P. Stringer

Summary

Studies of how people view their environment are needed to help solve problems that arise in architecture and urban design. Some recent studies using grid technique are reviewed. Two concern students' university choices, two their use of shops, and one concerns housewives' perceptions of the environmental features of the city of Bath. Emphasis is placed on the importance of relating attitudes expressed by informants in their grids to independent evidence of their behaviour. The author goes on to describe a comprehensive research of his own into attitudes towards alternative plans for the redevelopment of a shopping centre expressed by women in the neighbouthood. Maps of the existing situation and six alternative plans were used as elements, and constructs were elicited by comparing the elements in pairs. Finally, they were ranked in order of preference. The experiment was replicated by showing different informants' maps which had been drafted in different ways. Much encouraging evidence was obtained of the validity of grid technique in this context. The advantages of using efficient methods of analysis are indicated. (P.S.)

The need to study how people construe their environment

Interest in personal construct theory (PCT), and more particularly in the repertory grid method of measurement, has developed rapidly in the field of environmental studies. The relevance of PCT for architects and the emerging breed of environmental psychologists was first pointed out early in 1969 at a conference on architectural psychology (Stringer, 1970). The interest which they have subsequently shown is described by Honikman elsewhere in this volume. Shortly afterwards, a number of human geographers (e.g. Downs and Horsfall, 1971; Harrison and Sarre, 1971) also became involved with Kelly's ideas. This chapter will concentrate on describing a number of studies that have developed within the fields of geography and planning.

Because most of this work has been and is being carried out for masters and doctoral theses, the account can only be indicative. Much is in progress, and the majority of theses are unpublished. The studies discussed converge on the topics of university choice, images of shopping provision and urban perception. In the first part of the chapter, I shall focus on the investigators' rationale for using PCT and repertory grids, and indicate a number of shortcomings which are apparent in these early forays. The remainder of the chapter sets out some of my own work in greater detail. I shall attempt to demonstrate the potential richness of repertory grids and their analysis into principal components, when they are examined from more than one viewpoint.

The reason why geographers should have developed an interest in PCT are not altogether clear, even if one can sympathize with the beginnings of a trend. They have anticipated that it may be a particularly apt organizing framework for the study of the way in which the individual views his environment, a study which has emerged as one of the central concerns of contemporary human geography. As Stea and Downs (1970) put it (pp. 4—5):

Many geographers, interested in the prediction of human environmental behaviour, found that so-called 'rational models' taking into account only ecologically 'objective' pushes, pulls, opportunities, and the like failed to explain a large portion of the variation in the behavioural response. At one time this portion was attributed to 'irrational' factors. As our knowledge progressed, these irrational factors, the 'noise' of earlier research, became the 'signal' — the subject matter — of environmental behaviour . . ..

Elsewhere, one of the same writers (Downs and Horsfall, 1971) suggests that this interest in PCT is not quite like the previous flirtations of human geography with the social sciences, which have involved borrowing syntactical systems admired principally for their apparent mathematical rigour and sophistication (such as an interpretation of spatial behaviour through classical learning theory) or attractive semantic measuring devices. The advantages of Kelly's emphasis on Man as an individual is stressed:

. . . the behavioural approach has championed the role of the individual over the mass as being the fundamental analytic unit for the development of spatial theory. However, we have a total lack of a necessary theoretical stance with respect to the characteristics of the individual since we have discarded Economic Man and have never felt comfortable with Psychoanalytic Man. Instead we have adopted Plastic Man who, chameleon-line, changes his characteristics according to the demands of the research problem in which he is placed.

Kelly's postulates are seen as offering an alternative and encompassing framework of constructs about individuals which can be tested, developed and interpreted within the context of spatial behaviour. An additional advantage is seen in the elaboration of a methodology for data collection, which:

. . . presents an elaborate form of scaling which allows investigation of the nature of constructs about the spatial environment as our subjects see it. Thus, we can arrive at valid constructs for use in theory building. At the same time, the analysis procedure is sensitive to subtle forms of individual differences which *may* become crucial components in building theory about extremely small-scale, non-recurrent spatial situations such as residential site selection, or industrial and office location.

University choice

The first of two studies on university choice (Reid and Holley, 1972), was carried out within an educational rather than a geographical framework. The purpose was to move toward a better understanding of the factors affecting university choice and to develop more appropriate techniques for advising university candidates and making decisions on their applications. The images of universities and their relation to environmental factors and to applicants' actual choices were explored with thirty boys and forty girls. A grid technique recommended itself, apparently as a means of identifying potential idiosyncracies in the applicants' constructs, though the main focus was on isolating stable construct patterns within the group.

The possible outcomes of this individual/group bipolarity were expressed in an intriguing way. If stable construct patterns were not forthcoming, it was anticipated that results would be of interest primarily to counsellors in the context of individual psychology. Generalizable conclusions would not be possible and the findings would be of limited relevance to public and institutional policy-makers. This pre-emptive line of reasoning shows a curious notion of the way in which policy-makers operate and a failure to appreciate the possibilities of the phenomenological approach.

Rather more validly, however, the repertory grid is seen as being peculiarly appropriate to the investigation of a choice situation (p. 53): 'As choice is based on discrimination of some kind, a test involving actual comparison of the items to be discriminated seemed to afford a useful approximation to the "real" situation.'

One of Reid and Holley's main conclusions was that the major component of the image of a university was something 'given' rather than being derived from individual viewpoints, and that university applicants are heavily influenced by stereotypes. They inferred this from the observation that the largest factor of a grid aggregated across subjects was unrelated to biographical and educational variables and to university choice. However, if this largest factor is taken to define the stereotype, then applicants are *not* influenced by it in their choice of university, contrary to Reid and Holley's conclusion. Furthermore, the aggregation of grids was only possible because a common set of nine constructs had been *supplied* to subjects. This effectively begs the whole question of stereotyped images. By contradiction one of the main tenets of PCT and repertory grid technique (see Adams-Webber, 1970; Stringer, 1972c), the study aborts one of its major objectives. Like so many other studies, it demonstrates both the attractions of the theory and grid technique, and the difficulty of fully incorporating their assumptions into a research design.

A somewhat different approach was adopted by Rowles (1972) in his thesis, *Choice in Geographic Space: Exploring a Phenomenological Approach to Locational Decision-making*. His intention was to see whether one could usefully consider spatial choice situations from within the cognitive system of individuals rather than in terms of the external economic and sociocultural variables traditionally used in research on locational questions. He chose to adopt a phenomenological viewpoint which acknowledges Man as the controller of his destiny rather than as the inevitable subject of a controlling environment, and saw Kelly as exemplifying this philosophical viewpoint. In addition, PCT was seen as providing a thorough and coherent psychologically based theory of cognitive organization which could provide the underlying rationale for a dynamic model of decision processes. And thirdly, a methodology was available in the form of the repertory grid technique.

The basic aims of Rowles' study were to test the operational worth of the grid technique and the validity of his cognitive decision-making model. Like Reid and Holley, he anticipated that his results might point the way for guidance counsellors in schools. But as a geographer he also saw that information on the spatial component of university choice, even from a phenomenological viewpoint, might be related to policy issues in the matter of regionalized university intake. University choice was selected as the framework for this study, in preference to many other perhaps more crucially locational decision fields (e.g. the siting of industry, shops or housing developments). Students applying for admission to university comprise a relatively homogeneous population, are faced with a finite set of locational alternatives and express their choices under the simplifying constraints of a formalized application procedure, administered by the Universities' Central Council on Admission (UCCA). Rowles lays emphasis, consistently with PCT, on the importance of measuring locational images in the context of an individual's 'real life' construing of them. The research design was intended to give maximum scope to the expression of individual idosyncracies of university evaluation, at the same time as allowing for aggregation of data for purposes of inference. The potential conflict between these two goals was side-stepped by the observation that, even if substantive information presented difficulties of aggregation, as for Reid and Holley, the task was more straightfoward for structural and process information.

The basic hypothesis was that the rank order of the six UCCA choices would reflect a preference ordering of the same six universities in each individual's grid. The preference ordering was basically derived from the sums of the raw differences between each appropriate element vector and the vector representing the 'ideal university'. Raw data were used and no attempt was made to 'clean' or order it structurally by such a procedure as principal components analysis. Six variations of the preference ordering were used. It was derived either from the complete grid, or from the personal constructs alone, or from only the first seven personal constructs elicited. And in each case the construct vectors were either weighted by their 'importance scores' or left unweighted.

Although one might have expected that weighted, derived preference orderings would correspond more closely to the UCCA choices than unweighted, in general this was not the case. Nor were there any marked or consistent differences between orderings derived from differing amounts of the total completed grid. Averaging results across the six methods produced a corresponding derived preference order within ± 1 of the first UCCA choice for 52 per cent. of the individuals, of the second for 44 per cent., of the third for 28 per cent. and of the fourth 27 per cent. The success rate was, in all cases, far in excess of chance. Grid information was able to replicate previous commitments to university application.

Detailed examination of individual grids, supplemented by interview data, enabled Rowles to explain many of the failures to replicate. For example, eight individuals had been pressured to apply to Oxbridge, though their grids and interviews showed that they were not eager to attend; and seven other individuals, although greatly favouring Oxbridge in their grid, did not apply because they construed, superordinately, that it was too difficult to gain admission. For others, their local university seemed highly attractive, but was construed as 'too near to home' and so rejected. The lower success rate in replicating the third and fourth UCCA choices was accounted for by a frequent lack of commitment to all but the first two choices, since it is known that these are the only ones that many universities consider seriously. Although Rowles was primarily concerned to establish the validity of the grid technique through routine correlation of grid structure with behavioural information, the chief benefit of his study was perhaps the light it threw on the grid's power to explain choice behaviour more fully than is usual. We are not normally led to ask what is behind the invalidatory part of our data, once we find our null hypothesis can be confidently rejected.

Shoppers and shopkeepers

Although Rowles emphasized the probable importance of temporal aspects in locational preference and decision-making, and was attracted to PCT by its own dynamic emphasis, he was unable to deal with them in relation to university choice. Hudson (1974a, 1974b), however, came a little closer in an investigation of shopping behaviour. He related the grid to data on repetitive choice behaviour.

He was interested in the ways in which immigrant societies adjust to their new environment. Enlisting the aid of a number of postgraduate students in their first term at Bristol University and of undergraduates who had just moved from halls of residence into 'digs', he had ninety-six students complete a food shopping diary for a ten-week period. Interviews were subsequently conducted with twenty-six of them.

A grid was administered consisting of, as elements the eleven most commonly visited food shops — a 'preferred shop' and any others used by the individual — and of between seven and seventeen elicited constructs. It was hypothesized that there would be a relation between the position of any shop in an individual's cognitive space, relative to the 'preferred shop', and the frequency with which he visited it. The Euclidean distance between each shop and the 'preferred shop' in the construct space was calculated (the space being defined by constructs rather than by their principal components). The ratio of this distance to the sum of distances for all shops visited during a time period (the distances being expressed as reciprocals) was used to define an expected probability of visiting each shop during the time period. The expected probabilities were correlated with actual choice probabilities as derived from data in the shopping diaries.

When the actual probability of patronizing each shop over the ten-week period as a whole was used as the dependent variable, the twenty-six correlations ranged from −0.96 to 0.95, eight of them being negative and half of them being greater than 0.40. Weighting constructs for their adjusted importance improved the correlations very slightly in these and subsequent calculations. Although neither Rowles nor Hudson found that individuals' weights helped to relate grid to behavioural data, they appear not to have tried to derive optimal weights by a regression method. The discrepancy between subjective and statistical weights would have made an extremely interesting and appropriate discussion point with those who had done the grids.

The actual probabilities were also calculated for each of the ten weeks separately and aggregated, in view of the possibility that each week was the relevant shopping unit to be considered. In this case, the correlations between expected and actual probabilities increased. They ranged from zero to 0.96; all but four were higher than 0.40 and eighteen were over 0.60. One might have anticipated that taking the average pattern of shopping choices over a ten-week period would have smoothed out irregularities in the shopping demands on particular weeks and produced a closer fit to the grid data, assuming that the grids essentially measure an average image of the shops in an individual's activity space, independent of any specific food shopping needs. However, the model seems to be particularly powerful, in that it relates the grid images of shops to actual week-by-week shopping choices.

There is not unimpressive evidence in this study for the possible correspondence between aspects of grid-measured construct systems and independently observed behaviour — a point about which Kelly himself tended not to be explicit. Where a correspondence was not found, it was suggested that features of the decision process were the responsible factors rather than the grid distance model.

A rather different perspective on images of the shopping environment has been taken by Harrison (1973; Harrison and Sarre, unpublished mimeo). He wished to assess the feasibility of a behaviourally based cognitive theory of retail location to replace the traditional limited economic approach of central place theory. Central place theory was developed to explain the location, size, nature and spacings of groupings of retail and consumer activity. It rested upon assumptions as to a perfectly informed, rational and infinitely sensitive 'economic man', and attempted to give a normative and prescriptive explanation of consumer spatial behaviour. By contrast, a cognitive behavioural approach would concentrate on the individual and the nature of his perceptual and decision-making processes. This contrast underlies the choice of PCT as a framework for both these studies of retail activities.

Harrison examined shopkeepers' perceptions of their retailing environment for a sample of forty-one small shopkeepers — butchers, grocers, chemists and menswear and shoe retailers. The elements on the grids, rather than being geographically located events, were twenty-seven attributes of shops supplied by Harrison. The selection of the elements and of eight supplied constructs was made primarily on *a priori* grounds in relation to aspects of central place theory which were to be tested. A further six to seventeen personal constructs were elicited and used on an eleven-point rating scale.

An interesting opportunity was missed here by not using the shopping environment attributes as constructs as well as elements. In the context of a reflexive theory such as PCT, it would also have been nice to explore the construct systems of individuals as shoppers as well as of shopkeepers. In none of the studies described here do the investigators explicitly share *their* construct systems with the individuals who complete the grids, even though they presumably have both specialized and day-to-day sub-systems to deal with university and shopping choices. Their concern for a phenomenological stance rarely extends to enlisting the individual as a colleague in a shared and mutual investigation. One of the main facets of the 'experimenter effect' is the subject's desire to know what the experimenter is thinking about. PCT offers a rationale for satisfying that desire.

Analysis of grids demonstrated little more than that it was possible to collect from shopkeepers in the field psychological data of the kind that might be required in formulating or testing a behaviourally based theory of retail location. No evidence was found of a hypothesized relation between shopkeepers' perceptions and the distance of their shop from the city centre or the size of composition of the shopping centre where it was located. A contrast was suggested between shopkeepers who perceived their situation primarily in terms of their shop's environment and those who perceived it in terms of the internal features and operation. It was assumed that these differences would be reflected in differences of behaviour, but disappointingly no evidence of this was offered.

Urban images

Sarre (1973; Harrison and Sarre, unpublished mimeo) also failed to relate constructs to behaviour in his study of twenty middle-class women's perception of environmental features of Bath, though he did assume that perception makes an important contribution to the genesis of the environmental behaviour in which geographers are interested. Sarre's study is chiefly interesting because of the alternative methods he adopted of analysing his data.

Twenty-five standard locational elements were derived from pre-tests and the investigator's personal knowledge of the city, to which individuals added another fifteen to twenty elements which had some personal significance. Similarly, nine bipolar constructs were supplied from pilot interviews and the literature on environmental perception and evaluation, with a further nine-to twelve personal constructs being elicited. The elicited constructs were not always bipolar in form; this was left to the individual's discretion. It was noted that she often had considerable difficulty in giving an adequate definition of the implicit pole of a construct. Although unipolar constructs decrease the amount of available inform-ation and give rise sometimes to difficult questions of interpretation, they are usually simpler for people to handle and avoid the possible non-linearity and problematic mensural assumptions of bipolar constructs.

Analysis of each complete grid (generally of the order of 17 x 40 approximately) by principal components analysis yielded some consensus and meaning in the construct definition of the first two components. They were identified as an 'aesthetic-functional' dimension, and one describing the extent and ways in which the women identified or not with places in Bath. These results were reflected, but in a somewhat attenuated form, when the grids were aggregated into a 'supergrid' (25 x 333), omitting the elicited elements. A 'supergrid' analysis was also performed on all the elements in terms of the supplied constructs (a 9 x 745 matrix). Forty-seven places which were construed by at least three subjects were given mean values for their loadings and plotted in the space defined by the two largest components (see Figure 12.1). The plot confirmed that these two components discriminate among places in Bath in an intelligible way.

It was also possible to combine the plotting of element loadings with the elements' existing topographical mapping in a rather interesting way. Figure 12.2(a) shows the contour surface based on loadings for the first component. Negative scores, signifying that an area is disliked and seen as ugly, occur along Bath's main roads, particularly to the west where there are two industrialized routes. Less blight is seen on the roads leading south and east, due to a heavier concentration of, often, period housing. The city centre is well located, with three peaks occurring around the parks and main concentrations of Georgian architecture. In Figure 12.2(b) contours indicate the degree of involvement which the women felt with parts of the city. They felt rather out of place everywhere, particularly in the Georgian enclaves, but not in the city centre nor in three middle-class residential areas.

Figure 12.2(c) contrasts areas which have been known a long time with those

190

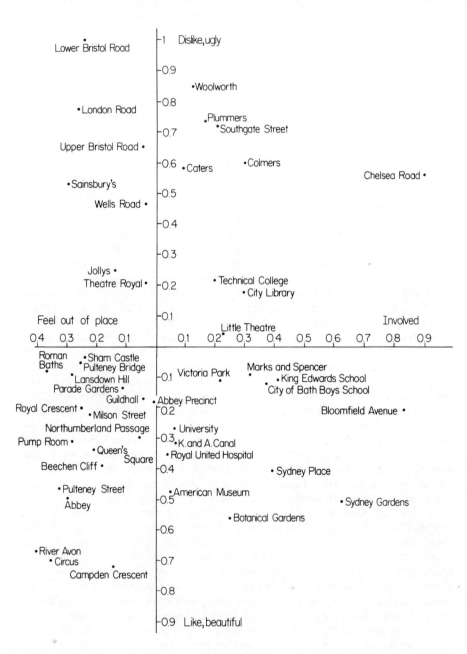

FIGURE 12.1

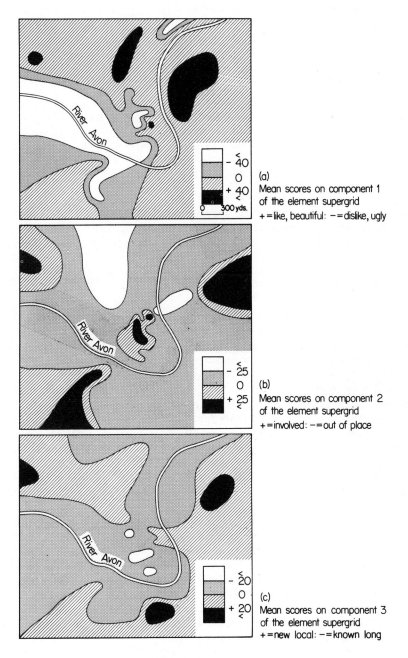

(a)
Mean scores on component 1
of the element supergrid
+ = like, beautiful: − = dislike, ugly

(b)
Mean scores on component 2
of the element supergrid
+ = involved: − = out of place

(c)
Mean scores on component 3
of the element supergrid
+ = new local: − = known long

FIGURE 12.2

recently discovered by individuals and of local significance. The former, not surprisingly, are in the city centre. Sarre discusses this third component in relation to temporal aspects of people's response to Bath:

During their early residence in the city their activity is largely in the centre. This has led to a lasting involvement with city centre places. In time it appears that the city centre and other areas near main routes were recognized as inferior aesthetically to the Georgian areas and other residential zones on the higher land. However the most aesthetic areas resisted colonisation by people like those interviewed, and they took up residence in middle class suburbs. Residence in these peripheral areas led to the discovery of small features of only local significance which reinforced liking for them. Contact with people of similar status in other parts of the city may also have contributed to the high scores of other middle class residential areas than the one actually inhabited by the particular subject.

Sarre concludes as a result of these speculations about behavioural processes in the city that image measurement procedures in future studies must be linked to overt behaviour and that appropriate theoretically derived hypotheses should be formulated and tested.

Evaluating alternative planning proposals

The main study to be reported in this chapter, carried out by myself in 1971–2, was also concerned with urban images. It was done in the field of planning rather than geographical studies. The grid was used not primarily to test its feasibility or validity, as in some of the previous studies, but because PCT and the grid measure seemed appropriate to the content and aims of the experiment.

Under legislation introduced in 1971 local authorities in this country are now obliged to give 'adequate publicity' to their planning proposals. In addition, there is a general movement toward permitting and even encouraging the public to participate more fully in local government affairs, and particularly in environmental matters. One of a number of mechanisms suggested for helping this process forward is the publication of alternative development plans (Skeffington, 1969). The consideration of environmental futures by laymen, in an atmosphere of participation rather than of the more traditional paternalism, is a very Kellian object of study.

Two aspects of this situation concerned me. The first was that planning proposals should be published in such a form as to enable people's construct systems to discriminate between them to the full, and make representative and meaningful evaluations of them. The second point was that people should not be asked to give their opinion of the proposals simply in terms of the planners' constructs, which is a temptation frequently succumbed to, nor by means of some rather simple-minded voting procedure, perhaps by making a simple rank ordering of preferences (Stringer, 1972a, 1972b). A repertory grid technique using personal constructs enabled me to tackle both points directly.

Five aspects of the grid data that emerged will be discussed here, in the hope of demonstrating the richness of analysis that is possible with the principal components procedure. The analysis has considerable implications from the planning viewpoint, but for the present purposes attention will be directed primarily to the intrinsic significance of several different but highly interrelated aspects of the information in a collection of repertory grids.

1. Hypotheses are tested regarding the effect of plan format on the capacity of people's construct systems to discriminate different planning proposals.
2. Some relations between such variables as age, education, familiarity with elements and structural aspects of construct systems are examined.
3. The structural aspects are studied in greater detail in isolation.
4. The content of personal constructs is analysed and shown to vary between individuals in different age groups, etc., and between construct systems which have different structural characteristics.
5. The measurement of environmental preferences by a grid technique is exemplified and related to the previous considerations.

These five viewpoints make up a part of the total complex dynamics of a personal construct system as seen through the grid.

The study was carried out under field conditions in the context of an ongoing planning situation in South London. Six alternative proposals had been put forward for the redevelopment of a medium-sized Victorian shopping centre (Westow Hill 'Triangle', Upper Norwood), which was suffering from severe traffic congestion, deterioration in its building stock, poor access and economic decline. There was a good deal of public interest in the proposals. The general opinion seemed to be that something should be done about the problems as quickly as possible, although two large and energetic local amenity groups were pressing for conservation of some of the Triangle's Victorian character.

A randomly selected sample of 197 women, approximately one in forty of those living within the shopping 'catchment area' of the Triangle, was contacted by unannounced house visits. The sample was restricted to women for economic reasons (to avoid introducing an extra factor in analysing and so increasing sample size), because a shopping centre redevelopment was at issue (range of convenience) and because women are reputed in the psychological literature to have relatively poor spatial ability (if this component of map-reading skills, the map-format evaluation would thus be affected under more stringent conditions). In addition to completing a grid in which the six planning proposals and the present situation were presented in map form as elements, they answered a number of questions which gave information on background variables. The answers (see Stringer, 1974a) showed that the sample was generally representative of the area's female adult population, as described in the 1966 census.

Contacts were made by a female interviewer. Only six women refused to be interviewed. Three others, who were of advanced years, proved unable to cope with the grid. Constructs were elicited by having individuals compare pairs of plans. The elicitation was facilitated by asking for implications of each construct produced and recording them as further constructs. On average, fifteen constructs emerged, their frequency varying between eight and twenty-six. Individuals ranked the seven elements on each personal construct and on a supplied construct — 'the proposal I would most like to see put into effect'.

The grid was generally done with seriousness and interest. Sometimes as much as two or three hours were devoted to the task. Many women spontaneously expressed their pleasure with the interview; they appreciated receiving information about possible changes to their shopping centre and being encouraged to think concentratedly and in depth about alternative future environments.

Map-format evaluation

There are a number of ways of describing planning proposals. I confined myself to comparing the communication effectiveness of different sorts of map. Because planning authorities have to communicate their proposals to central government in map form, there is a tendency for this to be the most common medium of communication to other groups of people. Planning maps varying in chromaticity and the extent of their Ordnance Survey base were compared, since these two factors have, respectively, economic and sociopolitical implications. Black-and-white maps are much cheaper to reproduce than coloured ones. Publishing planning proposals on a full Ordnance Survey base enables an accurate identification of affected property to be made, which brings with it the consequences of 'planning blight'. Central government has suggested that planners might avoid this by omitting or distorting the Ordnance Survey base.

Four different sets of map, each consisting of the same seven land-use plans and proposals, were shown to four separate randomly drawn sub-samples of the total sample. It was hypothesized that perception and evaluation of the proposals through individual's construing processes would be richer and more discriminating in the face of coloured as opposed to black-and-white maps, and that there would be a similar effect when an Ordnance Survey base was provided in the map, as against there being a partial base or no base at all. Many of the details of the map evaluation part of this study have been published elsewhere (Stringer, 1974b). The results will only be summarized here.

The extent to which the seven plans were discriminated was estimated by a number of measures taken from a principal components analysis of each grid. A relatively large first component was taken as an indication of lack of discrimination in the construct system, and contrariwise for subsequent components. An even spread of variance across the seven plans would indicate good differentiation, as would a small 'element distance' in the construing of two rather similar pairs of plans in the set. On all three of these types of indicator the first of the two hypotheses failed to be invalidated. The women who saw the coloured maps showed significantly more differentiation in their grids than those who saw the black-and-white maps. However, in relation to the second hypothesis, results were not so clear. Map formats with a complete Ordnance Survey base or no base at all appeared to permit richer discrimination than maps with a partial base (the base was obscured in those parts where redevelopment was proposed). The latter format appeared to confuse map reading by omitting the base at just the area of maximum concern and to lack the clarity of figure and ground which the baseless set had. Overall, the coloured maps with full Ordnance Survey base afforded the best discrimination of the plans in terms of personal constructs.

Grid measures and background variables

In comparing the grid structure measures across the four sub-samples who saw different map sets, seven 'biographical' variables were used as covariates in an attempt to minimize unwanted variation between the sub-samples. These were: the woman's reported age, her age at the termination of formal education, social class (by the Registrar General's classification), length of residence in the catchment area of the Triangle, the distance from her home to the Triangle, the extent of her knowledge of the redevelopment proposals before she was shown the plans and the frequency with which she reported using the Triangle. (The relations between a wider range of background variables and the grid measures are reported elsewhere — Stringer, 1974a.)

The seven plans each woman saw consisted of the current land-use situation (N), three proposals by the London Borough of Croydon (C_1, C_2, C_3), two by Lambeth L.B. (L_1, L_2) and one by a private individual (P). The three Croydon proposals, particularly C_1 and C_2, tended to be rather similar, suggesting comprehensive redevelopment of the area. The Lambeth proposals were also more like one another than any other of the plans; they concentrated on rerouting through traffic, while retaining as much as possible of the Victorian and 'village' character of the Triangle.

It was the element distance between two of the Croydon proposals ($C_1 - C_2$) which significantly discriminated the map-set groups, and not that between the Lambeth proposals; and it was in the former case that significant covariate effects emerged. Those who had lived longer in the area and those who lived closer to the Triangle construed more differences between the two Croydon proposals.

When it came to examining the amount of the total variance of the grids accounted for by each of the seven plans, it was again the Croydon plans which revealed differences between the four groups. Those who saw the black-and-white maps had a less even spread of their grid's variance shared between the three Croydon plans. In the case of C_1, the younger women in the sample and those who used the Triangle less frequently construed the plan more extremely. Significantly, more emphasis was placed on the Lambeth proposals by the older women. The relative amount of variance attributable to the current land-use plan tended to be negatively related to age, educational level, distance of the home from the Triangle and frequency of use of the centre; and positively to length of residence in the area.

The relative sizes of the first three components also had significant covariate effects. The first component, defined by Croydon's comprehensive redevelopment plans, tended to be larger in the case of women who used the Triangle less frequently and lived at a greater distance from it. The third component, defined by the current land-use plan, was larger for the women who use the centre more frequently. The size of the second component, defined by Lambeth's 'conservationist' proposals, varied positively with both age and residential proximity to the Triangle. These relations seem to be intuitively quite meaningful and interesting in the light of the way in which each component is defined.

A final structural measure, not referred to before, was the number of functionally distinct constructs in a grid. That is, any construct yielding the same rank ordering of elements as a previous construct was omitted from the count. Not only were more distinct constructs elicited from those who saw the coloured as opposed to the black-and-white maps, but their frequency was also higher in the case of those who already knew something about the redevelopment proposals, the younger women and those from a higher social class.

These associations, and others not reported here, between measures of grid structure and background variables do not go so far as to establish relations between construct systems and overt behaviour in the way that the geographical studies clearly intend to move. But they are encouraging evidence of the validity of the technique in a somewhat unusual context and for a fairly large and representative sample.

Measures of grid structure

The structural measures used in the map evaluation exercise are obviously highly interrelated. Their use for hypothesis testing involves an inelegant amount of redundancy. However, the point to be made here is that, if construct systems are to be viewed in a systematic light, their interrelated features must be explored in detail without fear of such apparent redundancy. In addition, if the discussion that follows were conducted with more extensive references to the planning situation than are feasible here, it would be clear that the structural details can give considerable insight into the way the plans were being construed by the public, over and above the insight afforded by the grids' content and by particular evaluatory constructs.

The extent of interrelatedness of the structural measures is indicated by there being only ten statistically insignificant correlations in the total matrix (see Table 12.1). Not surprisingly, the relative sizes of the first three principal components are related at a high level of significance to all the other measures. The size of each of the first two components is related positively to the percentage variance of the particular component-defining elements, as one might expect. That this is not an invariable association, however, is evident in the case of the third component, which though defined by high loadings for plans N and P shows larger correlations with the percentage variance attributed to plans L_1 and L_2. Insofar as the component sizes are used as indications of differentiation in construct systems, one should note that the extent of differentiation can be related specifically to the salience of particular elements in an individual's system.

Element distances were also treated as differentiation measures. Consistently they show marked inverse relations to the size of the first component, but are positively related to the second and third. The size of the second component is more markedly associated with distance L_1 and L_2, these being the component-defining elements, than with $C_1 - C_2$. The size of the third component, defined by elements N and P, however, is positively related to an equally marked extent with both distance measures.

Although the second and third components are relatively small in size (on average accounting for 16 per cent and 9 per cent of the total grid variance respectively), they do contain valuable information. The size of the third component, in particular, discriminates between the four map-set groups at a higher level of significance than the two larger components. We have seen that the second and third components are significantly and positively related in size to the reported frequency of use of the Triangle and to the length of women's residence in the area. The size of components after the first has been taken here as a direct indication of differentiation within a construct system. It is not unreasonable that greater differentiation should be shown by those individuals who may have been more familiar with the elements being construed.

The two element distances ($C_1 - C_2$ and $L_1 - L_2$) show quite distinct patterns

TABLE 12.1 Product moment intercorrelations for thirteen grid measures

	(1)	(2)	(3)	(4)	(5)	(6)	(7)	(8)	(9)	(10)	(11)	(12)	(13)
Number of functionally distinct constructs	1.00	0.30	0.16	-0.22	-0.24	0.16	0.23	0.18	0.29	-0.26	-0.47	0.29	0.41
Distance between plans													
C_1-C_2		1.00	0.13	-0.20	-0.22	0.27	0.14	0.06	0.14	-0.10	-0.44	0.27	0.45
L_1-L_2			1.00	-0.29	-0.34	0.03	0.36	0.53	0.17	-0.26	-0.51	0.44	0.48
Percentage variance plan													
C_1				1.00	-0.00	-0.32	-0.35	-0.47	-0.15	0.13	0.54	-0.50	-0.44
C_2					1.00	-0.60	-0.39	-0.36	-0.17	0.17	0.62	-0.53	-0.57
C_3						1.00	0.19	0.11	0.01	-0.17	-0.35	0.22	0.39
L_1							1.00	0.35	-0.13	-0.37	-0.55	0.52	0.46
L_2								1.00	0.01	-0.38	-0.63	0.65	0.54
P									1.00	-0.51	-0.31	0.23	0.26
N										1.00	0.35	-0.28	-0.34
Percentage variance component													
1											1.00	-0.89	-0.86
2												1.00	0.60
3													1.00

$r \geqslant 0.14, p \leqslant 0.05, r \geqslant 0.18, p < 0.01; r \geqslant 0.23, p < 0.001; \text{d.f.} = 195$

of relation to other variables. Only the former discriminates between the four groups of women. And whereas it is negatively related to the percentages of variance of elements C_1 and C_2, $L_1 - L_2$ is positively related to the element percentages of L_1 and L_2. Thus, only in the second case is the apparent salience of two elements in the sample's grids associated with their being construed in a more highly differentiated way. The differentiation between C_1 and C_2 seems to depend rather more on the number of functionally distinct constructs an individual is using than in the case of $L_1 - L_2$. Furthermore, differentiation in different parts of the grid space may have varying relations with biographical characteristics. As we noted above, distance $C_1 - C_2$ is positively related to the proximity of an individual's residence to the shopping centre and the length of time she has lived there, while $L_1 - L_2$ is positively related to age.

Age is also positively related to the relative salience of the Lambeth plans in the grids, as well as to their differentiation and, consequently, to the size of the second component. Plans C_1 and N have less salience for the older women, and their grids' first component tends to be smaller. The only strong positive correlation within the element variance percentages is that between the percentages for the Lambeth plans. Although C_1 and C_2, and to a lesser extent C_3, are very similar plans in appearance, particular attention to one of them does not seem to imply equal attention to either of the others. There is a zero correlation between the percentages for C_1 and C_2, and marked negative correlations between C_3 and both C_1 and C_2.

It is the number of functionally distinct constructs, rather than the total number of constructs elicited, which shows a pattern of significant relations with the other measures of grid structure. The latter total is positively and significantly related to the percentage variance of the private plan, but to no other measures. The number of functionally distinct constructs varies inversely with the size of the first component and directly with the size of the third component. It is also negatively related to the percentage variance of C_1, C_2 and N, the three plans which tend to orientate the grids; and positively to the other four. It is positively related to both distance measures, and in particular to $C_1 - C_2$. These obsevations tend to reinforce the notion that the number of constructs which lead to a unique rank ordering of elements may reflect the extent of differentiation of grid structure.

Construct content

Several of the human geography studies made an attempt to categorize the constructs elicited from individuals, but the use of the categories was limited either to the simplest descriptive purposes or to arriving at a hopefully representative set of supplied constructs. The most carefully worked out method to date for categorizing constructs is that of Landfield (1971). He reports a variety of relations between content and improvement or change in long-term psychotherapy.

In the present study, the majority of the constructs were concretistic rather than psychological, which to some extent simplified the task of categorizing them. Here I shall relate the information derived from the content categories to those aspects of the map evaluation exercise discussed above. More detailed analysis of the relation of content to background variables may be found elsewhere (Stringer, 1974a).

Two independent mathods of categorizing constructs were explored. Since some 60 per cent of all constructs referred explicitly to aspects of land use, one method adopted seven substantive categories:

1. Shops (e.g. 'shops compact', 'bad shopping layout'),
2. Traffic (e.g. 'easier traffic flow', 'good car parking'),
3. Roads (e.g. 'wider roads', 'good for pedestrians'),
4. Industry (e.g.'more industry', 'industry well located'),
5. Housing (e.g. 'more local housing', 'housing in wrong place'),
6. Public buildings (e.g. 'more public buildings'),
7. General (e.g. 'little change', 'good atmosphere', 'a bad plan').

For the purposes of analysis, the frequency with which an individual used constructs in a particular category was expressed as a percentage of the total number of constructs elicited from her.

An individual tended to produce either mainly substantive constructs or miscellaneous, general ones. Those who produced several constructs referring to 'traffic' and 'roads' produced fewer of the other substantive constructs. The frequencies of the categories 'industry', 'housing' and 'public buildings' were positively interrelated.

No hypotheses were formulated about possible effects of map format on the content of constructs, though several were, in fact, observed. Women who saw the black-and-white maps produced significantly fewer constructs referring to specific land uses, and in particular to shops (shopping) and to industry. On the other hand, they produced markedly more 'general' constructs. This may have been due to their difficulty in discriminating the different patterns used on the black-and-white maps to denote land use, and consequently having to resort to less specific, and frequently evaluative, constructs.

Significant covariate effects were found in the analysis of covariance in the cases of 'traffic', 'housing' and 'general' constructs. More constructs referring to traffic were produced by those who had a higher level of formal education or had lived longer in the area. The percentage of 'housing' constructs, although only accounting for 1 per cent of the total, was negatively related to age and positively to the frequency with which the Triangle was visited. Housing, in fact, was not a very noticeable feature of the centre, although several of the redevelopment proposals dealt with it in crucial ways.

There were marked relations between the substantive content of the grids and their structural characteristics. In particular, the distance measure $C_1 - C_2$, which I have already discussed in some detail, was significantly and negatively related to the frequencies of 'general' and 'shopping' constructs, the two most common categories, and positively to 'housing', 'roads' and 'traffic'. Distance $L_1 - L_2$, however, was significantly related, and positively, only to the frequencies of 'roads' and 'shops' constructs. The road pattern was perhaps the most obvious differentiating feature between the two Lambeth plans. The number of functionally distinct constructs was related to content measures in rather the same way as distance $C_1 - C_2$. Those who used a greater number of constructs produced fewer in the most common categories ('general', 'shopping') and more referring to 'traffic', 'roads' and 'industry'. Three of these five relationships were not apparent in the case of the total number of constructs elicited, once again suggesting the superior validity of functional uniqueness as a defining characteristic of constructs.

The second method of categorizing the constructs distinguished between different ways in which the references to substantive land use were qualified. Once again, seven categories were used:

1. Distributive (e.g. 'shops compact', 'everything separate'),
2. Inferences from distribution (e.g 'quicker for shopping', 'you know where you are'),
3. Quantitative (e.g. 'more industry', 'narrow roads'),
4. Inferences from quantity (e.g. 'more employment opportunities', 'not so much a shopping centre'),
5. Qualitative (e.g. 'more pleasant to shop in', 'less worry from traffic'),
6. Inferences from quality (e.g. 'would increase trade', 'would be unpopular with the local people'),
7. General (e.g. 'a good idea', 'expensive', 'quicker to build').

This categorization was performed entirely independently of the substantive method. The qualifying categories appeared to polarize between the distributive and qualitative; individuals tended to produce the one sort or the other. 'General' constructs showed a marked negative relationship in frequency to the distributive.

From the relations between the two sets of categories (see Table 12.2), it can be seen that the quantitative constructs referred most often to housing, public buildings, roads and particularly to industry; distributive constructs referred noticeably to shopping facilities, and inferences from distribution to the traffic solution, while qualitative constructs, as one would expect, had a strong tendency to be non-substantive. The differing map formats had a larger apparent effect on the content of constucts elicited for the four groups in the case of the qualifying categories than for the substantive categories. Those who saw the black-and-white maps produced fewer distributive and quantitative constructs than the other groups, and more qualitative constructs and inferences from quality. The latter result, of course, reflects the correlation between quality and general constructs. The degree of Ordnance Survey base present appeared to have little interpretable effect on the construct frequencies.

Significant effects for individual covariates were found for four of the qualifying content measures. Age was positively related to the frequencies of both quantitative and qualitative constructs, and negatively to 'inferences from distribution'. The latter measure was also positively related to the distance of an individual's home from the shopping centre. Qualitative constructs were produced more frequently by those with a higher level of formal education, and 'inferences from quality' by those who used the centre less frequently.

There were somewhat fewer significant relations between the qualifying content of constructs and the measures of grid structure than for the substantive content. Eighteen of the twenty-three significant correlations included either distributive or qualitative categories, and they showed an opposed pattern between categories. Although 'inferences from distribution' accounted for more than one-quarter of the constructs, it was not significantly related to any structural measures.

Although it is difficult to convey the flavour of these observations on construct content without a fuller description of the planning situation and physical

TABLE 12.2 Percentage frequencies of constructs within categories

Qualifying categories	Substantive categories							
	Shops	Roads	Traffic	Industry	Housing	Public buildings	General	Totals
Distributional	8.4	1.6	1.0	2.2		0.1	13.7	27.0
Inferences from distribution	6.2	8.8	6.7	0.8	0.4	0.2	4.2	27.3
Quantitative	3.7	4.2	0.9	1.9	0.7	0.4		11.8
Inferences from quantity	1.2			0.4				1.6
Qualitative	1.1		0.3				9.7	11.1
Inferences from quality	1.3						1.8	3.1
General	0.9	1.4	6.0				9.8	18.1
Totals	22.8	16.0	14.9	5.3	1.1	0.7	39.2	100.0

environment to which they related, they do nevertheless give some indication that the constructs which individuals produce in the grid technique are neither random nor meaningless. The methods of categorization adopted here were simple ones arrived at by inspection. It might be that alternative methods would be worth exploring. Those who produced the constructs might even be asked how they could be categorized.

Environmental preferences

In the context of public participation in planning the content of the constructs would probably tend to be looked at for the light they might throw on the public's environmental preferences or their evaluation of alternative proposals. Planners are more interested in information which might appear to validate their actions, than simple descriptions of how people perceive the world around them.

In the present study, the use of a supplied construct — 'the proposal I would most like to see put into effect' — made it possible to treat people's preferences in a more dynamic way than usual. The construing of the proposals on this construct was only carried out after all the other constructs had been elicited and used to rank-order the proposals. By the time an individual came to express preferences, she had been thinking about and reporting fairly intensively for an hour or two on what she saw in the plans. From the point of view of the individual, the preference judgements were probably far more informed than if they had been made 'cold', without the relevant part of her construct system having been externalized.

It is possible to infer the basis on which the preference judgements were made by referring to the associations of the supplied with the personal constructs, rather than by mere conjecture, as is often the case. Following a principal components analysis, other constructs with high loadings on the same component as that on which the preference construct has its highest loading together define a domain of meaning for the preference. Unless there are other important relevant constructs which a person has not revealed, and this must always be considered a possibility, one can assume that the basis for the preference is given by those other high-loading constructs.

For example, those who tended to prefer Croydon's proposals (the supplied construct having its highest loading on the component defined by Croydon's plans) seemed to base their judgements on the compact appearance of the land use, and the consequent inferred ease and convenience of shopping. They liked the modernity which they saw in the proposals and the sweeping environmental changes implied. Those favouring Lambeth's proposals expressed their preference apparently in terms of conservation of aspects of the Triangle's existing atmosphere.

These inferences are drawn from analyses of 'supergrids' for each of the four sub-samples of women, aggregate grids with seven elements and 700 to 800 constructs. It is convenient to define each component in terms of the highest loading constructs, positive and negative, for each individual whose preference construct also has its highest loading on that component (see, for example, Table 12.3). In general, one might expect its highest loading to occur on the first component, since in applications of such instruments as a grid or semantic differential the largest amount of variance is usually accounted for by an evaluatory

TABLE 12.3   Individuals' highest positive and negative loading personal constructs

Highest positive loading construct	Highest negative loading construct

1+ For individuals with supplied construct loading highest on component 1, and positive

Know where you are going	Not much change
Might encourage trade	Don't like it
Safer	The Triangle is smaller
Everything is together	Headache for shopping
More shops	Will be a lot of traffic congestion
Does away with the shops	More like a village shopping centre
Nice neat pattern	Bitty
Good pedestrian routes	No change
More modern	More or less the same as now
Shops all in one area	Shops have not changed place
More shops	Car park in a better position
Good solution for pedestrians	Not much change
A lot of difference	Not much of a change
More convenient for shopping	Some shops should decline
Looks less dangerous	Shops spread out
Completely different	An economic plan
Things more grouped together	Looks rather muddled
Shopping in one area	Not much improvement
Easier for shopping	Seems similar
Easier for shopping	A bit messy
More compact	Shops similar
Safer solution	Dangerous
Compact plan	All jumbled up

1− For individuals with supplied construct loading highest on component 1, and negative

Very modern	Pleasant to shop in
Turned into a Whitgift Centre	Rebound sort of shopping
Car park similar	Doesn't look different
Would mean multi-storey high-rise buildings	Not much change
Would lose the atmosphere of the Triangle	Not so much destruction
A lot of demolition	Not so sweeping a change

2+ For individuals with supplied construct loading highest on component 2, and positive

Looks neater	Would encourage congestion
Easier access for shopping	More roads
Less residential	More public buildings
Viewing platforms a great idea	Don't like industrial location
Easier to cross the road	
More choice in shopping	Keeps the atmosphere of the place
Market better for shopping	Don't like delivery facilities
Better for pedestrians	Seems more closed in
Shops are better situated	Difficult to get about
Safer	Confusing for traffic
Attractive to local people	Don't like it
Roads wider	Shops in a bad position
Better for delivery	Shops have changed place
Less residential	Not so good access to shops

TABLE 12.3   *continued*

Highest positive loading construct	Highest negative loading construct
3+ *For individuals with supplied construct loading highest on component 3, and positive*	
Area will be cleaner generally	Looks similar
The space is a good idea	Less industry
3− *For individuals with supplied construct loading highest on component 3, and negative*	
Routes seem unnecessary	Shops more scattered
More traffic	Inadequate car parking
Easier for delivery	More convenient for shopping

1. Data derived from 'supergrid' analysis (Slater's PREFAN) of individuals' grids who saw the coloured full-base maps.
2. Highest loading personal constructs are listed for each individual only for that component on which her use of the supplied construct had its highest loading.
3. Positive loadings on component 1 indicate an inferred preference for plans C_1, C_2, as against N; on component 2 for L_1, L_2 as against N; on component 3 for P as against N, L_2.

component. This proved to be so for 71 per cent of the present sample. The first component was defined by a contrast between Croydon's comprehensive redevelopment proposals and the current state of the Triangle, and 61 per cent of women had their supplied preference construct loading in the same direction as the Croydon proposals.

Those whose preference construct had its highest loading on the second (20 per cent of subjects) or third (8 per cent) component present an interesting case. They represented minority preferences for, respectively, Lambeth's proposals and the private solution. These individuals' preference construct usually had a low loading on the first component. One may infer from this, perhaps, that other of their constructs which did have a high loading on the first component were more descriptive than evaluative in content. When an attempt was made to sort out descriptive and evaluative constructs in this way, the most striking finding was that they were often nominally identical. Thus, constructs such as 'more shops' or 'safer for pedestrians' might lead to very similar or quite different rankings of the proposals as against rankings on the preference construct. There would seem to be little justification for ever assuming *a priori* that any particular construct was or was not evaluatory for an individual. Some cases were even found where a construct like 'it's a good idea' was independent of a person's preference construct.

In the 29 per cent of cases where the preference construct did not have its highest loading on the first component, this occurred in the analysis both of 'supergrids' and individual grids. Thus, for nearly one-third of the sample, preference, or the evaluation component, did not coincide with the major dimension of discrimination, neither in relation to an individual's construct system nor the systems of others. This is clearly a function of the particular set of elements being construed. But it is important to note that evaluation by no means always accounts for the greater part of the construing process.

How far does the pattern of supplied construct loadings reproduce information that one might get from examining the preference rankings alone? Table 12.4 summarizes the position. The only major discrepancy is a greater emphasis on the

TABLE 12.4 Percentage preferences for plans as derived by two methods

Plan	C_1 or C_2	C_3	L_1 or L_2	P	N
Most preferred plan on ranking of supplied (preference) construct	57	8	24	8	3
Plan(s) defining component pole on which supplied (preference) construct has its highest heading	61	—	21	6	12

present land use in the construct loadings. This is probably misleading, and is a result of the fact that the present land use accounted for the largest part of the grids' variance and served to define one pole of each of the first three components.

Just one indication of the validity of the inferred preferences can be taken from a comparison of the evaluation of Croydon's comprehensive redevelopment proposals by four groups of women (seventy-seven in all), who showed a marked like or dislike for the Triangle as it was and who also reported visiting it very frequently or very rarely. The four groups can be ordered according to the degree of 'involvement' one would suppose they had with the Triangle:

(a) Those who disliked it and visited it never or very rarely,
(b) Those who disliked it, but visited it several times a week,
(c) Those who liked it, but visited it never or very rarely,
(d) Those who liked it and visited it several times a week.

The percentages of these groups, respectively, who were inferred to express a preference for the sweeping changes of Croydon's plan were 78, 62, 50 and 39.

The preferences can also be related to the map-format effects discussed earlier and to the content of individual's constructs. Although a distinct overall preference was shown by the sample for Croydon's proposals, many more of the women who saw the coloured full-base or baseless maps showed a greater preference for Lambeth's proposals. The opportunity to express this minority opinion seems to have been a function of the greater differentiation of construing afforded by these particular map formats. The form in which elements are presented to people can crucially effect their response to them.

It was the frequency with which 'road' constructs and qualitative constructs were used which had the strongest relations to the preferences expressed. Significantly more 'road' constructs were produced by those who preferred Lambeth's proposals — not surprisingly in view of the fact that Lambeth's solution to the Triangle's problems focused on redistribution of the traffic flow. Many more qualitative constructs, which were often of a general evaluative content, were elicited from those who subsequently expressed a preference for the current land use disposition or for the very similar private proposal. Significantly fewer such constructs came from those favouring comprehensive redevelopment, who had rather more specific points to make, and in particular referred more often to the inferred results of distribution of land uses. Again, this is entirely reasonable, since the major feature of Croydon's proposals was to keep each land use (e.g. shopping, traffic, housing) in a separate zone. Women found it much easier to make inferences about the possible effects for them of such a distribution.

General remarks

These results have been laid out in some detail in order to indicate the range of information which can be obtained by using the grid technique. The grid was used for a perceptual evaluation exercise which would previously have been tackled by methods of the classical experimental psychology laboratory. Measures of both the structure and content of grids can provide valuable and mutually reinforcing information on construing processes. These measures can be shown to be associated in a reasonable way with individual differences on background variables such as age, education and social class. Aggregations of public opinion about the elements being construed may be derived with no difficulty, even though individuals express their opinion in terms of personal constructs.

In conclusion, a number of general points should be made about this study. Because of its empirical framework the alternative elements construed were in no sense representative, except of those proposals which had actually been produced. It might have been preferable to have had a set of artificially generated proposals, which were evenly spread through the universe of possibilities. As a result, any of the measures used may have been affected through an incomplete or unduly weighed elicitation of individuals' construct systems. The distinction between the current land use in the Triangle and Croydon's proposals was so sharp that it tended to dominate the construing. Construing may also have been affected by the method of construct elicitation. Initially contrasing the present situation with each of the proposals may have suggested to some people that there was a virtue in a proposal being as different as possible from the present situation.

There are other variants on the procedure which might have led to different, and possibly more valid, results. The women might profitably have been given some form of briefing or other preparation so that they could consider the proposals in a more informed light. This would be similar in some ways to supplying constructs, but in addition to trying to ensure that people understood the supplied constructs.

It is often complained that public opinion, while interesting, is too uninformed to be of much use to planners. But the fact that the public's viewpoint does not mesh with that of people with highly specialized concerns does not thereby invalidate the viewpoint. It is a set of data to be taken into account in formulating a planning proposal. Within PCT one might expect the planners' construct system to be able to subsume that of the layman. One of the things missing in planning theory is an account of the relation between value systems at different levels of expertise, and how these can be translated into decisive action.

These considerations point to a gap in the studies discussed in this chapter. Nowhere is there any evidence of the grid or a derived technique being used as the framework for a dialogue between two parties. The attempt to understand a construct system is only made explicit as a one-way process. There is particular scope in the context of public participation for development of such a dialogue. The public, perhaps, have more curiosity about how a planner views the world than a geographer. As in most other areas of recent PCT research, there has been a failure to conceive of the social scientific process as being a two-way affair.

Two other principal shortcomings of uses of the grid in investigations of environmental perception have been referred to at several points in the previous discussion. They have to do with the relation of construct systems to other forms of behaviour and the evolution in time of construct systems and associated phenomena. Neither of them were dealt with by my study. Temporal aspects of environmental images have been seen as something which PCT is peculiarly suited to deal with. If these issues have not yet been properly grappled with, it must be because the studies I have described represent the earliest attempts to view environmental perception through Kelly's system. And in no area of PCT research has progress been remarkable for its speed.

References

Adams-Webber, J. R. (1970). 'Elicited versus provided constructs in repertory grid technique: a review'. *Brit. J. med. Psychol.*, 43, 349—354.

Downs, R. M., and Horsfall, R. (1971). *Methodological Approaches to Urban Cognition*. Association of American Geographers, Sixty-seventh Annual Meeting, Boston, Massachusetts (Mimeo.).

Harrison, J. A. (1973). *Retailers' Mental Images of the Environment — An Exploratory Study with an Evaluation of the Repertory Grid as a Method of Measurement*. Unpublished Ph.D. dissertation, University of Bristol.

Harrison, J. A., and Sarre, P. V. (1971). 'Personal construct theory in the measurement of environmental images: problems and methods'. *Env. and Behav.*, 3, 351—374.

Harrison, J. A., and Sarre, P. V. (Mimeo.). *Personal Construct Theory in the Measurement of Environmental Images: Applications*.

Hudson, R. (1974a). *Consumer Spatial Behaviour: A conceptual Model and Empirical Investigation in Bristol*. Unpublished Ph.D. dissertation, University of Bristol.

Hudson, R. (1974b). 'Images of the retailing environment: an example of the use of the repertory grid methodology'. *Env. and Behav.* (In press.)

Landfield, A. W. (1971). *Personal Construct Systems in Psychotherapy*, Rand and McNally, Chicago.

Reid, W. A., and Holley, B. J. (1972). 'An application of repertory grid techniques to the study of choice of university'. *Brit. J. Educ. Psychol.*, 42, 52—59.

Rowles, G. D. (1972). *Choice in Geographic Space: Exploring a Phenomenological Approach to Locational Decision-making*. Unpublished M.Sc. dissertation, University of Bristol.

Sarre, P. V. (1973). *Personal Construct Theory in the Measurement of the Perceived Environment*. Unpublished Ph.D. dissertation, University of Bristol.

Skeffington, A. M. (1969). *People and Planning*. Report of the Committee on Public Participation in Planning, HMSO, London.

Stea, D., and Downs, R. M. (1970). 'From the outside looking in at the inside looking out'. *Env. and Behav*, 2, 3—11.

Stringer, P. (1970). 'Architecture, psychology, the game's the same'. In D. V. Canter (Ed.), *Architectural Psychology*, RIBA Publications, London.

Stringer, P. (1972a). 'A rationale for participation'. In N. Cross (Ed.), *Design Participation*, Academy Editions, London.

Stringer, P. (1972b). 'Some remarks on people's evaluation of environments'. In A. G. Wilson (Ed.), *Patterns and Processes in Urban and Regional Systems*, Pion, London.

Stringer, P. (1972c). 'Psychological significance in personal and supplied construct systems: a defining experiment'. *Eur. J. soc. Psychol.*, 2, 437—447.

Stringer, P. (1974a). 'Individual differences in the construing of shopping centre redevelopment proposals'. In D. V. Canter and T. R. Lee (Eds.), *Environmental Psychology*, Architectural Press, London.

Stringer, P. (1974b). 'A use of repertory grid measures for evaluating map formats'. *Brit. J. Psychol.*, 65, 23—34.

13

A GRID INVESTIGATION OF
LONG-TERM PRISONERS

J. P. Watson, J. C. Gunn, Jean Gristwood

Summary

In the main study, ninety long-term prisoners were asked to rank different ways of responding to a set of stressful situations, described in vivid detail. Their responses were used to construct a consensus grid and then the individual grids were compared with it. The characteristics of the consensus grid are reported. Unpleasant affective states, rather than aggressive or negativistic actions, were found to be the commonest consequences; there were subsidiary tendencies for being depressed, and thieving to be seen as specific responses to lack of accommodation, money and work; for punching out and smashing up to be associated with being laughed at, rudeness and fights; and getting drunk with rows. Characteristic patterns of deviation from consensus were found in the grids of problem drinkers and compulsive gamblers, but not in those of professional thieves and men with records of violence. (P.S.)

Interviewing prisoners

A consecutive series of long-term prisoners was studied during 1969. The violent propensities of these men, other aspects of their criminal behaviour and some of their other characteristics are discussed elsewhere (Gunn and co-authors, 1973). We were interested, among other things, in the prisoners' reported responses to environmental stress. This could have been investigated by means of structured interviews, but this technique is time-consuming, tends to be unreliable, unless interviewers are thoroughly trained, and is rarely applicable outside a research setting. On the other hand, the usual alternative, the questionnaire method, did not seem to us to provide satisfactory rapport or flexibility. We therefore used a very unstructured interview, yielding data which could be tabulated in grid form and analysed as such.

Method

Pilot work

Questions and responses which could be evaluated reliably were determined in pilot work. Random groups of prisoners were found to be extremely consistent in their evaluation of some types of grid element, including photographs of people and named real persons, even when these were chosen by themselves or (as pictures of prison officers or policemen) were related to their penal and criminal experiences. Nine constructs and nine elements were finally chosen which appeared to produce responses which were stable over a few days.

The test procedure

Each subject was asked to rank nine 'elements' in terms of nine 'constructs' (Table 13.1). The 'constructs' were situations which a recidivist prisoner might meet in his stress-filled life. These were portrayed to each subject by narrative, as vividly as possible, and each man was asked to imagine himself in each crisis situation. For situation 1, for example, the subject was asked to 'imagine that you are working well at a job you like and then one morning, for reasons you don't know about, the foreman or boss comes up and says "I'm sorry, but you've got to leave, please collect your cards from the office"; you ask why but he won't give you any information'. If the subject indicated that for some reason (such as that he had never had a job he liked) he could not imagine such a scene, then a story was developed by discussion to indicate the same type of stress but in his own individual life context. The subject then looked at a series of nine cards with one 'element' printed on each and chose what he thought was the likeliest consequence for him of being in the imagined situation. The appropriate card was removed and its number noted. The next most likely consequence was then chosen from the remaining eight and the procedure repeated until only one element remained. After this, the next situation was given and the subject began with the nine elements once more. The whole procedure usually took about 15—20 minutes; once the subject understood it and knew what the elements were he could work fairly quickly.

We were, then, assessing the extent to which subjects perceived certain behaviours and feelings as occurring in response to selected environmental events. The chosen 'constructs' were situations regarded by us as possible precipitants of antisocial conduct. The 'elements' were chosen to include three negativistic actions (thieving, drinking and gambling), three negative feelings (depression, tension and anger) and three aspects of aggressiveness (punching out, smashing up and swearing). Care was taken to describe them in terms meaningful to prisoners.

TABLE 13.1   The elements and constructs used in each grid

Constructs		Elements	
1	Getting the sack	1	Punch out
2	Being unemployed	2	Feel depressed
3	Getting caught by the police	3	Get drunk
4	Having no money	4	Feel angry
5	Witnessing a bloody fight	5	Feel tensed up
6	Being laughed at	6	Go thieving
7	Others being rude to me	7	Smash up
8	Having rows	8	Go gambling
9	Having nowhere to live	9	Swear

Reliability

Thirty-two male prisoners were selected at random from the prison we were going to use in the main enquiry, excluding grossly uncooperative and possibly psychotic men, and were given the test twice, seven to ten days apart. Each subject's two grids were then compared, using the DELTA program of the M.R.C. service for analysing repertory grids (Slater, 1968); indices of consistency (measuring the overall correlation between pairs of grids) varied (between subjects) between 0.30 and 1.00, with a mean of 0.74 and a standard deviation of 0.17.

The study proper

Our sample consisted of ninety consecutive male prisoners admitted to the South Eastern Region Long Term Allocation Centre at Wandsworth prison, each of whom had been sentenced to five or more years of imprisonment. Each man provided one grid by the procedure already described.

Hypotheses

We thought it possible that subjects might not see themselves as consistently responding to situations in the ways indicated or that prisoners might see action rather than internal feeling states as responses to environmental events. We thought there might be subgroups of prisoners who did, and subgroups who did not, see themselves as responding to problem events in particular ways. Lastly, we sought to derive a measure of aggressiveness or violence from the grids which might correlate with one or more of the other violence measures used in the associated study (Gunn, 1972).

Analysis

The grids were analysed by the M.R.C service for analysing repertory grids (Dr. Patrick Slater). A 'consensus' grid was prepared by calculating the mean ranking for each cell in all the grids taken together, placing, as it were, the original grids in a pile and dealing separately with each of the eighty-one columns in the cube thus formed. A principal component analysis was carried out on the consensus grid, and the deviation of each cell mean from the general cell mean (=5.0) was calculated, as well as the amount of variation about it. The overall level of correlation between each grid and the consensus grid was also evaluated.

Results

Characteristics of the consensus grid

Principal components. The distribution of the consequences in the 'construct' space in terms of the first two principal components of the consensus grid is shown in Figure 13.1. The first component accounts for 71.4 per cent of the consensus grid variance and the second for 21.1 per cent, so that other components are clearly of relatively little importance, although the third component (2.9 per cent of the total grid variance) merits mention.

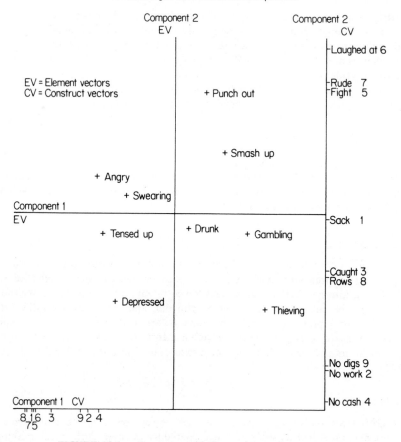

FIGURE 13.1   Consensus grid: first and second components

Figure 13.1 is readily interpreted. All the constructs (situations) have sizeable loadings at the negative pole of the first component, with the three social situations (having no money, being unemployed and having nowhere to live) being less prominent than the remainder. The distribution of the element (consequences) vectors in terms of this component indicates that emotional consequences (feeling angry, depressed or tensed up, or swearing) were rated on consensus as more likely possible consequences of being in all the situations than the remaining consequences, which appear at the positive pole of the first component, implying that their average rankings were all greater than 5. There was thus a general tendency for subjects to perceive unpleasant affective states as more likely consequences of being in particular situations than selected overt behaviours.

The second component of this consensus grid describes sources of variation in the matrix which remain after the removal of that part of the scores in the original consensus grid attributable to the first component. Three social situations (lacking accommodation, work and money) were associated with thieving and feeling depressed, and contrasted with being laughed at, witnessing a fight and rudeness, which were deemed likely to lead to punching out and smashing up. This means that, apart from the general tendency for all situations to be judged as leading preferentially to emotional rather than behavioural consequences, there was a tendency for lack of money, accommodation or work to be associated with thieving and feeling depressed, and not with violence. There was a contrasting tendency for interpersonal events (being laughed at, rudeness and witnessing fights) to be seen as leading to violence and not to depression or thieving.

The third component includes very large contributions from having rows and getting drunk, with thieving marking the opposite pole, implying that rows tended to be seen as leading to drunkenness and not to theft.

In summary, the three principal components accounted for 95.9 per cent of the variance in the consensus grid, the first component being very large. The main finding was that emotional states were the most likely perceived consequences of being in all the situations rated. There were subsidiary tendencies for being depressed and thieving to be seen as specific responses to lack of accommodation, money and work; for punching out and smashing up to be associated with being laughed at, rudeness and fights; and getting drunk and not thieving, with rows.

Large individual cell means. The general mean of all the rankings in all the cells of all the individual grids was 5.0. The difference between the mean for any cell in the consensus grid and this general mean reflects the magnitude of the general tendency for a particular element to be ranked higher or lower than the average. Table 13.2 gives all the cell means which differed from the general mean by more than +2.0 or −2.0, which respectively indicate rankings numerically greater than 7 and less than 3, i.e. relatively unlikely consequences and likely consequences.

Table 13.2 is, in part, a restatement of the main implication of the principal component analysis that feeling states were seen as relatively likely consequences of

TABLE 13.2　Consensus grid: large differences of cell means from general mean

	Possible consequences	
	Likely	Unlikely
	(cell mean < general mean by	(cell mean > general mean by
Constructs	at least 2.0)	at least 2.0)
1　Getting the sack	Feeling tensed up	Thieving
2　Being unemployed	Feeling depressed	Punching out
3　Getting caught	Feeling tensed up	
4　Having no money	Feeling depressed	Punching out
		Smashing up
5　Witnessing a fight	Feeling angry	Theft
		Gambling
6　Being laughed at	Feeling angry	Theft
		Gambling
7　Rudeness	Feeling angry	Theft
		Gambling
8　Having rows	Feeling depressed	Punching out
	Feeling tense	Theft
9　Having no digs	Feeling depressed	Punching out

being in any of the problem situations. It also shows, however, that feeling angry was seen as an emotional consequence of being in interpersonal problem situations and feeling tense and depressed as following social difficulties. 'Having rows' is anomalous in this respect. The finding that theft and gambling were markedly unlikely consequences of interpersonal stress and punching out unlikely to follow the others implies that theft and gambling sometimes followed social difficulties and punching out interpersonal ones, as indicated by the characteristics of the second principal component.

Large amounts of variation about individual cell means. The amount of variation about a cell mean in the consensus grid reflects the extent to which rankings in that cell in the individual grids differed from the overall cell mean. A large amount of variation indicates that some rankings were much higher and some much lower than the mean, implying in turn that some subjects ranked the cell consequences as particularly likely to follow exposure to the cell situation, while others ranked it as particularly unlikely. Table 13.3 shows all the cells for which the level of variation was greater than 500.

Table 13.3 indicates that there were groups of subjects who saw getting drunk as a very likely response to getting the sack; thieving or gambling as associated with lack of work, money or digs, and getting caught; and punching out as likely to follow three interpersonal problem situations. The cell means in all these instances approximated the general mean, indicating that there were other subjects who saw these particular consequences as very improbably associated with these situations.

TABLE 13.3   High levels of variation about cell means

Constructs	Consequences for which level of variation in consensus grid was <500 (and hence including numbers of high and low rankings)
1 Getting the sack	Getting drunk
2 Being unemployed	
3 Getting caught	Thieving Gambling
4 Having no money	
9 Having no digs	
5 Witnessing a fight	
6 Being laughed at	Punching out
7 Rudeness	

Relationship of eccentricity or other variables. The index of consistency between any one grid and the overall consensus grid could be taken as a measure of the eccentricity of that grid. Intercorrelations were examined to see if such a measure related to other data collected about our prisoners. The only significant correlation was with IQ ($r = 0.35$, $p < 0.01$), suggesting that the most eccentric grids came from the dullest men.

Validation of the grid

It has been pointed out that high levels of variation about cell means in the consensus grid indicated that some subjects associated particular consequences and situations together. Inspection of the matrices of differences between individual subjects' grids and the consensus grid enabled us to identify those subjects who saw getting drunk as likely to follow getting the sack; thieving and gambling as associated with lack of money, work or accommodation; and those who ranked punching out as a likely consequence of witnessing a fight, being laughed at or rudeness. All the twenty-nine subjects who ranked getting drunk as likely to follow getting the sack had been independently identified as problem drinkers, and there were no known alcoholics unaccounted for by this means. Similarly, all the seven known inveterate, if not compulsive, gamblers were identified from these grids by their high rankings for gambling as a consequence of social stress. There were, however, some clinically incorrigible thieves who were not identified by high rankings for thieving as a response to a situation. This would be expected of 'professional' thieves whose illegal activities were planned rather than impulsive, and who might see themselves as deliberately bettering themselves rather than as responding to disagreeable events in their environment.

The fact that we could identify alcoholics and gamblers from their grids gave us grounds for looking for violent or aggressive prisoners along similar lines. There was a very weak but significant association ($r = -0.253$, $p < 0.05$) between a high total number of violent convictions recorded against a man and a low sum of his rankings for 'punch out' (which was a more likely perceived consequence when this sum was low). Also, both these 'punch out' scores and similar ones for 'smash up' correlated significantly with the scores obtained on the Buss—Durkee test, a paper-and-pencil aggression questionnaire completed by each subject (Buss and Durkee, 1957, 1957).

	Buss—Durkee assault scale score
	r
Sum of ranks for 'punch out'	−0.506
Sum of ranks for 'smash up'	−0.340

The Buss—Durkee questionnaire itself correlated better with the number of violence offences and our scale of violence than did either of the grid scores.

	B—D assault scale score	'Punch out' score	'Smash up' score
Number of convictions for violence	0.409	−0.253	−0.105
Overall violence scale score	0.458	−0.195	−0.081

This seems to indicate that as far as violence is concerned the grid technique was a better indicator of responses to other questionnaires than of behavior.

There are several possible explanations for this. Firstly, a minority of persistently violent men might report themselves as such in test situations like this; and, secondly, our violence measures, like all such scales, had to take into account both severity and frequency of violence, which have recently been shown to be positively associated at the r +0.608 level. (Nicol and co-authors, 1972.) In other words, a man who under severe stress has an outburst of rage when he seriously hurts somebody may only rarely succumb to such behaviour (Megargee, 1966), but would collect a high score on our violence scale and a violence conviction if he is caught. It would be understandable for such a man to see himself as usually making non-violent responses to criminogenic stress. It is relevant in this regard that violence scores derived from the grids correlated better with the number of previous convictions than with the score on the overall violence scale. It is also, of course, possible that a particular individual's violence might be very situation-specific, but related to situations which were not included in the test list.

Discussion

The procedure described in this paper can be construed as a structured interview or test which can be analysed by methods applicable to repertory grids, is reliable, at least in the short term and for those of at least average intelligence, and is relevant to the problems of a prison population. Our results also suggest that the procedure is valid with respect to drinking and gambling problems, but may be less helpful in assessing 'violence'.

Does the technique, or the instrument, have any value? It would certainly be foolish to advocate its use for the identification of drinkers and gamblers when this can be tackled by simpler means. However, we were impressed that a grid constructed in this way enabled prisoners to communicate about reactions to stress experienced in the past, matters on which such persons can rarely articulate easily. The finding that it is the brighter prisoner who conforms to the group norm in terms of his reported reactions to stress is interesting, as it can be taken either as a limitation of the test or as indicating that dull prisoners do diverge widely from their brighter prisoner brethren in their affective and antisocial responses. The present experiment does not distinguish between these possibilities.

As the consensus grid was constructed from the collective responses of a consecutive sample of long-term prisoners, a general statement can perhaps be made that unpleasant affective states were seen to be more likely responses to stressful situations than antisocial behaviour. This will not surprise anybody working in the criminological field, but it does illustrate that it is possible to interview groups of people with this technique and meaningfully analyse their collective responses. Its short length is a further advantage. Another non-controversial finding from the consensus grid (and perhaps again therefore giving confidence in its validity) is that a lack of material things (money, accommodation and work) is seen as leading to thieving and depression, whereas interpersonal frustrations lead to violence. Drunkenness is also seen as related to rows.

The failure of the technique to produce any close relationship with violence behaviour is an important negative finding, and it calls into question the whole process of labelling a person as 'violent' or 'non-violent', or of placing him at a point X on a unitary violence scale. It is probably much more meaningful insofar as the individual is concerned to describe in what circumstances he is violent, what severity of violence he exhibits in those particular circumstances and how often such things happen. Most human beings can be violent, and extremely violent under some circumstances, and chance events partly determine whether or not those particular circumstances arise; and men are sometimes, as in war, expected or even compelled to be violent.

Summary

Formally identical grids were obtained from ninety prisoners. Each subject ranked nine possible consequences of being in situations in order of likely occurrence for each of nine situations. A consensus grid was obtained from all ninety grids taken together and subjected to principal component analysis. Emotional consequences were judged on consensus as the more likely responses to all the rated situations than selected problem behaviours. Grid entries concerning excessive drinking, gambling and violence were related to other known characteristics of the subjects and the implications of the findings are discussed.

Acknowledgements

We would like to thank the Home Office for the facilities provided, especially by Dr. Lotinga and his long-suffering staff at Wandsworth prison. Dr. Patrick Slater very kindly analysed the grids for us using the M.R.C. grid analysis service which he has developed, and he also gave statistical advice. The project was made possible by a grant by the M.R.C. to Professor T. C. N. Gibbons in the Institute of Psychiatry, London. The prisoners participated freely, cheerfully and willingly; without them the project would have been impossible.

References

Buss, A. H., and Durkee, A. (1957), 'An inventory for assessing different kinds of hostility'. *J. Consulting Psychol.*, 4, 343—349.

Gunn, J. C. (1972). 'Research into aggression among long-term prisoners'. *Prison Medical Journal*, April, 3—12.

Gunn, J. C., Nicol, R., Gristwood, J., and Foggitt, R. (1973). 'Long term prisoners'. *Brit. J. Criminol.*, 13, 331—340.

Megargee, E. I. (1966). 'Undercontrolled and overcontrolled personality types in extreme anti-social aggression'. *Psychological Monographs, 80*, No. 611.

Nicol, R., Gunn, J. C., Foggitt, R., and Gristwood, J. (1972), 'Quantitive assessment of violence in adult and young offenders'. *Medicine, Science and the Law*, 12, 275—282.

Slater, P. (1968). *Summary of the Output from DELTA*, obtainable from Dept. of Psychiatry, St. George's Hospital Medical School, London.

14

THE USE OF GRID TECHNIQUE
IN SOCIAL ANTHROPOLOGY
John Orley

Summary

In studying another culture, the anthropologist first immerses himself in it in order to understand the opinions and beliefs that sustain it and then endeavours to translate them into the language of his own culture. He collects his information through informal conversations with representative members of the community at times when they feel completely at ease, and defers to their customary ways of expressing themselves. He may be content to report prevalent beliefs on a topic in a literary manner without attempting to measure how widely or strongly they are held. But once good rapport is established, it may not be difficult to apply grid technique and thus quantify a current system of beliefs. Different ways of obtaining the data are discussed.

Two examples are given of quantified studies in rural Buganda. The first concerned the position of mad people and epileptics in the community and the beliefs which governed the behaviour of the rest of the community towards them. The second was a study of the way in which the Ganda see their spirit world. Both produced definite and informative results. A well-established sophisticated system of beliefs concerning the spirit world is demonstrated by the consensus grid. (P.S.)

The subject matter of social anthropology

One aspect of anthropological work is to describe concepts held by a group of people, including their 'world view'. The groups usually studied are small-scale societies who share most of their beliefs, so that it is possible to say, for instance, that all of a particular tribe believe something to be true or think that it is right to do certain things. The information that an anthropologist collects is of different sorts.

(a) There are those beliefs which the people studied feel are certainly true. They are often thought to be held by all mankind and are considered obvious facts.

(b) There are those things that are believed, but are thought of as traditional beliefs, peculiar to the people themselves. These could include beliefs relating to their gods. Many people may not know these traditional beliefs very well and they can refer the enquiring anthropologist to experts within the society for their knowledge of the tradition.

(c) There are things which people believe, but they are uncertain of the extent to which others believe them, and on investigation they may either be found to be widely held or idiosyncratic.

(d) Some 'beliefs' may not be expressly stated by the people themselves, but may be elicited by the anthropologist who looks for themes which can bring his data into some unity. These superordinate beliefs may explain many other beliefs or ways of behaving.

In the discipline of anthropology, the concepts investigated have often concerned the ways in which people view their own social organization. In many small-scale societies, the people do this in terms of kinship relations, so that the study of kinship has been important in anthropology, although other fields such as religious beliefs have also been studied.

In the study of another culture, the anthropologist has first of all to immerse himself in this new culture so that he can really understand the thinking and experience of the people he studies; he then has to withdraw himself from this in order to translate what he has understood into the language of his own culture. This translation has always been an important aspect of the work and is why it is sometimes stated that anthropology is the study of other cultures. The anthropologist should really begin, therefore, by learning the language of those people he studies, for without this he will find it difficult to understand how they think and experience life. In his actual fieldwork, he may just record what he observes and what he is told the tribe believes, and translate this, taking care to convey the full meaning of the words. He should use several informants to ensure that what he has been told are fairly widely held beliefs. If he obtains much of his information from an expert in the traditions, as he often does, he should then try to find out the extent to which these beliefs are held by the rest of the population, or at least make sure that they are compatible with what little they do know.

The anthropologist thus builds up a consensus grid for certain areas of knowledge and experience in the society he studies. He will usually select particular topics which interest him or possibly he will be drawn to these topics because they seem of particular interest to the people themselves. Within that topic, he will select a group of things that seem important and will learn in what ways these seem to the people to be alike and in what ways they are seen to be dissimilar. Thus, in the field of religion, he may collect together the names of various spirits or categories of spirits. He can then describe each one and in doing so will see how the people think that certain ones resemble each other and differ from others, and will thus define the categories used by the people. Much of this work is done in very informal conversations with informants, but essentially it is a similar process to defining the key elements that the people perceive and eliciting the constructs that are used to define these elements.

Many anthropologists are content to describe certain collective representations obtained from an uncertain number of informants or, possibly, just a few experts, without ever going on to determine the extent to which these beliefs are widely held. Some do go on to prepare questionnaires which can be administered to a large sample in order to validate their initial observations. It is suggested, however, that not only can the formal methods suggested by Kelly for eliciting constructs be used in the anthropological setting but the repertory grid technique could be a useful and very appropriate addition to the methods used in anthropology.

The first study

The author carried out fieldwork in rural Buganda in 1967–1968, working about 40 miles from Kampala, the capital of Uganda. The fieldwork mainly concerned the position of mad people and epileptics in the community and the beliefs associated with this. During this, he built up a list of constructs which were frequently used by the people. He then took a sample of eighteen men, none of whom had more than seven years' schooling, with most having four of five years, and none knowing much English, and asked them to rate certain elements on the constructs using a five-point scale. The whole procedure was done in the local language (Luganda), the translation of the elements supplied being 'man', 'woman', 'child', 'thief', 'madman', 'epileptic', 'sorcerer' and 'hero-spirit' (Lubaale). The constructs, roughly translated, were:

1 Happy/sad	10	Male/female
2 Industrious/lazy	11	Poor/rich
3 Weak/strong	12	Fast/slow
4 Old/young	13	Health/death
5 Cruel/kind	14	Warm/cold
6 Sort/hard	15	Dirty/clean
7 Honest/dishonest	16	Dangerous/safe
8 Wise/foolish	17	Many/few
9 Bad/good	18	Fear/brave

Answers were obtained from eighteen male adults, ten of whom repeated the procedure one week later in order to test reliability, thus giving twenty-eight sets of responses in all.

The responses were analysed for each subject separately using the INGRID program and a consensus grid was prepared from all twenty-eight sets of responses; this, in turn, was analysed using the INGRID program. It is recognized that the technique used is that of the Osgood Semantic Differential, and it is interesting to note that the first principal component obtained by an analysis of the consensus grid is an 'evaluative' one accounting for 80 per cent. of the variability and defined by the constructs 'happy', 'good', 'safe', 'wise', 'healthy', 'honest', 'kind', 'rich' and 'clean'. (All of these had loadings over 2.0 on the component; those with the highest loadings are mentioned first.) The elements were ranged along this component from 'good' to 'bad', with their loadings in brackets, as 'woman' (4.6), 'child' (3.8), 'man' (3.6), 'hero-spirit' (−1.0), 'epileptic' (−2.4), 'sorcerer' (−2.5), 'thief' (−3.0) and 'madman' (−3.2).

The second principal component of the consensus grid accounts for 10 per cent. of the variability. The constructs defining it concerned potency and activity, and in descending order of loading were 'brave', 'fast', 'strong', 'hard' and 'industrious' (all these had loadings over 1.0). The elements ranged along this component from 'brave' to 'fearful' as 'man' (2.0), 'sorcerer' (0.8), 'thief' (0.7), 'madman' (0.4), 'hero-spirit' (−0.5), 'child' (−0.5), 'woman' (−1.1) and 'epileptic' (−1.9). Only these first two components were found significant on the Bartlett test, although the third, which accounted for only 4.5 per cent. of the variability, did distinguish the sorcerer from the other elements, the defining constructs being 'cruel', 'dishonest' and 'old'.

The scores are interesting when looked at in the cultural context and almost all are understandable, thus validating the method. The analysis of the results was all done after the writing of the anthropological monograph with which it is compared (Orley, 1970). Thus, the anthropological monograph and the grid results were prepared quite independently and any agreement is good evidence of the validity of the technique.

The epileptic in Buganda, whose plight was described in the monograph, is stigmatized, ostracized and despised, much like the position of the lepers described in the Christian Bible. The epileptic can be seen from Table 14.1 to occupy the extreme position on the constructs 'weak', 'slow', 'cold', 'young' and 'lazy' (this latter equally with the thief). Epilepsy is thought to be catching, and for this reason the epileptic is only exceeded in the extent to which he is dangerous by the sorcerer.

When a person becomes mad, he is thought to possess superhuman power and is very much feared. The scores on the consensus grid are compatible with this since the madman is the strongest and hardest of all elements but also the dirtiest and most foolish. Interestingly enough, although the thief is the most dishonest, he is also the poorest and is the most lazy (together with the epileptic). This is not just because they are seen as weak people who cannot succeed in other ways, because they tend to be seen as relatively strong and cruel. On asking directly about this result subsequently, it was explained that to call someone rich is praise and thieves cannot be praised. The contructs 'rich/poor' and 'good/bad' correlated with a coefficient of 0.964. Although the madman and thief are viewed in very similar ways, nevertheless they differ in that the thief is more dishonest (significant at 1 per cent) and the madman is more dirty and foolish (significant at 1 and 5 per cent. respectively). It might be added that the woman is seen (in descending order of distance) as significantly more fearful, female, slow, soft, happy and less industrious than the man, but it should be remembered that all respondents were men! Although their being seen as more female may seem obvious, nevertheless it helps to show the validity of the technique and would indicate that the men do really see the women in the ways they have marked.

These few results indicate the obvious validity of the technique, even though it was used by people with a fairly low level of literacy. Some of the respondents found it interesting to complete the forms since they said that they had not previously thought in quite these terms. It might be that they had never before realized that they had thought in these terms.

Apart from this very obvious face validity of the technique, there is also a fair degree of consistency between the individual responses which also helps to validate it. Each of the subjects' grids was analysed seaparately using the INGRID program. In twenty-three out of the twenty-eight outputs, 'good/bad' was strongly represented in the first principal component, in association with 'happy-sad' and 'safe-dangerous'. Of those five in whom 'good/bad' did not form a very important part of the first principal component, 'safe/dangerous' was important in all except

TABLE 14.1

Constructs		Man	Woman	Child	Epileptic	Madman	Thief	Sorcerer	Hero-spirit	General mean
1	Happy/sad	-1.1	-2.2	-2.1	1.3	1.4	1.3	0.9	0.5	3.4
2	Industrious/lazy	-1.4	-0.4	-0.2	0.7	0.5	0.7	-0.3	0.4	2.8
3	Weak/strong	0.5	-0.1	-0.1	-0.9	0.6	0.3	0	-0.5	3.7
4	Old/young	-0.4	-0.5	0.2	0.6	0.3	0.5	-0.6	-0.1	2.6
5	Cruel/kind	1.0	0.9	1.1	0.3	-0.8	-1.0	-1.3	-0.2	2.7
6	Soft/hard	0.1	-1.2	-0.6	-0.4	0.9	0.5	0.4	0.2	3.5
7	Honest/dishonest	-1.1	-1.4	-0.9	-0.2	0.6	1.4	1.3	0.3	3.2
8	Wise/foolish	-1.5	-1.2	-0.9	1.2	1.5	0.8	0.1	0.1	3.1
9	Bad/good	1.4	1.7	1.4	-1.0	-1.0	-1.0	-1.2	-0.4	2.5
10	Male/female	-0.6	1.0	-0.1	0.2	-0.1	-0.2	-0.1	0	2.9
11	Poor/rich	1.2	0.9	0.8	-0.6	-0.8	-0.9	-0.4	-0.1	2.8
12	Fast/slow	-1.2	0.3	0.2	0.6	-0.3	-0.4	-0.4	0.3	2.8
13	Health/death	-0.9	-1.4	-1.3	1.0	0.8	0.7	0.8	0.3	3.5
14	Warm/cold	-0.7	-0.7	-0.5	0.6	0.3	0.2	0.3	0.5	2.8
15	Dirty/clean	0.9	1.2	0.7	-0.8	-1.2	-0.3	-0.3	-0.2	2.8
16	Dangerous/safe	1.4	1.5	1.6	-1.1	-0.9	-0.9	-1.2	-0.4	2.4
17	Many/few	-0.1	-0.5	-0.1	0.4	0.4	-0.3	0.2	-0.1	2.6
18	Fear/brave	1.0	-0.1	-0.4	-0.5	0.3	0.5	0.4	-0.3	3.7

The results were scored from 1 to 5, 3 representing the mid position. The mean of all respondents ratings for each element (element mean) is given as its distance from the general mean for all elements on that construct. A negative result indicates that it is in the direction of the first of the pair.

one. With most people, the first principal component accounted for over 50 per cent. of variability, a notable exception in which the first principal component accounted for a small amount of the variability was the one for whom the component had an abnormal composition not including 'bad' or 'dangerous'.

As was mentioned earlier, ten of the eighteen subjects repeated the procedure one week later. Analysis of these ten pairs of responses using the DELTA program showed that the general degree of correlation between the two occasions on which it was used was over 0.6 for seven out of the ten subjects, another was 0.55, but there were two which were rather low at 0.21 and 0.03. There were no particular elements or constructs which consistently accounted for the change occurring between the two occasions. The subject with the test—retest correlation of only 0.03 was the same one with the principal component which was different from all others and which accounted for only a small amount of the variability. His results have been included in the subsequent analysis, however, despite the unusual responses.

Of the five positions available to mark, the extreme ends (1 and 5) were used 45 per cent. of the time, the mid point (3) was marked 32 per cent. of the time and the intermediate positions (2 and 4) were used 23 per cent. of the time. This would seem to indicate a good use of the intermediate positions, which justifies the use of a five-point scale rather than a three-point one.

Problems of method

Since this method of rating on a five-point scale requires only a little supervision in a population sufficiently literate to use it, it is particularly useful. The author has tried other methods but has not had time yet to evaluate them all properly. He can, however, make some preliminary observations. In the example cited, the constructs used were defined by two words having approximately opposite meaning, such as 'good/bad' or 'strong/weak'. Subsequent work using a word and its negative, such as 'strong/not strong', seems to diminish the amount that the intermediate positions are used. The scale can be defined by a more explicit phrase rather than single words, and in one grid concerning deviant characters such as 'murderer', 'drunk' and 'sorcerer' the constructs used included 'he can kill', 'he should be made an outcast' and 'he should not marry'. The five points on the scale can be defined as 'I agree very much', 'I agree a little', 'I do not know', 'I disagree a little' and 'I disagree very much'. This method could then be administered verbally by a researcher.

Hoorweg and McDowell (1972) used a similar method in research on attitudes to food for children amongst some mothers in Uganda. They were presented with the names of certain meals and were asked if they thought a meal was, for example, 'strong' or 'weak'. Assuming they chose one of these, they were then asked whether they thought it was 'very strong' or 'a little strong'. The five-point scale could then be filled in by the questioner accordingly.

There are times when elements will be grouped too closely together if a rating method is used, since it is unreasonable to expect a barely literate population to master seven- or nine-point scales. Thus, in the example given, 'epileptic', 'madman' and 'thief' are all seen as equally bad although they do score differently on the first principal component.

Where elements are rated closely together or where the investigator is looking for changes occurring over time, then ranking rather than rating may provide a better method. Hoorweg and McDowell (1972) were looking for changes in the way that the mothers perceived various foods as a result of nutrition education. The way they built up a ranked grid was by using paired comparisons, asking which of two foods had more of a certain property, such as being good for their child. The present author has had some success in using this method in a study of the way in which the Ganda saw their spirit world.

The second study

There are six classes of spirits in Ganda mythology and it was decided to compare the way in which these classes of spirits were seen on various constructs. Most of these constructs were elicited by informal methods of interviewing in the course of anthropological fieldwork. A study in which two of these classes of spirits had been rated on the scales described previously had indicated some constructs that were used in discriminating between those two, and led to their inclusion in this study. Some of the spirits have individual names within their class (just as some Christian 'angels' are known by name), but this study was done by just comparing classes, not individuals. Before giving details of the methods and results, these six classes of spirits will be described, much as they have been previously in the anthropological monograph (Orley, 1970).

1. *Lubaale* (hero-spirits). These are the spirits of heros who figure in Ganda tradition, some being people who were involved in the origin of the Ganda and others being the ghosts of dead kings. These spirits possess people at ceremonies and use these people as mediums through whom to speak. Although other spirits do this, the *Lubaale* do it most typically. The fact that they need people through whom to speak and have no voice of their own is seen as a weakness.

2. *Mayembe agëkika* (horn-spirits of the family). These often belong to a family and are kept for protection and help. Their origin is thought as being a medicine that was carried by a warrior in a horn for protection. If the owner died, the medicine would in some way continue with his ghost to produce a horn-spirit. Some of these spirits have a national status, such as Nambaga, and these really only differ from *Lubaale* in that they live in horns or gourds, since they possess people at ceremonies in much the same was as the *Lubaale*.

3. *Mayembe ag'ekifalu* (horn-spirits of sorcery). (*Ekifalu*, from Swahili, literally means a rhinocerous, and by extension means any large, powerful, noisy thing, such as a military tank.) This is a quite different horn-spirit fron that of the family. Whereas all other spirits need a person to act as a medium for them, these have an existence quite independent of people and have a voice of their own. They can be controlled by evil people and sent to injure or kill others. They are the most feared of all spirits and many traditional healers claim not to deal with them, since anyone who has the power to control them enough to cure people could also use them for evil purposes. These spirits may be owned by sorcerers, and can be sold to others or their services can be hired.

4. *Mizimu* (ancestor-spirits or ghosts). Apart from the spirits of dead kings, these are usually remembered, respected or feared only for as long as anyone living can remember the whereabouts of the grave. There are no shrines (or no very permanent ones) to the dead, except for kings and princes. The ghosts of commoners sometimes attack if they become annoyed at having been neglected, particularly if their graves have not been weeded and kept clean. They may also have an evil nature if the person himself had not been treated well in life, but apart from acting for themselves they can also be sent to attack people by putting a medicine on the grave. In order to avoid the wrath of the ghost of someone who died in misfortune, such as an epileptic, a leper or someone who commited suicide, the bodies of such people are buried in the bush away from the home, since ancestor-spirits do not usually travel far from their graves. The ancestor-spirits do occasionally possess people at ceremonies and in some respects resemble hero-spirits, but their ability to be sent to attack people is more like the property of a horn-spirit of sorcery.

5. *Misambwa* (nature-spirit). These are usually benign, although they have a malicious streak which easily comes to the fore if they are offended in any way. They reside in natural objects such as trees, animals, stones or rivers. Those residing in woods can cause a person to get lost if he enters and may kill him if he takes firewood from it. These spirits are sometimes the ghost of a mythical hero who gave origin to the object or animal species, or they may be the ghosts of people who, for instance, died in that forest or river.

6. *Bitambo* (cannibal-spirits). These spirits are associated with certain families and they can enter a member at times causing him to become an *omusezi*, who walks or dances naked at night, eating dead bodies and even killing people, thus resembling sorcerers as often described from many parts of Africa. The practice tends to run in families, with a father teaching his sons, and in some sense a person chooses to serve these spirits and is not regarded as ill or mad, and if caught walking naked at night should be killed. These spirits do occasionally possess people at ceremonies without leading them to become night dancers. They are said to have come into some families by being bought to use against others, rather like a horn-spirit of sorcery, but because of some mistake they may cause their owner to be a night dancer.

It was observed during fieldwork that the spirits of most importance in everyday life were the hero-spirits (together with the similar horn-spirits of the family) and the horn-spirits of sorcery, and that these two differed from each other in important ways. The hero-spirits do not kill their victims, but wish to enter into some form of relationship with people; they therefore attack or upset people only in order to draw attention to themselves and are placated by offerings and the establishment of a relationship. Thus, they tend to produce a chronic illness or a series of misfortunes, whereas the horn-spirits or sorcery are more dangerous. They attack people, sometimes spontaneously, or, more frequently, are sent by people against their enemies producing a sudden and disturbing illness, killing quickly rather than producing a chronic illness like leprosy. Ancestor-spirits can be sent in a similar way and produce a sudden fatal illness, but they can at times resemble the hero-spirits and require placating in a similar way. Madness is in an ambiguous position as an illness, since it can occur as violent or excited outbursts in someone who may be chronically disturbed. Thus, it may be attributed to either sorcery or a hero-spirit.

At ceremonies where spirit possession occurs, it is the hero-spirits who are the main focus of attention, with the horn-spirits of the family playing a similar but less important part. The author has observed the ancestor-spirits, nature-spirits and cannibal-spirits manifesting themselves at these ceremonies, but the horn-spirits of sorcery attend ceremonies in a different way and can only talk in the dark, which is not surprising, since they do not talk through mediums, but out of the air, and the presence of light might in some cases reveal deceptions by the doctors organizing the proceedings.

In an attempt to verify and quantify these observations, it was decided to compare these six classes of spirits using the repertory grid technique. With as small a number as six, it was feasible to obtain rankings on constructs, the ranking being obtained by paired comparisons. All fifteen possible pairs of the six were presented in turn to the subjects, asking them which of the two was best described by the construct. When all fifteen pairs had been dealt with on one construct, the interviewer moved on to the next construct. By giving a score of 1 to an element each time it is chosen in a comparison, a ranking from 0 to 5 for the spirits on each construct should be obtained. In practice, inconsistencies arise because the construct may be multi-dimensional and different pairs are judged on different criteria, or because the elements are so similar in that respect that the forced choice is unreliable. The subject should be given the opportunity to say that the comparison is not valid for certain elements, so that whereas spirits a, d, e and f may possess people, spirits b and c may never do so, and thus neither will be more likely to possess someone if compared for that property. There should also be some mechanism for recording that the subject does not know about one of the elements or that two may be equal on certain constructs. It would seem best to give a score of 0.5 to each of a pair if they are seen as equal or if one is not known well enough to the subject to make a comparison. If the subject is emphatic that the description applies to neither of the pair, then each should score zero. In this study, these suggestions for scoring were not always followed at first, since they were developed during the course of the study.

The subjects in the study were Ganda villagers, either interviewed at their homes or occasionally at the teaching hospital where they were patients or visitors. There were fourteen subjects, chosen only on their willingness to answer the questions. They were asked to compare the six classes of spirits on eighteen constructs. Half of the eighteen constructs used were of a more general kind, while the others tended to describe particular characteristics known to be relevant to spirits. Of the more general kind, some were evaluative, such as 'dangerous', 'saddens', 'very bad' and 'cruel'; others related to potency and activity, such as 'strong' and 'works quickly'; while 'kills quickly' combined the two properties. 'Wise' and 'many' (referring to their relative numbers) were also of a general kind. The remaining constructs referred particularly to attributes of spirits. These were 'sent' (sent against people), 'of sorcerers' (*bya balogo* — this refers to those used maliciously against others, but also to other forms of sorcery such as night dancing), 'possess' (*bisamirwa* — are served in ceremonies at which they speak through mediums), 'come on the head' (*ebirinnya ku mutwe* — although referring primarily to speaking through mediums, this can refer to any control of a human by the spirit), 'talks by itself' (not through mediums), 'is bought' (either for protection or malicious purposes), 'makes mad', 'met in the home' and 'has its proper owner' (*bya bwa nnanyini*).

The anthropological fieldwork had indicated that the horn-spirits of sorcery could be sent against others and were evaluated as the worst of all spirits and the most dangerous, strong and quick. They differed in these respects from the hero-spirits and the horn-spirits of the family, the latter having a primarily protective function. The cannibal-spirits are regarded as fairly bad and the nature-spirits are not particularly bad. The ancestor-spirits were known to be very bad and cruel at times, but certainly not always, and it was presumed that they are seen as lying between the horn-spirits of sorcery and hero-spirits in this respect. Perhaps because the ancestor-spirits, cannibal-spirits and nature-spirits were not so important in everyday life, the fieldwork had given no very clear idea of the more general properties by which each is distinguished from the other spirits.

Results

The measure of agreement between subjects was calculated for each construct and fourteen of the eighteen were highly significant ($p < 0.01$). Those agreeing less significantly were 'met in the home' and 'makes mad' ($p < 0.05$) and 'talks by itself' and 'saddens' ($p > 0.05$). The best agreement was obtained on 'many', and after that were 'comes on the head', 'kills quickly', 'is bought' and 'has a proper owner'. The INGRID analysis of the consensus for components showed the first four components all to be significant on the Bartlett test. The percentage of the total variability for which each component accounted and the composition of the components is given in Table 14.2.

Discussion

Component 1

The first component distinguishes between the horn-spirits of sorcery on the one hand, and the hero-spirits and horn-spirits of the family, on the other. In his fieldwork, the author had concentrated on what the later work with the grid revealed as the first principal component, rather to the exclusion of the other spirit classes, which show themselves in the other components. The constructs in this first component are concerned with evaluation, potency and activity, the bad being strong and quick. It is quite true that the author had the hero-spirit and horn-spirits of sorcery particularly in mind when choosing constructs, since they contrasted so markedly, and thus it is not surprising to see them appearing as contrasts in the first component.

Component 2

The second component describes the nature-spirits, contrasting them primarily with the hero-spirits and the horn-spirits of sorcery. The nature-spirits, cannibal-spirits and ancestor-spirits had been rather left to fend for themselves when the constructs were decided upon, and thus the nature-spirits appear in component 2 as almost

TABLE 14.2

	Component 1		Component 2		Component 3		Component 4	
Percentage variability accounted for	67%		14%		9%		8%	
Element loadings (of spirits), listed in order	Horn of sorcery	6.5	Nature	3.1	Cannibal	2.6	Ancestor	2.5
	Cannibal	1.4	Horn of family	0.5	Hero	0.1	Nature	0.4
	Nature	0.3	Cannibal	0.1	Ancestor	0.1	Hero	−0.3
	Ancestor	−0.7	Ancestor	−0.7	Nature	−0.2	Horn of sorcery	−0.4
	Horn of family	−3.5	Horn of sorcery	−1.1	Horn of sorcery	−1.2	Cannibal	−0.9
	Hero	−4.0	Hero	−1.9	Horn of family	−1.4	Horn of family	−1.2
Important constructs describing the spirits with the high positive loadings above, listed in order of loading irrespective of sign, but those which had a negative loading are prefixed with *not*	Kills quickly	2.8	Is not sent	1.6	Not wise	1.6	Is not bought	1.6
	Not many	2.7	Not many	1.6	Comes on the head	1.4	Kills quickly	1.2
	Do not possess	2.5	Have not a proper owner	1.3	Is not bought	1.1		
	Have not a proper owner	2.4	Does not make mad	1.3	Does not talk by itself	1.1		
	Cruel	2.4	Does not come on the head	1.3	Very bad	1.0		
	Of sorcerers	2.4	Does not work quickly	1.3				
	Dangerous	2.3	Is not met in the home	1.0				
	Does not come on the head	2.3						
	Strong	2.3						
	Is bought	2.2						
	Very bad	2.0						
	Sent	1.9						
	Works quickly	1.6						

totally defined by negative loadings for the constructs (in only three constructs does this spirit score more than the general mean for the construct, and then only by small amounts). The nature-spirits are not used in sorcery and thus can be seen to have less tendency to cause illnesses (such as making mad). They have neither the attributes that so clearly describe the horn-spirits of sorcery, such as being 'sent', nor those that describe the hero-spirits such as 'comes on the head'. Being nature-spirits associated with the wild, they are not met in the home and have no proper owner.

Component 3

The third component describes the cannibal-spirits, contrasting them with the two kinds of horn-spirit. They are more positively defined than the nature-spirits. Their strong association with foolishness must be a reflection of the way it induces people to walk naked, like a madman. The way in which it controls people is reflected in the expression 'comes to the head' (as opposed to attacking people), even though it seldom possesses people at ceremonies. Any similarity between these spirits and the horn-spirits of sorcery is brought out in the first principal component.

Component 4

The ancestor-spirit is described by the fourth component and contrasted with the horn-spirits of the family and the cannibal-spirits. The ancestor-spirits can kill quickly, like the horn-spirits of sorcery, but, unlike them, are not bought for this purpose. They contrast strongly with the horn-spirits of the family, which have a protective function and can be bought.

General comments

A few general comments can be made about the Ganda spirit world which are brought out by this analysis. On the whole, it is a bad world in that the bad spirits are the strongest, whereas the horn-spirits of the family, which have a more protective function, are the weakest. A consoling thought is that the bad spirits are fewer in number.

The author is a little uncertain as to the meaning of the important construct 'has a proper owner', which seems to imply not so much having a person who controls it as having a place, home or family of its own. The horn-spirits of sorcery, although bought and used by people, resemble a prostitute or vagrant with no real home.

It was surprising to see that the construct 'many' was the one on which there was highest agreement between subjects, since in his fieldwork the author had not elicited that there was a consistent opinion about their relative numbers, having been more concerned about evaluation and potency.

The analysis of the principal components indicates that five out of the six classes of spirits are clearly and significantly distinguished from each other by these constructs, and only the hero-spirits and horn-spirits of the family are less clearly differentiated, with very similar loadings on the first component. They are, however, clearly separated on components 2, 3 and 4. It would thus appear that the Ganda, in their thinking, clearly differentiate between these six classes of spirits, and the fact that four components are statistically significantly distinguished, each being related to particular spirit classes, indicates a considerable complexity of thought in this field.

It is interesting to note that, although, in the anthropological fieldwork, the author took more note of the information about spirits obtained from experts, yet the grid was administered to a group not chosen for their knowledge of these matters. Nevertheless, a consistent and meaningful pattern of responses was obtained. It would be interesting, however, to compare grids obtained from experts with those from the general population.

Apart from the paired comparison technique used in this study on the spirits, other methods of ranking can be used. In a sufficiently literate population, the names of the elements can be written on cards which can be placed in a row according to the degree to which they are described by the construct. With illiterate subjects, the elements might be portrayed as pictures on the cards. Ranking differs from rating in tending to minimize large differences between elements and exaggerate small differences, thus distorting the grids obtained. Ranking may be a better method when measuring differences which are small, particularly when these are being compared between two groups or on two occasions. There are times, however, when it forces a score on a construct when there would be a tendency not to use it. This is illustrated in another study from Uganda. It was postulated that the Ganda use certain constructs in defining diseases. namely '*kiganda/kizungu*', 'strong/weak' and 'sent by sorcery/comes by itself'. It was postulated that these were interrelated in that those illnesses that were regarded as traditional ones (*kiganda*), rather than European ones (*kizungu*), were those that were strong, and these were not amenable to the usual European treatments and were thus thought to be due to sorcery (Orley, 1970). Subsequent work has shown that these are by no means the only constructs used, and that, although they form a pricipal component in a less medically westernized group, they were hardly used by a group of trained Ugandan nurses (Orley and Leff, 1972). This result was easily detected because the subjects used rating scales and the trained nurses tended to use the mid points when rating on these constructs, whereas they could not have done so if they had been forced to rank the illnesses.

It is, of course, not true that these techniques can somehow replace traditional anthropological methods. In most cases, these old established methods are essential in eliciting the constructs used by the people under investigation, although the formal methods can also be used. Similarly, without the relationship of trust that develops between the anthropologist and the people he studies, it is less likely that the subjects will respond with the care or ability that gives consistent and valid results. It is probably not very useful to send bundles of forms to be filled in by people quite unknown to the investigator.

It might be thought that this way of approaching anthropological problems resembles the structural approach of Lévi-Strauss, which also emphasizes the contrasting symbols which represent various aspects of society. The 'constructs' which Lévi-Strauss postulates are not obtained directly from the people themselves, but are postulated as being the organizing principles of the people's thought. Thus 'raw/cooked' and 'nature/culture' can be thought of as superordinate constructs. The people themselves are postulated as selecting certain symbols to form constructs, so that 'only a few of its elements (symbolic forms) are retained — those suitable for the expression of contrasts or forming pairs of opposites' (Lévi-Strauss, 1969, p. 341). Lévi-Strauss, however, is more concerned about the contradictions implied in these contrasts and the way traditional folklore is used to overcome this or reintegrate it. It is doubtful if many of the pairs he talks about are, in fact, very important in people's everyday lives and thoughts. It is possible, however, that myths force people to rethink their established relationships between constructs. Thus, 'quick' and 'clever' might normally be thought of as related, but by comparing the tortoise and the hare in Aesop's fable, the relationship of these constructs is called into question. Whether this or Lévi-Strauss' rather tortuous explanations are more satisfactory is debatable. Although he is acknowledging the fact that contrasting pairs, like constructs, are important in analysing ways of thought, his approach is of an analytic nature quite unlike that of the repertory grid technique as described here.

To return to the present study, although many anthropologists accept that part of their work is the analysis of the 'collective representations' of a people, they are seldom inclined to go on and explore this and test or measure their results by means of the semantic differential and repertory grid techniques. In some case, the information can only be expressed in a descriptive way such as a piece of history or myth, but at other times the information obtained can be translated into terms which could be explored by the repertory grid method. It should be emphasized that a perfectly good ethnographic description can be given of a people or some aspect of their culture without any recourse to these methods. It is merely suggested that this method may help in the exploration of their concepts and, more importantly, may be of value in measuring and validating the impressions obtained by the anthropologist. It should be of particular value in comparing beliefs held in two geographical areas or by two classes of people (providing they use the same language), or it may be used on different occasions to measure changes over a period of time. If some of the 'collective representations' can thus be expressed as a 'consensus grid', then the technique provides a valuable addition to the investigations available to the anthropologist.

Acknowledgements

I would like to thank Dr. P. Slater for his help and encouragement and the M.R.C. for providing, through him, a service for the analysis of the grids. I would like to thank the Nuffield Foundation, London, for funding the fieldwork in 1967—68 and again briefly in 1972, during which most of the data discussed in this article were collected.

References

Hoorweg, J., and McDowell, I. (1972). *Nutrition Education and Changes in Knowledge and Attitudes Among Mothers of Malnourished Children*. Makerere University, Kampala (Mimeo).

Lévi-Strauss, C. (1969). *The Raw and Cooked* (English Trans.), Harper and Row, New York.

Orley, J. (1970). *Culture and Mental Illness — A Study from Uganda*, Nairobi.

Orley, J., and Leff, J. (1972). 'The effect of psychiatric education on attitudes to illness among the Ganda'. *Brit. J. Psychiat.*, 121, 137—141.

15

MEASURING THE MEANING
OF FERTILITY CONTROL

John Simons

Summary

This is a thought-provoking analysis of the confrontation between two construct systems, an indigenous one and a cosmopolitan one. The study of the confrontation, which arose in the attempt to persuade village midwives in Central Java to promote fertility control, is used to demostrate a new theory-based methodology for eliciting the significance, subjective and sociological, of fertility control. The methodology is contrasted with conventional procedures which are held to produce findings more consistent with the researcher's own beliefs and values than with those that could be plausibly attributed to their respondents. In the midwife study, questionnaire responses suggested that many of the forty midwives interviewed did not share cosmopolitan beliefs and values, and were unlikely to be vigorous advocates of fertility control. This inference was supported by a study of the midwives' subsequent performance in recruiting clients for family planning clinics. (P.S.)

Assumptions made in constructing conventional questionnaires

It often seems easier to understand the construction and use of a conventional 'attitude' questionnaire if it is construed as a representation of the investigator's beliefs about his own conduct. Questions that might otherwise seem impossible to justify then have an obvious rationale: the investigator believed they could have elicited his own sentiments and inclinations. Similarly, the puzzle of how he chose among alternative interpretations of the personal significance of responses is solved: he attributed to them the meaning he imagined they would have had if he had given those responses himself. For example, he may have included a question about intended family size if he believed this was or could have been a motive of his own behaviour, and he may have interpreted all responses of, say, 'three children' as indicating a strong determination to have at least three children. Finally, it may be supposed that he included questions on religious affiliation, education and other classificatory variables because he believed they might explain differences between responses he would have given and those given by other respondents.

Although clearly a caricature, the foregoing account probably does explain much of the apparent ethnocentrism and many of the apparently arbitrary assumptions underlying conventional surveys of attitudes to fertility control. It is not surprising that a widely discussed characteristic of these surveys is the incompatability of their findings with the behaviour they purport to explain or predict. The results of some of these surveys in developing countries are summarized and discussed in Mauldin (1965) and Fawcett (1971). Major improvements are unlikely without radical changes in methodology, entailing a better understanding of the requirements of conceptualization, theory and technique. The nature of these requirements and their implications for methodology are the subject of this paper. Much of what follows comprises a detailed exposition of a particular study in which an attempt was made to develop some of the required changes in methodology. The study was an investigation of the meaning of fertility control among a group of indigenous midwives in Central Java. Although this example is especially relevant to the problems of investigating the meaning of fertility control in developing countries, the principles and procedures are applicable to similar problems in developed countries.

Subjective and sociological meanings

To make clear the distinctive characteristics of the procedure described, it is necessary to be explicit about the senses in which the term 'meaning' and related terms are used here. The term 'subjective meaning' or 'subjective significance' is used of an experience and refers to an interpretive construction, in the mind of the person concerned, connecting the experience with other experiences, real or imagined. The construction is a product of an individual's construing system, a system that defines and applies similarities and distinctions among experiences. For example, the birth of a seventh child may mean to the child's mother that God has been kind to her or that she will have support in her old age. Depending on her construing system, the experience may have both these subjective meanings and many others to her.

An observer, attempting to explain the mother's sentiments, may construe them as evidence of a poor education. In this paper, the term 'sociological meaning' or 'sociological significance' is used to refer to such a construction. Thus, a sociological meaning of an experience is an interpretive construction, adduced by an observer, connecting properties of a person's construing system with properties of its social environment. For an analysis bearing on some aspects of the relationships between subjective and sociological constructions, see Schutz (1953).

Subjective and sociological meanings may coincide. A common example is when a subjective meaning of an experience constitutes someone's motive and when this same motive is proposed by a sociologist to explain the individual's observed behaviour in seeking the experience. For example, subjective and sociological meanings of a seventh child may be that the mother will have security in old age. In this case, and in general, there would be other subjective and sociological meanings that would not coincide.

A system of interpretive constructions used to interpret variation among the properties of personal construing systems is a sociological theory of variation in subjective meanings. A theory of this kind is used below to examine differences between (a) constructions of the personal system typical of a traditional community and (b) constructions of the personal system implicit in national family planning programmes.

As mentioned above, subjective and sociological meanings sometimes coincide. However, a sociological theory is needed to determine the explanatory status, if any, of subjective meanings. For example, the statement 'I love children' may be offered as a mother's explanation of her own large family. In the light of a sociological theory, her explanation may be categorized as simply an indicator of her sentiments, of no explanatory significance. On the other hand, such statements as 'I love children' may, be used to test a theory. For example, the theory may generate predictions of the form: if some specified explanation of particular large families is correct. mothers of these families will, in specified circumstances, be likely to apply to themselves the description 'I love children'. Conventional surveys are heedless of these considerations. Responses about, say, 'ideal family size' are accepted at their face value as indicators of subjective meanings, to be used either as explanations of conduct or as dependent variables with respect to education, religion or other background variables. For comments on the interpretation of responses about 'expected family size' in a major American study, see Simons (1974).

In order for an individual to function as a member of a community, it is necessary for his construing system to be congruent with the sytems of other members, thus permitting intersubjective understanding, shared meaning. Generally, individuals' systems can be regarded as variants of a system typical of members — a community construing system. The concept of a typical construing system can be usefully linked with some versions of the concept of a reference group. Important among these versions is one developed by Shibutani (1962), summarized in his phrase 'a group whose culture constitutes one's point of view'. The term 'typical construing system' could be used instead of the term 'culture' in this phrase.

As mentioned earlier, the study to be used for the purposes of this paper concerns the meaning of fertility control to some indigenous midwives in Central Java. It was one of several enquiries undertaken to guide policy for the use of these midwives in the national family planning programme. Attempts to involve the indigenous midwife in such programmes have been made in several countries (Verderese, 1973). It was generally argued that she was well placed, physically and socially, to act as an agent of the programme within the community. It was assumed that she would be willing to cooperate, or could easily be persuaded to cooperate by training or by some form of incentive.

The essential task of the midwife study in Java was to establish whether the subjective meanings of fertility control to midwives were compatible with their proposed role in the family planning programme. The problem can now be expressed as that of determining whether the personal construing system typical of supporters of the family planning programme was, in respect of fertility control, congruent with the construing system typical of midwives in the study area. Alternatively, the problem could be expressed as that of determining whether protagonists of the programme were the midwives' reference group in respect of the midwives' proposed role in the programme.

The next section of the paper reviews the role and status of the traditional midwife and contrasts the subjective meaning of fertility control implicit in the family planning programme with the subjective meaning of fertility control and related behaviour typical of the community in which the midwives live and work.

Subjective meanings of fertility control

The subjective meanings of fertility control underlying family planning programmes have become common knowledge and need not be elaborated here. In brief, it is asserted that family health and welfare and national prosperity are impeded by high fertility in many countries. It is claimed that large proportions of births in these countries occur contrary to the wishes of the parents, and merely because they lack means to exercise effective control over their fertility. Therefore, the argument proceeds, if parents are given access to modern techniques of contraception, the desired fall in fertility will occur. Some recent versions of this doctrine appear to have been influenced by the fact that, in the event, family planning programmes have failed to have much effect on fertility. This failure is generally not attributed, by exponents of this doctrine, to intractable social or cultural barriers. Instead, the problems are seen as ones that will yield to suitable techniques of information and persuasion.

For data on the subjective meanings of fertility control to members of the midwives' community, the principal source was a previous enquiry into the role and status of the midwife in the area (Djuarini and co-authors, 1971). This had been conducted by a team of social scientists from the University of Indonesia, partly as a foundation for the subsequent specific enquiry into the meaning of fertility control. (The published report just cited drew also on interview data obtained during the subsequent specific enquiry.) A total of fifty midwives and thirty of their clients were interviewed in their homes. A further twenty interviews were conducted with village leaders, both formal and informal. The following account is based on the findings of the study.

The study area was a sub-district of the regency of Temanggung in Central Java. This is a rice-growing area. Most of the population of the sub-district live in its forty-five villages (average population 1760), each surrounded by rice fileds. Life styles make few demands on modern amenities. A typical home has walls of bamboo and timber and an earthen floor, and is sometimes shared with a buffalo or a goat. Birth invariably takes place in the home. The dead are buried in unmarked graves in a cemetery field adjoining the village.

Family and community appear to be the dominant concerns of village women: 'Basically people would feel happy to have many children' and 'Many children are considered a blessing'. Older children help with the care of younger siblings, and often with neighbours' young children. Most houses are close together and are without dividing fences. Personal relationships among neighbours are similarly close. Owing to the simplicity of the dwellings and of the village diet, household duties are not onerous. The women may help in the rice fields at the time of planting or harvesting, but there are few other opportunities for employment outside the home. Some efforts are being made to include women in schemes to hasten the rate of rural modernization. Special meetings are arranged, under the auspices of women's organizations, to give instruction in such subjects as hygiene, cooking, child care, family planning and beauty care. Some kindergartens have been established. The investigators from the University of Indonesia concluded from their interviews that people in the village felt that life was becoming increasingly difficult. Rice fields were being divided between more farmers. Most children attended at least elementary school, adding to the financial burdens of parents.

The administrative centre of the sub-district is the small market town of Temanggung. A health centre there and a subsidiary clinic in one of the villages are responsible for all public health services in the forty-five villages, including maternity care and family planning. The two doctors and small supporting staff are unable to offer comprehensive health care for the 79,000 individuals of the sub-district. For several reasons, even the limited services available are probably substantially under-used. The people are poor and unaccustomed to seeking modern treatment for their ills. They are especially unaccustomed to the idea that modern treatment includes help with methods of birth control. Many villages are distant from a health post. Good roads are rare and so is public transport. In addition to these reasons for the under-use of public services, another is the existence of a long-established alternative service. This is the locally generated health care system provided by several types of indigenous practitioner known as *dukuns*, each type specializing in a different craft.

The indigenous midwife, or *dukun baji*, is one of the types. Another type specializes in massage, a craft occupying an important place in the treatment of illness in Java. Other specialisms are the treatment of broken bones and the treatment of snakebites. Not all specialisms are therapeutic. Some *dukuns* are consulted for advice on the best moment for doing something important, such as starting the harvest. Others are consulted for religious guidance. In some cases, the *dukun baji* started her career as a *dukun pijat*, a specialist in massage. She became a *dukun baji* after discovering she had the required aptitude and vocation. Often the first experience was acquired by helping a mother or grandmother who was a midwife. In other cases, the village head had recruited her from among the village women and sent her for training to the health centre.

Whatever her specialism, religious beliefs (predominantly Moslem) usually shape the way the midwife and her clients understand her work. Divine will is felt necessary to a successful outcome. Special prayers and rituals are part of normal practice. Not only her craft but her behaviour and experience in general are construed in terms of Divine purposes. To illustrate this, the investigators report the comment of an old midwife when they mentioned to her the possibility of a shortage of midwives: 'Should the village be blessed with many children, then surely God would provide the necessary *dukuns*'. However, there is also evidence of a conviction that has something in common with the notion summarized in the English adage, 'God helps those who help themselves'. The local version might be expressed as 'God helps those who help themselves in ways that conform to God's will, but disappointments should be accepted serenely, because God's purposes are being fulfilled'. Although spiritual aspects of the midwife's work are emphasized by many of them, there are some who see their work as primarily secular in character.

The indigenous midwife is regarded with affectionate respect by villagers. She is invited to weddings and other ceremonies and is generally treated as a member of the family by former clients. Whatever her age, she is called 'grandmother'. In fact, she often is a grandmother. Sometimes her client is a woman she had delivered.

The midwife is the authority on pre-natal and post-natal care. She recommends medicinal herbs for the pregnant mother and foetus. She advises against certain foods in case their characteristics are passed on to the child. For example, it is believed that eating a particular type of fish can make the baby slippery and difficult to hold. Post-natal care consists of massage, advice on diet and care of the body, prayers and the performance of various rituals such as shaving the baby's hair. The midwife visits the home daily for five days after the delivery and then regularly over the next thirty days. As her fee she might receive up to US $1 or a gift of some kind. Two or three deliveries a month seem to be the typical case load. Asked whether fewer babies would mean a reduced income, some midwives intimated that their work was not motivated by financial considerations but by a desire to help people.

Massage and other traditional methods of influencing the number and spacing of children may be prescribed or provided by the midwives. It is believed that massage so alters the position of the uterus that sperm are unable to enter. Another method is to take special herbs. All the midwives questioned thought abortion was sinful, though some admitted that it did occur occasionally. For women who wish to enhance rather than diminish the chance of pregnancy, traditional methods are also employed. These comprise: massage to put the uterus in a favourable position, herbs, certain foods and intercourse on specified days of the week.

As mentioned earlier, many indigenous midwives in Indonesia have received some training in midwifery practice at a health centre. In Temanggung continuous training was started in 1952. Midwives are encouraged to attend a half-day training session once a week for as long as they continue to practice. The main purpose of the training is to eradicate such potentially harmful practices as abdominal massage during labour and the use of unsterilized instruments to cut the umbilical cord. Attendance is made attractive in a number of ways. Teaching is informal. Meals are provided free. Trainees regularly entertain themselves and the staff with songs and plays. Those who reach a certain standard of proficiency are presented with a certificate or a small kit of simple midwifery equipment. Many of the midwives live a three-hour walk away from the health centre and they cannot afford to pay for transportation, even when it is available. Yet two-thirds of the midwives in the area, including many of the oldest, attend the training sessions regularly and appear to enjoy doing so.

Instruction in modern methods of birth control was included in the curriculum of the *dukun* training course in Temanggung from 1969. The midwives were urged to bring to the clinics any villagers who wished to avoid pregnancy. Response was poor. By the time of the study, the sixty-seven midwives in the sub-district had been responsible for a total of only thirty-four referrals.

The foregoing account of the *dukun baji*'s social world suggests that she is a valued member of the community, that the community's construing system is a traditional one and that the midwife helps to sustain this system in her work. It is a system that appears to differ substantially from the modern system underlying the family planning programme. Her work does sometimes include giving help with birth control, although she usually recommends or supplies traditional methods. On the other hand, many of the midwives seem to value their affiliation to the health centre, the local source of modern methods and ideas.

Sociological meanings of fertility control

The knowledge that two construing systems differ in respect of the subjective meaning of fertility control does not in itself reveal whether they are incongruent. For example, in a traditional system large families may subjectively mean poverty, and both large families and poverty may mean the will of God. In a modern system, large families may be regarded as calamities that can and should be avoided, precisely because large families mean poverty. Although these systems seem to differ fundamentally, they would be congruent if what is expressed as the will of God in the traditional system included (or could include) both small families and the practice of birth control. (A belief in the possibility of accommodations of this kind would be needed to justify many current attempts to induce changes in fertility behaviour.) It is not a specific meaning but properties of the meaning system as a whole that determine whether it is congruent with another system in respect of fertility control.

In order to reveal incongruency, it is necessary to start not with personal systems or meanings but with a sociological theory that can provide putative answers to the following two questions. First, what characteristics of a personal construing system determine whether it is congruent with other systems in respect of fertility control? Secondly, which of these characteristics are possessed by the two systems of interest here? This study drew on the development of a theory that has entailed the integration of an existing classification of 'value orientations' with models of family-building conduct.

The existing classification of value orientations was developed by Kluckhohn and Strodtbeck (1961). The value orientations are different ways of construing fundamental human issues, such as that of the relation of Man to nature. Kluckhohn and Strodtbeck extracted five such issues from the writings of philosophers and social scientists. By postulating a range of three possible orientations for each of the five issues, they constructed a scheme for categorizing any community's value orientations. It is a fundamental assumption underlying the scheme that all orientations are always present in all societies but are differentially emphasized. In the terminology defined above, the scheme is a way of classifying construing systems by distinctions among some of their fundamental properties.

One of the five issues included in the original scheme was the character of innate human nature: whether innate human nature was construed as good, or as evil, or as a mixture of good and evil. For the purposes of this paper, the character of human nature is replaced by the character of the human capacity for reproduction. This issue and the other four, and the possible orientations for each, can be conveniently summarized as a series of questions. These are questions that can be asked about the construing system characteristic of a community or of some group within a community. The questions are formulated in a way that adapts the issues and orientations to the theoretical framework adopted for this study. In treatment and function, the use of the scheme here differs fundamentally from its use in other fertility studies, such as a study by Clifford (1971).

The series of questions starts with the issue of human reproduction. Does the construing system tend to construe the capacity for reproduction as benign, as burdensome, or as a mixture of both? Secondly, does the system tend to construe Man's relation to nature as one of subjugation to nature, or as one of harmony with nature, or as one of mastery over nature? Thirdly, does it tend to attribute the significance of contemporary events to other contemporary events, or to past events, or to future consequences? Fourthly, does it tend to construe human activities as means of self-expression, or of self-development, or of achievement? Finally, in constructions concerning Man's relationship to others, does it tend to emphasize the independence of individuals, their interdependence, or the continuity of their interdependence over time?

The expression of general orientations may be assumed to be stronger in some spheres of conduct than in others. The next operation was therefore to convert the general scheme into one specific to fertility control by re-defining all the orientations except the one to reproduction. Given the fundamental and complex ways in which reproductive behaviour necessarily influences, and is influenced by, the careers of individuals and societies, it should not seem surprising that different subjective meanings of fertility control could readily be postulated to express each of the three orientations for each of the issues. The second operation required to convert the general classification of construing systems into a theory of variation in the subjective meaning of fertility control was to associate this variation with variation in environmental variables. These two operations may be illustrated by the treatment of the orientation to nature. The first operation entailed adopting the assumption that an orientation of mastery over nature was being expressed by those who valued the prudent and competent control of fertility. The second operation entailed adopting the assumption that this orientation was likely to be dominant in the circumstances of developed countries, but unusual where the intractability of nature was emphasized by high mortality, the unreliability of food and water supplies, and the general uncertainty of the future. Assumptions about some other orientations about each of the issues are revealed below, where the theory is used to suggest whether, and in what respects, the construing system typical of the village may be incongruent with the system underlying the family planning programme.

Incongruent meanings

For the purposes of this section, it was assumed to be at least possible that the indigenous midwife had adopted the construing system underlying the family planning programme and rejected the system typical of the village. The procedure used to determine which system did, in fact, apply to her is the subject of the succeeding section.

Judgements about the meanings prevailing in the village are based on the account, summarized above, of the enquiry into the role and status of the midwife in the area. (Since it was not the purpose of that study to obtain data for this exercise, some judgements required a liberal use of imagination.) In the following paragraphs, each category of orientation is applied in turn, starting with the orientation to reproduction.

From the standpoint of the family planning programme, the capacity for reproduction is regarded as burdensome. The programme exists to discourage a generous exercise of the capacity. From the villager's standpoint, in contrast, the capacity for reproduction seems to be regarded as benign. Probably sustaining this orientation are the positive opportunities to prosper offered by large families and the security they provide against misfortune. In other words, the village construing system appears to be incongruent with respect to the orientation to reproduction.

With regard to the orientation to nature, strict control of fertility represents an orientation of mastery over nature. From the traditional villager's point of view, however, it is probably important that motives and methods of fertility control seem to be in harmony with nature and with God's purposes. As well as finding the general theme of the programme unnatural, the villager may have specific reservations about the practice of providing family planning services at a health centre. To associate fertility with disease may seem especially unnatural. In short, the two systems appear to be incongruent with respect to the orientation to nature.

The 'time' and 'activity' orientations also pose the possibility of incongruency. The villagers probably look to the past for the rationale of their present family-building behaviour. The major change in circumstances that would impose the need for a new rationale has yet to occur. For the programme, the rationale lies in the presumed future consequences of family limitation for family welfare. The postulation of differences in the 'activity' orientation requires a reference to self-concepts. Among villagers, it is likely that much activity expresses or pursues a self-concept founded on a social status ascribed at birth. The tenure of this status may be conditional on the capacity to produce several children. The assumptions of the programme reflect an attachment to the view that status is not ascribed but achieved, and that children need not be important to the achievement of a valued status.

Finally, the programme and the villager are likely to be incongruent with respect to the 'relational' orientation also. From the standpoint of the programme, potential clients are seen as independent and autonomous individuals. They have reason to see themselves, however, more as participants in a collective enterprise in which family-building provides for the continuity of interdependence over time. They may also regard themselves as subject to community views of the propriety of using family planning services.

The meaning of fertility control among midwives

With respect to fertility control, does the midwife share the traditional construing system attributed to the village or the modern system underlying the family planning programme? If she shares the former system, is this why she had not brought many clients to the family planning clinics? Or does the reason for that lie not in her construing system but in deficiencies in her information about modern methods of birth control? Or is it simply that she cannot persuade villagers to adopt the ideas she shares with the family planning programme? Answers to these questions were sought with a specific enquiry among a group of midwives. The enquiry sought data on the meaning conferred by midwives on fertility control, on their circumstances and background, and on their knowledge of methods of birth control. The study relied heavily on the collaboration of the social scientists who had previously undertaken the general enquiry into the role and status of the midwife. The new study was essentially a test of the proposition that the meanings the midwife assigned to fertility control would, irrespective of her knowledge of methods, be incongruent with the subjective meanings implicit in the programme.

A questionnaire was developed and administered to forty of the sixty-seven midwives working in the study area. The interviews, which took place at the health centre in Temanggung, were conducted by the team which had previously undertaken the general enquiry. This arrangement had substantial advantages. The investigators were experienced and gifted interviewers. They were already familiar with the community and were especially practised in interviewing midwives. They had participated fully in the construction of the questionnaire, for which task their experience had been invaluable. A disadvantage was that these were senior staff who could not be spared from their posts in Djakarta for the time needed for adequate piloting or for adequate practice to ensure uniformity of technique in administering the questionnaire.

The mean age of midwives interviewed was 57.8 years. Their ages ranged from 40 to 88 years. All but four were Moslem. All had been married at least once, and over a third had been married three or more times. They had had an average of 5.8 live births. None had had fewer than five children. Of the twelve who had attended school, six said they could not read. Over half said they engaged in other types of work (usually farming or peasant labouring) as well as midwifery.

From the questionnaire responses it seemed that most midwives had heard of modern as well as traditional methods. Few seemed to believe traditional methods were very reliable. According to their responses, fewer than half thought oral contraceptives and condoms were very reliable, but a majority thought this of the intrauterine device. In most cases, midwives who had used a method themselves appeared to have relied on abstinence. Data on midwives' knowledge of family planning doctrine was obtained from a section of the questionnaire to be described now. Its function was to attempt to determine whether the midwife's construing system was modern or traditional with respect to fertility control.

The theory used above to distinguish modern from traditional construing systems can be used to distinguish modern from traditional models or types (ideal types) of midwife. The modern type can be invested with those characteristics which effectively distinguish the system underlying the programme from the villager's system. The specifications of the constructed type can then be used as a measure of the meaning of fertility control to midwives. For an analytical account of such procedures, see Schutz (1954).

One characteristic of the constructed modern type is her endorsement of the doctrine of the family planning programme. She necessarily believes that family planning is a legitimate part of midwifery practice, that modern methods of birth control are better than traditional methods, that comparatively small families and long intervals between births have advantages over comparatively large families and short intervals. These specific preferences are manifestations of the orientations that distinguish this type from the traditional type. Consistently with the distinctions proposed above between programme and village, the modern type of midwife is defined as one who regards the capacity for reproduction as burdensome, who believes that fertility should be stringently mastered, that the rationale of fertility control lies in its presumed future consequences for family welfare, that children are not important to a valued status and that potential clients can be treated as independent and autonomous individuals.

The constructed type was operationally defined by its presumed assent to a number of specific propositions and its presumed dissent from others. The propositions were based on the doctrine of the family planning programme and on orientations to three of the possible five issues: the orientations to reproduction, to nature and to activity. There were thirty-three propositions, each embodied in a direct question. For example: 'Do you think it is important to have many children in case some of them die?' A few of the questions sought information regarded as of immediate practical interest. For example: 'If there was a course about family planning for a week in a clinic, and you were invited, would you come?'

Interviewers were asked to present questions in the following way. First, the midwife was to be asked the question directly. If necessary, it could then be explained to her. If her reply indicated that she agreed or disagreed with the proposition, she could be asked whether she was 'half sure' or 'very sure'. Responses were to be scored from '1' (yes, very sure) to '5' (no, very sure). A score of '3' was to be given if it seemed clear that the midwife had no opinion. In every case, it was to be the interviewer, not the respondent, who decided which score was most appropriate.

The task of analysing the responses was conceptualized as a problem in the analysis of a repertory grid. In its conventional form (Bannister and Mair, 1968; Kelly, 1955), the repertory grid is a matrix with 'elements' (persons or things or events) assigned to columns and 'constructs' (attributes of any kind) assigned to rows. The cells of the grid are used for a respondent's ratings or rankings of each element with respect to each construct. The grid can then be analysed to seek relationships among constructs and elements.

For the purposes of this study, the propositions (questions) were assigned to columns of the grid as its elements. The constructs, assigned to rows, were thought of as being in the form 'applies to m', where m was each midwife in turn. Thus, the grid had a column for each question and a row for each midwife. The cells of the grid accommodated ratings of the midwives' agreement or disagreement with each proposition. In principle, the required relationship between the ideas of real midwives and ideas distinguishing the modern from the traditional type were then available from an analysis of the grid.

There are various methods of analysing repertory grids. The choice of method in this case was guided by a concern with the following questions. Do sets of responses co-vary in such a way that the thirty-three propositions can be summarized in a few general propositions? If so, are the latter of such a kind that assent or dissent distinguishes the modern type from the traditional type?

To answer these questions, the completed grid was subjected to a principal components analysis, using the computer program INGRID 67. This was developed for the analysis of repertory grids by Slater (1964). The program allocates total variance in the data into amounts due to variation in independent components, starting with the component that accounts for most of the variance and ending with the component that accounts for the least. It was hoped that components accounting for most of the variance would be measuring characteristics that would distinguish between modern and traditional types of midwife. The method should not be confused with a type of factor analysis. For a pertinent comment on the distinction between these techniques, see Hills (1972).

Midwife loadings and question loadings show the contribution of each midwife and each question to the variance summarized by each component. Use of the two kinds of loading combines the advantages of analysis based on correlations among column variables (in this case, propositions) with the advantages of an analysis based on correlations among constructs (midwives) assigned to rows. Because the analysis is based not on row scores but on deviations of these from the respondent's means score, the effect of a general tendency to agree or to disagree is eliminated. Further, differences from the mean score are divided by the standard deviation of the row of deviations. The result is to allow equal weight in the analysis to the responses of each informant, whether she has a general tendency to respond strongly ('very sure') or cautiously.

The first four components located by the analysis account for 62 per cent of the total variation. The questions that have the highest loadings, positive or negative, on the components are shown in Figure 15.1. If a component is summarizing variation in one of the specified characteristics distinguishing the modern midwife type from the traditional midwife type, the identity of the characteristic should be ascertainable by studying the questions with the highest loadings. The procedure is subject to translations difficulties. Questions were originally formulated in English and translated into Javanese for the questionnaire. The Javanese versions were later translated back into English by a different Indonesian translator. Anglicized versions of the latter's translations are used in Figure 15.1. Also shown are the distributions of the midwives' loadings on each component.

The first component alone accounts for 40 per cent of the variation. As the distribution of the midwives' loadings shows, the component summarizes responses to the questions for which there is agreement among midwives. The dominant questions appear to be concerned with the ideas of the family planning programme rather than with value orientations. Questions about such matters as the merits of smaller families and God's providence contribute much less to the component than do questions about abortion, preferred birth intervals and the best source of birth control advice. Evidently all the *dukuns* are willing to affirm the ideas of the programme.

The questions that have the highest loadings on the first component produce little variation in response and large proportions of 'very sure'. The most extreme example is a question that asked: 'Do you think abortion is the best way of avoiding births?' All but one of the respondents were scored 'no, very sure'. This degree of unanimity and certainty is consistent with the possibility that the midwives were giving answers they had been taught during training.

The next three components show major dimensions of variation between the midwives and seem to divide them evenly. The second component accounts for 10 per cent of the total variance. The dominant questions shown in Figure 15.1(b) suggest that the component represents an important characteristic distinguishing the modern type from the traditional type — the orientation to nature. Questions at one end refer to God's providence with regard to child-bearing. Questions at the other end refer to ways of making family planning services more effective. Midwives resembling the modern type would answer 'no' to questions on the positive side of the scale, 'yes' to questions on the negative side. Just over half the midwives are on the traditional side of the scale.

The third component, Figure 15.1(c), accounts for 7 per cent of the variance. It could be interpreted, though not confidently, as measuring the 'activity' orientation of midwives. The midwife who accepts her status as immutable answers 'yes' to questions on the negative side of the scale. She thinks the wife ought to have the number of children the husband wants. She would attend the health centre for training in family planning, perhaps because it also represents established authority to her. However, she would answer 'no' where 'yes' would suggest a pragmatic view of child-bearing. Just over half the midwives are on the pragmatic (modern) side of the scale.

The fourth component, Figure 15.1(d), accounts for 6 per cent of the variance. Questions at both ends are about the significance of family size and the component can be interpreted as a scale measuring orientation to reproduction. Questions at one end offer respondents an opportunity to affirm a traditional view of the importance of procreation, while questions at the other end allude more to the view attributed to the modern type of midwife. Midwives resembling the modern type would answer 'no' to questions on the positive side of the scale, 'yes' to questions on the negative side. Just under half are on the side representing the modern type. The majority, on both sides, are clustered towards the centre of the scale. The most important feature of this component is that it exists. Responses to questions about restriction of family size were so poorly correlated with responses to other questions that an independent component was produced.

As a check on the analysis, the data were reanalysed, omitting responses to the six questions that had contributed the highest positive and negative loadings to the first component, those shown in Figure 15.1(a). The effect was to partial-out variation along its axis, and the axes of the first three components approximated to those of the second, third and fourth components in the original analysis, accounting for 16, 11 and 9 per cent of the variation respectively. The result tends to confirm the interpretation given above of the main sources of variation in midwives' opinions.

There were some grounds for believing that midwife loadings on some of the components might be related to age or other variables. In the event, no significant relationships were found with age or education or with intelligence, as assessed by the health service midwife. An analysis of variance did show a significant interviewer bias in the midwife loadings for the first three components. However, the general character of each component and the distribution of midwives between positive and negative sides were probably not much affected. The possibility of interviewer effects on responses seems invariably to be ignored in accounts of surveys of fertility, and of other phenomena. In cases where they have been investigated (Lapham, 1971; Visuri, 1969), the results show clearly that interviewers can sometimes exert a substantial influence.

Taken together, the four components offer the programme administrator no foundation for optimism about the midwife's potential contribution. Unanimity among midwives is confined to questions with high loadings on the first component, questions referring to ideas that had been the subject of instruction at the health centre. It seems probable that in answering these questions they were reciting what they had been taught rather than expressing opinions consistent with their beliefs and values. In the second analysis, the one omitting responses to questions that produced the first component in the first analysis, all but three midwives have a score on the traditional side of at least one component. Sixteen of them have a score on the traditional side of at least two components. In other words, most of them appear to differ from the modern type in one or more major respects. On the other hand, twenty-four of them have a score on the modern side of at least two components. However, a pessimistic interpretation is reinforced by reports of the interviewers that a number of respondents seemed to be striving to give acceptable rather than true answers. Perhaps truthful answers in all cases would have meant more scores on the traditional sides of the scales.

Performance of the *dukuns*

Subsequently, groups of midwives, including most of those interviewed for this study, were given special training for their projected work as agents of the family

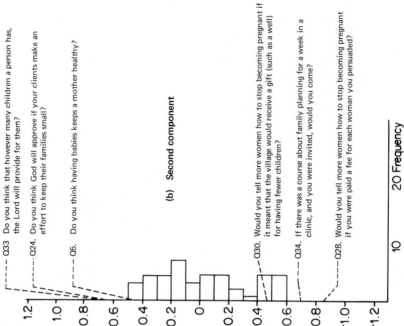

Q21. Do you think that the best interval between one birth and the next is from one to two years?*

Q32. Do you think that if a client of yours wants to stop becoming pregnant, you should send her to the maternal and child health centre?

Q23. Do you think a large family means many burdens if the parents are poor?

(a) First component

Q16. Do you think that if one of your clients wants to stop becoming pregnant, you should make her unable to conceive?

Q31. Do you think that helping to prevent pregnancies will mean less work for you?

Q18. Do you think that abortion is the best way of avoiding births?

Q33. Do you think that however many children a person has, the Lord will provide for them?

Q24. Do you think God will approve if your clients make an effort to keep their families small?

Q5. Do you think having babies keeps a mother healthy?

(b) Second component

Q30. Would you tell more women how to stop becoming pregnant if it meant that the village would receive a gift (such as a well) for having fewer children?

Q34. If there was a course about family planning for a week in a clinic, and you were invited, would you come?

Q28. Would you tell more women how to stop becoming pregnant if you were paid a fee for each woman you persuaded?

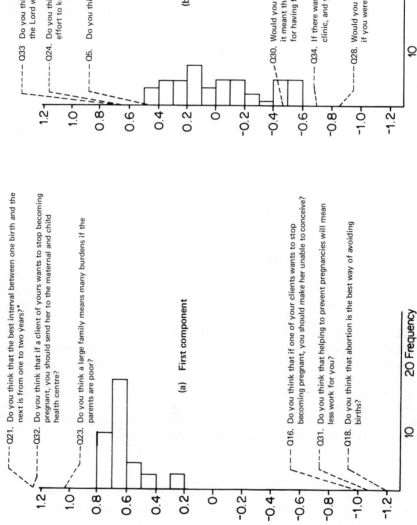

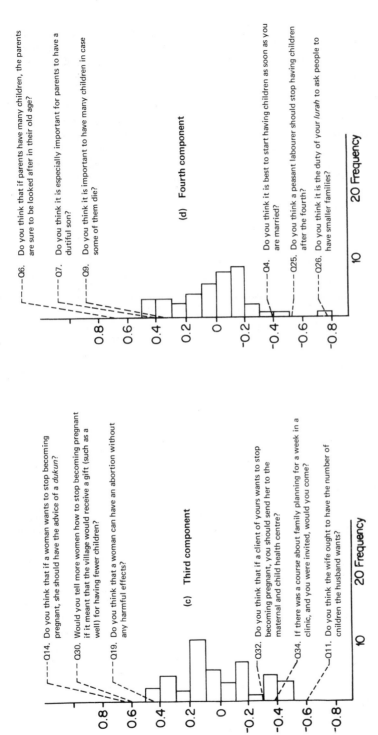

FIGURE 15.1 The first four components: questions with high loadings and the distribution of midwife loadings

*Original versions of questions were formulated in English and translated into Javanese for the questionnaire. The Javanese versions were later translated back into English by Indonesian translators. Anglicized versions of the latter translations are used here and throughout the paper.

planning programme. They were given basic instruction intended to enable them to answer questions about birth control methods and clinic services. They were encouraged to discuss family planning with their clients and others, and to make positive arrangements for clinic visits in the case of women who were persuaded to use oral contraceptives or the intrauterine device.

Two groups of midwives were trained in Temanggung, at six-day residential courses conducted by the health service midwife. After training, members of one group were supervised from the health centre in their new task. Members of the other group were not supervised. A third group received no training but were merely encouraged to recruit clients for the service. (When recruiting members to groups, no attempt was made at random allocation. Suitability and availability were the principal considerations.)

A fourth group of midwives was trained in Setjang, which is a few miles away in the neighbouring regency of Malagang. Here the midwives were trained at four-hour sessions held once a fortnight. Like the midwives in Temanggung, those in Setjang had been attending training sessions in midwifery. However, the latter were reported not to have the formers' close ties with the health centre. The performance of all groups was assessed in the middle of 1972, some months after most of the midwives had been trained. The findings are summarized below.

The achievement of all groups had been undramatic. In Temanggung, the specially trained midwives, working under the supervision of clinic personnel, referred an average of three women per month over the six-month period reviewed. Although modest, this was twice as many as the unsupervised midwives, and three times as many as those who were both untrained and unsupervised. In Setjang, trained but unsupervised midwives achieved a monthly average, per midwife, of about two referrals over a four-month period.

The averages conceal substantial differences in individual performance. Of the total of 666 referrals for all groups, 393 (59 per cent) were referred by only twenty-one (29 per cent) of the seventy-two midwives involved. Further, a decline in achievement over time was a characteristic of all groups. With the exception of the Setjang group (assessed over four months only), the average was below one referral per midwife in the final month. One possible reason for poor and declining performance, a reason consistent with the findings on beliefs and values, is that recruiting efforts tended to be restricted to women who already had large families or who were in some respects (their education, for example) untypical of village women. To investigate such possibilities, clinic records of women referred by midwives were examined. The enquiry used records in Temanggung for the middle two months (March and April, 1972) of the assessment period and records in Setjang for the whole period. The analysis revealed that overall mean family size (living children) of women referred by all groups was 3.9. Only 7 per cent of these referrals had all three of the following characteristics: fewer than four living children, wife illiterate and husband illiterate. This suggests that the midwives may have drawn heavily for referrals on couples whose family size or educational level probably reduced problems of recruitment. It is not possible to draw firm conclusions in the absence of data on the population from which referrals were drawn. According to an estimate based on the 1971 census, the total fertility rate in rural Java was 5.3. In 1973 the crude birth rate in Java was estimated to be 42 (Suwardjuno Surjaningrat and Haryono Suyono, 1974).

The midwives routinely report their deliveries to the health centre, and the numbers reported were inspected and compared with registration data for the area as part of the evaluation. This comparison suggested that the reported number of deliveries was probably a modest percentage of total births. It is possible that midwives were simply not reporting all their deliveries. Another possibility is that midwives associated with the health service were used less by the community.

It would have been interesting to measure the association between the number of acceptors recruited and midwife loadings on the components. Unfortunately, it was not possible to do this with the data available. One limitation was that the data on meanings were limited to the Temanggung groups. Another was that, in view of the unknown effects of supervision on the trained and supervised Temanggung group, measures of association for that group would have been impossible to interpret. In the case of untrained midwives, some of the necessary information was omitted from the data collected.

Apparently the performance of midwives in the study area was similar to the performance, at the time, of midwives in other parts of Indonesia. In 1972 a national conference was held in Djakarta to review experience of Indonesian researchers and health workers on the role of the indigenous midwife in the family planning programme. The Java studies provided the standpoint for this review. Other studies of performance discussed at the conference had produced results similar to those described above. The midwives were not capable of recruiting more than two or three acceptors per month, and performance declined over time. Participants at the conference concluded that, on the evidence available, there was no reason to suppose that the midwife could make more than a small contribution to the total number of clients recruited by the programme. On the other hand, her importance in the community might enable her to impede the programme if she was inclined to do so. It was therefore recommended that efforts should be made to ensure that the programme had at least her passive support, if it could not attract her active cooperation (Subagio Poerwodihardjo and others, 1972). Similar conclusions have been drawn from midwife studies in other countries (Simons, 1975).

Discussion and conclusions

The apparent implications of the enquiry into the meaning of fertility control were not contradicted by the subsequent performance of midwives as agents of the programme. Taking all the findings together, the following conclusions seem plausible. The traditional midwife does not merely profess traditional beliefs and values but is actively engaged in preserving them. Her dominant reference group is the village community. She uses and helps to sustain the community's construing system — its ways of making sense of the world, natural and social. Her identity, as understood by herself and others, is primarily a product of this system. It is as a member of the community that she knows what conduct may be legitimately expected of an authentic *dukun baji*.

Although it dominates her outlook, the community is not the midwife's only reference group. The health centre is another. She employs a construing system, or sub-system, she learned there to answer questions about the modern doctrine of family planning. But that system belongs to her life at the health centre. It has no roots in the system that gives meaning to her life in the village.

This schematic account is subject to important reservations. Firstly, there is considerable variation in outlook among the midwives. For some of them, the account is probably accurate enough in essentials. For others, it is equally probably a misrepresentation of their ideas. Secondly, the interpretation offered exaggerates the differences between modern and traditional ways of thought. The idea of controlling fertility, of attempting to make it consistent with values and circumstances, is not alien to villagers. Further, the situation is not static. The construing system of village society is under various pressures for change, probably including pressures due to the effects on social structure of rapid population growth. Finally, even if a midwife is unsympathetic to the programme, she may not be unwilling to guide to the clinic those women who wish to go. Nevertheless, the evidence suggests that the construing system currently *prevailing* over the midwives' conduct, including the conduct of dissenters, is probably summarized more accurately by the orientations attributed to the traditional type than by those applied to the modern type. One of the midwives interviewed in Djakarta when the questionnaire was being piloted epitomized some of the findings of the study. She sat in a flimsy hut, nursing her eighth child. She said she did not practice birth control herself, yet mentioned with pride that she had referred many women to the clinics. Asked for her views on birth control, she said it depended on the individual's fate. If the parents were strong, there was no need to worry about the number of children. Two of her children had been adopted, a fact which she regarded as a piece of good fortune. Another piece was that so many women used her midwifery services. Her husband listened to all this with pleasure and approval while children and hens wandered freely in and out.

In the introductory section, the methodology described in this paper was presented as an improvement on conventional procedures. The nature of this improvement can now be made more explicit by an examination of the essential differences between the Java study and a study of traditional midwives conducted in Pakistan. The latter study was conventional in type but was similar in purposes to the Java study. In the Java study, the function of questions was to test whether, and in what respects, the meaning of fertility control to respondents resembled the meanings used to distinguish between two midwife models or ideal types — the modern type and the traditional type. The construction of the types was grounded in a theory of variation in the subjective meanings of fertility control applied to data specific to the midwives' community. When the questionnaire was being prepared in Java, this theory was at an earlier stage of formulation than is the version described in this paper. In consequence, the distinctive characteristics of the two types were less clear than they may seem to have been from the account given above.

The Pakistan study was without a theory of the subjective meaning of fertility control to guide the formulation of questions and the interpretation of responses. The investigators followed the common practice of assembling a number of questions on issues that reason or experience had suggested were relevant to their purpose, which in this case, as in the case of the Java study, was to determine the midwives' sentiments and inclinations with respect to involvement in the family planning programme. For example, the midwives were asked whether and how much they thought family planning was against religion, and whether they thought modern contraceptives were successful in preventing births. Responses were accepted at their face value. For example, the investigators report that 26 per cent of respondents 'thought' family planning was definitely against religion (Gardezi and Inayatullah, 1969).

From the standpoint of the Java study, the fundamental weakness of the procedure adopted in Pakistan is that it offered respondents no way of revealing the subjective or sociological significance of their responses. A midwife who says she thinks family planning is against religion may possibly be expressing an orientation of subjugation to nature, an orientation that may be incompatible with enthusiastic support for the family planning programme. On the other hand, she may be indicating merely what she thinks is the opinion of religious leaders, an opinion that may have no importance for the beliefs and values guiding her own conduct.

There are three related problems here. One is that the referential meaning of questions and responses is not specific: it is not clear what proposition the respondent is supporting or rejecting. (In the Java study, the referential meanings of questions and responses were revealed by the ways in which answers to different questions were correlated to produce components that were interpretable in the light of theory.) The second problem is that, whatever the proposition, no formula is offered for interpreting the subjective significance of the response: there is no way of eliciting the interpretive construction in the mind of the respondent between (a) experiences that lead her to support or reject the proposition and (b) other of her experiences. The third problem is that, whatever the subjective significance, there is no way of interpreting its sociological significance: there is no system of interpretive constructions connecting subjective meanings with circumstances. Clearly the solution to these three problems are interdependent. A sociological theory is needed to specify types of subjective significance to be identified. The process of identification requires the use of propositions in a way that can distinguish between the types.

Had responses to all questions in the Pakistan study been subjected to a multivariate analysis, and had this revealed a systematic variation in responses to different questions, some inferences might have been made about underlying values. But the attribution of subjective meaning, *post hoc*, to the variation would have required reliance on questionable assumptions about the relationships between the responses and the expression of value orientations. In general, a want of theory when questions are being formulated cannot be remedied by attempts to theorize about responses. And a multivariate analysis that manufactures scales from response data is not a substitute for theory.

Another weakness of the Pakistan study, but one it shared with the Java study, was vulnerability to the tendency of interviewees to give answers they believe will be approved by interviewers. While people do not readily abandon sentiments and inclinations that express their basic value orientations, they are often very ready to modify what they say about their sentiments and inclinations in the light of their knowledge of what constitute 'approved' answers. For a review of studies of this phenomenon, and some further evidence, see Phillips (1973, Chapter 3). A tendency to give approved answers need not involve deliberate deception. For most questions in both studies, midwives probably regarded their answers as true in some respects and circumstances, untrue in others. It would not be surprising if they had chosen to give the answers they believed to be more acceptable from among those which were conditionally true. Without knowing the respects and circumstances in which they regarded their answers as true and untrue, the meaning of the responses is in doubt. The effects were ameliorated to some extent by the procedure adopted for the Java study. Alternative models of meaning were implicit in the questionnaire and conclusions were based on an analysis of all responses taken together. Improvements in procedure probably lie in the application of techniques, such as standard repertory grid techniques (Bannister and Mair, 1968), which elicit meanings indirectly in a manner not obvious to the respondent.

The Pakistan study was by no means unusual in its method of attempting to elicit sentiments and inclinations about fertility control. The absence of a theoretical foundation and the heavy reliance on individual questions typify most of the hundreds of enquiries over recent years into 'attitudes' to family limitation. Their procedures have probably been encouraged by the inclusion of suggested questions on attitudes in model questionnaires, such as those published in the Population Council's (1970) manual (a very useful one) on survey procedures. The findings of these enquiries have suggested fairly preposterous claims about the proportion of births that are 'unwanted' and the likely demographic effects of improved birth control facilities in developed and developing countries.

A reliance on answers to individual questions and an ethnocentric view of human culture have led to excessive dependence on questions and responses of the kind that produced the first component in the analysis of the midwife data from Java. Questions that might have elicited a more traditional view of fertility control have generally not been asked. On the other hand, some of the data produced by these surveys have been used as evidence of how little impact can be expected on birth control facilities owing to the relatively large families people say they want (Davis, 1967). The same kinds of data have also been used to examine trends in 'ideal family size' in America (Blake, 1966) and to provide support for the fertility assumptions made in population projections in Britain (Select Committee on Science and Technology, 1972).

There is a fundamental respect in which the description 'conventional' could be applied more aptly to the procedure adopted in Java than to what has been described above as conventional procedures. In common experience, expectations about a person's behaviour in given circumstances are based on patterns of behaviour believed to typify the individual. For example, a person construed as typically conservative will not be expected to wear flamboyant dress in a community where it signifies the rejection of traditional values. Whether he is, in fact, construed as typically conservative will depend on whether his behaviour signifies that he affirms a set of beliefs and values used to distinguish the conservative type from other types. In a similar way, whether the midwives were categorized as modern rather than traditional depended on whether their responses exhibited a set of beliefs and values believed to distinguish modern from traditional types. Thus, from the standpoint of everyday practices, the procedure adopted for the Java study seems quite conventional. From the same standpoint, conventional procedures seem, to say the least, quaint.

Acknowledgements

The research described in this paper was initiated by the Indonesian Planned Parenthood Association and supported by grants made under the British Government's technical assistance arrangements. The project required and received generous cooperation from the University of Indonesia (Faculty of Social Sciences), the National Family Planning Coordinating Board of Central Java and the health centres of Temanggung and Setjang. The author is indebted for much practical help and advice to Miss Sri Djuarini and Mrs. Nurdin of the I.P.P.A. and to Dr. Brooks Ryder of the Ford Foundation. The principal components analysis of the midwife data was provided by the Medical Research Council's service for the analysis of repertory grids, under Dr. Patrick Slater. The idea of analysing the data in this way was a consequence of much previous help received from Dr. Slater in the analysis of repertory grids.

References

Bannister, D., and Mair, J. M. M. (1968). *The Evaluation of Personal Constructs*, Academic Press, London.

Blake, J. (1966). 'Ideal family size among white Americans: a quarter of a century's evidence'. *Demography*, 3 (No. 1), 154—173.

Clifford, W. B. (1971). 'Modern and traditional value orientations and fertility behaviour'. *Demography*, 8 (No. 1), 37—48.

Davis, K. (1967). 'Population policy: will current programs succeed?'. *Science*, 158, 730—739.

Djuarini, S., Purbatin, S. H., Soejatni Surjotjondro, S. (1971). *Report on the Study of Dukuns in Central Java*, Indonesian Planned Parenthood Association, Djakarta.

Fawcett, J. T. (1971). 'Attitude measures in KAP studies: an overview and critique'. In *Conference Proceedings: Psychological Measurement in the Study of Population Problems*, Institute of Personality Assessment and Research, University of California, Berkeley. pp. 11—18.

Gardezi, H. N., and Inayatullah, A. (1969). *The Dai Study*, West Pakistan Family Planning Association, Lahore.

Hills, M. (1972). 'Factor analysis as a statistical method. Review of book by Lawley, D. N., and Maxwell, A. E.' *Journal of the Royal Statistical Society*, Series A, 135 (No. 3), 441—442.

Kelly, G. A. (1955). *The Psychology of Personal Constructs*, Vols. 1 and 2. W. W. Norton, New York.

Kluckhohn, F. R., and Strodtbeck, F. L. (1961). *Variations in Value Orientations*, Row Peterson, Evanston.

Lapham, R. J. (1971). 'Methodological and other issues in the assessment of attitudinal variables in family planning and population control'. In *Conference Proceedings: Psychological Measurement in the Study of Population Problems*, Institute of Personality Assessment and Research, University of California, Berkeley. pp. 19—32.

Mauldin, W. P. (1965). 'Fertility studies: knowledge, attitude and practice'. In *Studies in Family Planning*, No. 7, Population Council, New York. pp. 1—10.

Phillips, D. L. (1973). *Abandoning Method*, Jossey-Bass, San Francisco.

Population Council (1970). *A Manual for Surveys of Fertility and Family Planning: Knowledge, Attitudes, and Practice*, Population Council, New York.

Schutz, A. (1953). 'Common-sense and scientific interpretation of human action'. *Philosophy and Phenomenological Research*, 14 (No. 1), pp. 1–37. Reprinted in M. Natanson (Ed.) (1971). *Alfred Schutz, Collected Papers 1*, Martinus Nijhoff, The Hague. pp. 3–47.

Schutz, A. (1954). 'Concept and theory formation in the social sciences'. *Journal of Philosophy*, L1 (No. 9), pp. 257–273. Reprinted in M. Natanson (Ed.) (1971). *Alfred Schutz, Collected Papers 1*, Martinus Nijhoff, The Hague. pp. 48–66.

Select Committee on Science and Technology (1972). *Population Policy*, Fifth Report, Session 1971–72. HMSO, London.

Shibutani, T. (1962). 'Reference groups and social control'. In A. M. Rose (Ed.), *Human Behaviour and Social Processes*, Routledge and Kegan Paul, London.

Simons, J. (1974). 'The later years of childbearing. Review of book by Bumpass, L., and Westoff, C. F.' *Population Studies*, 28 (No. 2).

Simons, J. (1975). 'The indigenous midwife in Asia – supporter or opponent of family planning?' *IPPF Medical Bulletin*, 9 (No. 5), pp. 1–3.

Slater, P. (1964). *The Principal Components of a Repertory Grid*, Vincent Andrews, London.

Suwardjono Surjaningrat and Haryono Suyono (1974). 'Indonesia'. In S. M. Keeny (Ed.), *East Asia Review*, 1973. *Studies in Family Planning* (Population Council, New York), 5 (No. 5), 148–151.

Subagio Poerwodihardjo and others (1972). *The Role of the Traditional Midwife in the Family Planning Programme*, National Family Planning Coordinating board, Djakarta.

Verderese, M. (1973). *The Traditional Birth Attendant in Maternal and Child Health and Family Planning*, HMD/NUR/74.1. WHO, Geneva.

Visuri, E. (1969). *Poverty and Children: A Study of Family Planning*, Vol. 16. Transactions of the Westermarck Society, Westermarck Society, Helsinki.

NAME INDEX

SUBJECT INDEX